Meisner and Mindfulness

Meisner and Mindfulness: Authentic and Truthful Solutions for the Challenges of Modern Acting is the first book that reveals how Meisner and mindfulness can be united to create strong results for actors and help them navigate the challenges of the digital age.

The twenty-first century has created an entirely new set of demands and pressures on the working actor, including an acceleration of the digital age and the complications of COVID-19, which have led to auditions, rehearsals, and even whole performances happening entirely in isolation. This book combines a modern rethinking of the Meisner technique with a complementary set of tools from mindfulness meditation to offer profound solutions to these growing challenges, addressing the demands of a post-coronavirus industry as well as the pressures of acting in the digital era. In this ground-breaking expansion of the technique, readers will discover how it is possible to train some of the deepest values of living truthfully under a given set of circumstances, both with other actors and while alone. Since the 1950s, the Meisner technique has aided the actor in navigating the demands unique to their time. This book is a powerful reminder that, even in the midst of so many changes and challenges, the truthfulness that has defined outstanding performances across generations is still within reach.

Full of easily accessible mindfulness and Meisner exercises and principles for practice-based support, *Meisner and Mindfulness* will be illuminating to working actors, directors, students and instructors of acting, and practitioners of the Meisner technique looking to develop the authenticity, immediateness, and closeness essential to great acting.

The book also includes access to an online supplement featuring additional exercises and concepts, including new ways to incorporate Meisner exercises into training sessions, suggestions for how Meisner-oriented companies can use exercises such as repetition in rehearsals, and discussions for how to set up a facilitated Meisner group.

Royce Sparks is an internationally recognized teacher of the Meisner technique. He has taught it in Canada, Europe, and the United States at institutions such as UCL and the Royal Central School of Speech and Drama, and has presented his research on it and other approaches to acting at international conferences. His practice focus is on the interdisciplinary applications of Meisner to camera work, physical approaches including martial arts, classical texts, devising, and leadership development. He is also the author of *The Authentic Leader: Using the Meisner Technique for Embracing the Values of Truthful Leadership* (Routledge/Productivity Press 2020).

Meisner and Mindfulness

Authentic and Truthful Solutions for the Challenges of Modern Acting

Royce Sparks

NEW YORK AND LONDON

Cover image: Shutterstock

First published 2023
by Routledge
605 Third Avenue, New York, NY 10158

and by Routledge
4 Park Square, Milton Park, Abingdon, Oxon, OX14 4RN

Routledge is an imprint of the Taylor & Francis Group, an informa business

© 2023 Royce Sparks
Artwork © 2023 Sonia Martins

The right of Royce Sparks to be identified as author of this work has been asserted in accordance with sections 77 and 78 of the Copyright, Designs and Patents Act 1988.

All rights reserved. No part of this book may be reprinted or reproduced or utilised in any form or by any electronic, mechanical, or other means, now known or hereafter invented, including photocopying and recording, or in any information storage or retrieval system, without permission in writing from the publishers.

Trademark notice: Product or corporate names may be trademarks or registered trademarks, and are used only for identification and explanation without intent to infringe.

Library of Congress Cataloging-in-Publication Data
A catalog record for this book has been requested

ISBN: 978-1-032-18602-3 (hbk)
ISBN: 978-1-032-18600-9 (pbk)
ISBN: 978-1-003-25532-1 (ebk)

DOI: 10.4324/9781003255321

Typeset in Goudy
by Apex CoVantage, LLC

Access the Support Material: www.routledge.com/9781032186009

Contents

Acknowledgments	vi
1 When Pandemics Become Acting Teachers	1
2 This One Moment	15
3 An Audience Within	32
4 Miru Me, or The Eyes that See	48
5 The Ounce You've Been Waiting For	64
6 There's Wisdom in Forgetting Your Head	80
7 Riding the Non-Wave	105
8 Arising Before Thought	122
9 Floating Moments	139
10 Losing I Within You	163
11 Circle Without Beginning or End	183
12 What Burns Deeply Within	210
13 One Bright Pearl	242
14 The Two-Dimensional Reality	264
15 Maybe So. Maybe Not. We'll see	288
Index	294

Acknowledgments

This book was, to say the least, unexpected. I had never intended to write about Meisner and meditation together; in fact until I really began to think about it in my mind, they would be forever separate areas of my life. But the lessons of the coronavirus pandemic taught me something hard and true: we must always continue to assess what we believe to be true, in the event a greater discovery may lie beyond our older, preferred molds.

A project like this takes belief, and so I could not begin this without thanks to my incredible editor, Stacey Walker, and the dream team I worked with, including Lucia Accorsi. It has been a joy, and I am blessed to have walked this journey with you. A special thanks must be given to Kevin Otos who, more than just a great editor, became almost like a dear mentor in this process.

There are some individuals from whom I have been equally fortunate to learn these materials. On the Meisner front, two people invested years and hundreds of hours of time and effort into my development as an actor and researcher of this work: Scott Williams and Larry Silverberg. The knowledge, confidence, and joy you've infused into my work has given me courage to keep exploring the boundaries of this wonderful approach to acting. When it comes to meditation, I must offer humble thanks to the many kind souls whose lessons I have been fortunate enough to absorb over the years both directly and indirectly: Sensei Al Kaszniak, Henry Shukman, Reggie Ray, Thich Nhat Hanh and his sangha, Sam Harris, Richard Lang, Ken Vorndran, and Jerry Gardner.

Similar special thanks must also be given to the individuals who have poured support, kindness, and wisdom into my journey over the years: Steve Anderson, Eugenio Barba and Odin Teatret, Kathleen Bandaruk, Sarah Bauer, Ysabel Clare, Geoff Coleman, Complicite, Steve Comus, Gordon and

Acknowledgments

Olga Cruickshank, Megan Cunnington, Glenn Davis (the incomparable MrCologne76), Richard Dipple, Niki Flacks, Autumn Flint, Tamaya Gardner, George Goldman, Mo Goldman, Gail Gonzales, Nickolas Grace, Harry ter Haar, Ronan Harris, Sarah Davey-Hull, Gina Jones, Chance Kellner, Sarah King, Cameron Knight, Maike Koch, Tage Larsen, Teresa Lavina and Gavin Lennon, Kristine Mednansky, Howard Allen and Valerie Mustain, Nigel Fyfe, Shizuyo Okada, Brigid Panet, Chris Panoutsos, Kostas Poulakis, Marta Rubio, Lacy Padilla-Nunez, Georgia Fleury Reynolds, Lexi Sale, Paul and Joan Schumacher, Martin Juul Sorensen, Eleni Skarpari, Terence Stamp, Keith Stanovich, Tatsushige Udaka, Barbara Ujlaki, Taylan Uysal, and Robert Westenberg. A warm thank-you must be given for my second family in the UK: Clive Whitworth, Gary Alderman, and the ITG family. We'll all meet again one day, and I'll keep practicing poorly timed straight leads in the meanwhile despite my best efforts.

Thank you to my beloved family whose continued belief and support in me has kept me strong, including my parents Eric and Oksana. A special thanks must be given to Sonia, my beloved partner, guide and teacher, my other half. You have enriched my life beyond measure.

This book I dedicate to every actor whose hardships on an already uneasy journey have been compounded by the new world we've entered into. I hope this material brings a fresh breath on your path.

In memory of Roger Owen who, along with his partner India Osborne, made up one of the warmest, most generous teams I've ever met. Travel well, dear friend.

Zen is the opposite of withdrawal from the world. It's a radical acceptance of life, the pain and suffering no less than the beauty of the dawn skies, of the sea in rain, the mountain dark under morning clouds, and the shopping list . . . Making a cup of tea, fetching milk from the fridge, standing outside on the front step, watching the remains of a storm drift across the dawn sky, and hearing the *drip-drip* of rainwater into a puddle from a roof are miracles. The miraculous, in the end, is the fact of anything existing at all.

Henry Shukman
One Blade of Grass, Counterpoint Press

1
When Pandemics Become Acting Teachers

Three Plaits

Where were you when you first heard the news?

I was getting married when it was happening. Or planning to. I was back in the States by then, enmeshed in a chronic health battle that was nearing its second year. My fiancée, still living in London at the time, had just finished her dinner on WhatsApp video when we began to discuss it.

"I know we said January 7th I'd be landing," she said, "but work is really picking up right now."

"You want to wait an extra week or two?"

"Maybe a week, just to get some more in savings. Is that okay with you?"

"Wedding's the 31st so as long as you're there by, say, the 30th–"

"I will be. Smart ass."

"Yeah, it's fine. My only concern is the airports. I heard they were going to start doing temperature checks."

"At LAX? Jesus. That's going to back everything up even more."

"I know. It's probably just an overreaction, they're just playing it extra safe."

Like many other now-concerned people, I ate my words and more. But that was before I listened to a podcast in which Johns Hopkins researcher Amesh Adalja was interviewed about the spread of a variant of the SARS virus that would later come to be called COVID-19. That was also before toilet paper became worth more than gold, before lockdowns paralyzed the world, ICUs were flooded, and my friends working as nurses began to seek treatment for PTSD. It was before simple human errors such as not washing hands or

DOI: 10.4324/9781003255321-1

rubbing one's eyes when tired could come at a cost in life. It was also before the arts would take one of the biggest hits it had ever endured, changing the course of acting for years to come. Years we are still in the midst of.

Wherever you were when you first heard the news, we are both waiting for the same thing: the day we don't hear it anymore.

Two actors sit across from one another in chairs, engaging in a ritual that to any outsider would seem utterly bizarre. For some reason, they've been repeating the same phrase for several minutes now:

> "You're angry about that."
> "I'm angry about that."
> "You're angry about that."
> "I'm angry about that."
> Et cetera.

Though phrase remains the same, however, the behaviors around it are ever-changing. Over the course of these minutes, the actors somehow create effortless dialogue with delicious drama spiced throughout. They cry, push one another, roll on the floor laughing, and wind up forehead to forehead in a quiet embrace. They take us on a journey of the joys and pains of the human condition filled with raw, uninhibited, and spontaneous authenticity. When it finishes, we are breathless.

Is this a description of some Dada or absurdist play in performance? Not to my knowledge. This is what happens when two actors are working at a particularly high level of quality in a Meisner technique class.

Gensha, a monk living in the mountains, sits outside his room. It is summer, it's humid, and he's bathed in sweat. He's done the whole journey: shaved head, the robes that feel more like a water catchment system with how much moisture is in the air. But it's not working. He's been at this for years and nothing. The rituals, the chanting, sitting zazen for hours. It's all pointless. He doesn't feel any closer to awakening, whatever that might mean. He stands up, turns in the direction of the temple, and thinks to himself, "This is it. This is the day I tell Sensei to bugger himself and I go do something else." Cue Jerry Maguire quitting music.

As he begins to walk, a piercing screech suddenly rings throughout the air. He is completely caught off guard, and his foot jolts straight into the pointed end of a particularly sharp rock. Blood begins to stream from his broken nail as he screams and begins swearing. He looks to the source of what caused his misery. A bird sits on a branch nearby. The pain combined with the suddenness of it all stops him in his tracks. The bird has streaks of bright yellow in its plumage. Its call is as luminescent as any rising sun. The slight breeze he hadn't noticed before feels like silk against his wet skin. Everything, himself included, settles into a singular moment, and he realizes he is not, cannot even if he wanted to be, separate from anything else in this moment.

The smile that comes to his face envelopes the whole cosmos. A moment of true awakening.

The Hard Truths Always Come Home

As I write this we are currently in the midst of the coronavirus pandemic. Though the vaccines are working, problems are arising. New variants are emerging so quickly we are wondering if new letters in the Greek alphabet need to start being made up. Vaccine hesitancy has become the pleading ground of healthcare workers all over the country, and as the Delta variant takes its final bow before handing the mic to Omicron, fears of new surges and breakthrough strains rise. Seeing the world as it is, I turn my attention closer to home, my own industry, asking, "What is the future for acting?"

While attempting to find a career foothold in one of the lowest-income industries, often working multiple jobs just to survive, an actor's life is not easy. Constant scarcity of opportunity coupled with financial strain can push many talented, gifted individuals out of the field. This was life *before* the pandemic, before theatres shut their doors and films largely ceased production. Tens of thousands of precious, potential career-launching opportunities have been lost since. As much as we want to get back to "normal," whatever that was, we can't escape the persistent possibility that normal at any given time might mean more of the new norm: more lockdowns, suspended productions, anxiety, and sickness. Careers halted as precious time ticks away for the struggling actor.

The challenges created by COVID-19, however, are unfortunately going to persist long after its acute phase has ended. It is both these short- and long-term effects that we now have to consider. If the landscape of the industry is like an ecosystem, the natural pathways open to actors have been drastically altered in this new climate.

The first and most immediate ripple effect is going to be the financial fallout. Growing numbers of actors over the past two years have found it impossible to continue supporting themselves in major industry hubs. Socio-economic constraints, including mounting credit debt and evictions, are not going away overnight. Actors waiting for the industry to fully reopen will likely find the money coming in from acting work even more limited. Audience hesitancy about returning to theatres, for example, is a major concern for producers. In early 2021, the *New York Times* estimated that the New York tourism industry, of which theatre and the arts are an integral component, may not recover fully until 2025. One option on the table to aid major theatres in coping with these risks is reducing the standard eight-shows-a-week model, but fewer shows means less pay for performers – presuming, of course, there will be a show in the first place. While *The Lion King* may be protected from some of the concerns about smaller audiences, more experimental or social-issues productions are going to find themselves in a far more competitive search for audiences. Producers who would normally make these projects a part of their portfolio will be much more risk-averse. That translates to less desire to invest money into productions with higher risk margins, which is bad for both working actors and the transformative power the arts have within society.

If theatre isn't your concern, then it doesn't help to hear the film industry is being equally cautious. Investments in independent films are down significantly, and there is a growing interest in using smaller casts with opportunities to work digitally. Whether it's fewer roles or reducing performances, the news isn't sunny for actors. That's the United States, but is hard to imagine that London's West End and other major hubs across the world will be able to escape similar slow crawls back to some shred of normalcy, particularly with the pandemic dragging on far longer than expected. Fewer jobs plus financial burdens place near-suffocating pressures on actors attempting to navigate these challenges. If numbers help drive the scale of it home, a report released by UNESCO in early 2022 found that over 10 million jobs had been lost in the creative industries during the pandemic.

There's another side to this situation that expands beyond the immediate job market, which is what the makeup of our industry will look like in the coming years. Needing to work more hours in non-acting work means less time to audition, network, build relationships, train, and engage in the numerous other activities essential for thriving actors. In the next few years, I predict, we will begin seeing many more actors exiting due to burnout, re-shifting the landscape of both how to reach potential talent and how to find qualified actors. Groups already impacted by stratified socio-economic systems, as well as international actors seeking opportunity abroad, are going to find themselves forced to remain in their home countries, towns, or areas. What money they might have been saving up to enter the industry likely has been long since drained by lockdowns, rising costs of living and housing, and potentially caring for family members. For many the costs of relocating into industry hubs, as well as traveling for opportunities, will create obstacles too great to overcome. More than ever, the current conditions favor actors with the financial privilege to protect themselves, placing a chokehold on our ever-growing need for diverse voices.

Stepping outside the immediate financial crisis, there is a new pressure actors are dealing with from the outside, and that has to do with training. Universities and drama schools in a fair number of countries have a level of protection from governments and can stay afloat until they can resume classes. For training outside established schools, however, the story is different. Many acting coaches have had to re-shift their teaching priorities, canceling in-person classes altogether in favor of attempting to teach digitally. Extended study programs have had to be rethought. Some of these courses, such as the Meisner ones I am more familiar with, are coming back in various forms: a year-long course that met three times a week is now a three month "accelerated" course that only meets twice a week. That gives the actor a fraction of the time and attention needed to develop their craft. I mention Meisner but have also seen it happening within other channels of approaches to acting with which I am familiar.

The impacts on the teaching industry create a new, unique pressure on actors: when you are able to return to training, you may not be able to get as much of it. Sure, quality matters more than quantity, but only to an extent. Now, even if you can afford an extended training program it simply might not be available anymore. These are realities that are going to compound, the results being seen in weaker technique which makes it even more challenging to thrive in a highly competitive environment. Many acting teachers like to separate talking about the career marketplace from your development as an artist, but we need to start thinking of them alongside one another now. In these pages, we'll work on tackling these challenges by acknowledging two things: firstly, being able to maximize your time in training sessions, be it with other actors or a private coach, is going to become even more important in the future. Secondly, emphasizing tools to train at home some elements of your process ensures that, even if you cannot see other actors or access training as often, your technique will still be able to hold its own.

As we look to engage with the challenges created by a post-2020 industry in these pages, you'll notice there is an entire area thus far I've left out, and that relates to the consequences of stress and mental illness. Rates of depression, anxiety, and suicidality have skyrocketed in general. Post-traumatic stress from being sick, having lost loved ones, or career setbacks will create severe challenges for artists in the performance industry. The impact of such escalated levels of mental illness cannot be undone with just a few CBT sessions or six months of antidepressants. These are deeper obstacles that are going to create rippling effects in our industry for years to come. Actors utilize their minds and emotions in ways unique to their job, and when those faculties are hindered or compromised the rebound is severe. Approaches to training that provide tools to safeguard and support your mental health, and also make you aware of other practices that might not, is going to become especially relevant in the coming years. To be clear, this book isn't going to attempt to take the place of quality mental health treatment, but we will talk honestly about these situations to ensure training paradigms adapt to offer actors the support they may need today.

That's the rough news, but now let's look at what can be considered a helpful challenge. The industry has made some efforts to address issues of opportunity and finding talent. Before the pandemic, digital auditions were already growing in popularity. The self-tape is now its own art form, with actors creating entire mini-studios in their tiny apartments to give their videos a professional feel. For producers it is an excellent way to broaden access to entire channels of talent who couldn't make a particular date, location, or time for the call. Since the pandemic, the number of self-tapes as well as Zoom auditions, even for callbacks and screen tests, has exploded. Specialized articles, coaching, and training sessions now incorporate immensely specific contexts of Zoom auditions (one example that comes to mind is Backstage's article in 2021 on how to prepare children for a Zoom audition). Theatre companies as well are making use of digital platforms for finding talent. Beyond auditions, the role of online streamlining has significantly expanded. Not only castings but also production meetings, full rehearsals, and even entire performance runs are happening online. Whether it is theatre or film, you the modern actor cannot escape encountering and working with digital mediums.

The conveniences afforded by the digital era are here to stay. Benefits come with that: easier access to opportunities, as well as reducing your overhead costs by rehearsing anywhere or not traveling for a project. In a time of increased scarcity, we can't turn our nose up at this. At the same time, there are some drawbacks, the primary one being removing the ideal conditions for you to do your best work. Great actors feed on the immediacy of the moment. A lack of new environments, as well as the ability to work directly with another individual in the same room, poses a paramount shift that can be a disadvantage. Throughout this book we'll unpack why not being able to connect with another interpersonally, even if they just are a monotonous line reader for a take, is a major hurdle born of the accelerating digital age we are finding ourselves in.

Add all of these pressures onto the ones actors were already facing back when things were (again, I choose the word with all its shades of irony) "normal," and we can start to see the extent of havoc these butterfly effects will have for years to come. Long after the hand sanitizer stations are gone we are going to be dealing with these impacts. For the actor reading this in the near future, it may sound disheartening to hear the odds are even more complicated for finding your career pathway or growing it further. That, however, is why this book is interested in the modern challenges of acting, both to your technique and career development which we need to start considering hand-in-hand now. This is in many ways a newly changed world. These are the given circumstances of today.

From Roots to Wildfire

To help you tackle modern challenges, this book is going to offer tools, ideas, and support from the Meisner technique and mindfulness. In this introduction, let's explore a few clarifying points on how Meisner and its unexpected companion mindfulness can directly support your path in the industry. This gives us a meaningful starting point for this journey and training. It will also help answer some very basic questions about how this work will be valuable for you and meet your needs.

Let's start with Meisner, a word flooding the modern training scene today. For a long time this technique, created by Group Theatre member Sanford Meisner, was a largely underground approach to developing the actor's process. The reasons for this extend from everything to Meisner's health as well as the backseat his and other approaches took to the king of American acting – the infamous "Method" – for decades. After generations of incredibly successful names whose entire process was transformed for the better due to the Meisner technique (Gregory Peck, Diane Keaton, Philip Seymour Hoffman, Bryan Cranston, and Gene Hackman are just a few of these legendary individuals), the word is officially out: Meisner works. In fact, many would argue that it works not only well but is far better for the needs of the actor today than other name approaches to developing and honing your craft, both classical and contemporary.

Perhaps even more unique, the Meisner technique doesn't seem to be at odds with other tools in the contemporary actor's toolbox. It pairs beautifully with a vast range of elements and ideas about the actor's process, including physical approaches such as devising and contact improv, standard types of improvisation, Shakespeare tools, and more. Singers find it infuses their entire presence with a dynamic aliveness that is hard to look away from, and dancers discover the same results expressed entirely without words. Across multiple mediums of the industry there's something deeply relevant about it: it seems to want to fit your process, rather than ask you to conform to it.

One deep reason the Meisner technique transcends so many barriers other dogmatic approaches cannot is its main priority: Meisner places the interpersonal, the very core of the actor's experience, at the heart of its values. From day one the training asks that you forego attention on yourself and instead learn to invest it fully into another person. It is richly empathic at its core. Its practical exercises emphasizing the value of your partner's role in the acting process solve so many seemingly lifelong challenges for actors. In practical training, you not only get a shiny new set of skills but also realign your priorities and, in doing so, drop many of the burdens that seem like forever-elusive mysteries.

During the pandemic, the Meisner technique took a particularly nasty hit. As you'll soon discover, social distancing is nearly impossible in Meisner exercises. It's incredibly challenging to implement a six-feet rule and still absorb the many nuanced benefits this work confers. When COVID-19 came onto the scene, Meisner training found itself in one of the worst setbacks imaginable for a performance technique: when personal contact is such a premium value, what do we do when contact turns deadly? Of course it wasn't just Meisner training that felt the heat of this question first-hand. It's hard to find an acting technique that doesn't at one point or another place a high value on connection, touch, and the immediacy of being close to one another in training. I can't imagine contact improv found itself in a less devastating position.

Great acting always has taken on the immediacy of the moment. Even if it is the hundredth take or performance, acting celebrates the uniqueness of *this* moment. Despite how quick some Meisner teachers were to move their training onto digital platforms, thereby protecting the safety of their actors, it came with a cost: we know that losing the immediacy of touch and connection doesn't aid the actor but creates more challenges for them. There's no substitute for working with another actor, let's just be honest about that. If you could learn an entire creative process from just a book there wouldn't be any training institutions, drama schools, or private coaches. Acting is by nature relational. Relational with the text, with the entity you might label "the character," with the space you'll work in, and most importantly with other people. What Meisner offers to the actor is a means to train a healthy set of relational skills that equip you to juggle the chaos of the unknown, be fluid, and adapt on a second's notice when needed. That's the first set of results you can expect from engaging with, and applying, the concepts and exercises in this book.

Though Meisner works, almost all of its training happens with other people in the room. With not only less Meisner training around for the near future but also the lack of access you might now have to it, we have to branch out and ask what compliments the deeper values of Meisner that can be practiced alone. Whether you're new to Meisner or have been using it for decades, this question matters. Across skill levels, our task is to find a solution to this challenge. How do you practice at-home tools that depend on other people? In every chapter we are going to focus on answering this question through a variety of ways, both conceptual and in exercises, but let's start to get a sense of what that journey will look like.

The Magnificent Pressure of Urgency

This book is a hybrid approach. It blends classical Meisner with some modern takes on it, but even more impactful is that this unifies the technique with an entirely unique set of ideas and exercises found in meditation. Before we examine meditation's contributions, let's ask what the value of this more progressive approach is when it comes to your acting. A fair number of actor trainers love Frankenstein approaches to acting, more benignly known as the toolbox method. I have many colleagues in academia who relish combining different styles and approaches to training. They'll mix a little bit of Michael Chekhov in with some Viewpoints, throw in a dash of Laban, and then test it on actors just to see what happens. The results are often mixed, with a range that extends all the way from things not working one bit to the most wondrous outcomes. It's experimentation that may lead nowhere, or to profound discoveries and breakthroughs. It's valuable research my colleagues are doing, and for actors interested in exploring their own process, as well as creativity for its own sake, these training sessions are often a dream.

With respect to this way of training, it's an approach I'm not interested in. While I enjoy process development that can last for weeks or months with no clear outcome, in my teaching I'm much more focused on efficiency.

Which techniques deliver the best results, and which do it the fastest? I've been blessed to both teach and work with thousands of industry actors across the world and for me working actors are simply the most exciting individuals to teach. These individuals are directly grappling with the industry, where artistic tools have to answer to the trends of the job market. There is a tension between process and result, a practical edge that dominates both questions and which answers work. They need tools that work, and they need them now.

Training in this way is so exciting because what we are actively doing is testing possible solutions to real-world challenges. When an actor tries out a particular tool or idea in an audition, for example, there will be feedback on how well that works in the job market. Actors both get and lose jobs for many variables, of course, but we can apply this process of trial-and-error to techniques that target everything from close-ups to networking. Wherever possible, finding the quickest, most efficient tools to get the job done is of premium value. In economics terms, we look at what yields the best results with the smallest amount of effort. To some this might sound like an affront to both art and the ingrained idea that artists must devote years of pure training to their craft. Throughout this book you'll encounter many reasons why I think a hybrid approach interested in efficiency is far healthier for industry actors. An upfront vote for working smart, rather than working hard, has to do with how little time to spare working actors have, so if there are approaches that can yield the same results with less time, then this is what is worth pursuing. Some actors might happily spend years or decades devoted to their craft. The working actor who can only land two auditions a month, has an agent breathing down their neck, and needs to balance working with networking, is in a different position entirely.

Coming Home, Hand in Hand

As the exercises in this book will reveal, the Meisner technique prioritizes efficiency over many other values. It's a superb approach for acquiring strong industry skills with less time than other techniques demand. To ground it more concretely with our goals, given what the past two years has done to the training scene, it helps to ask how working actors can develop the same values of the Meisner technique by practicing complimentary exercises at home. Independent work may not be the same as working with another actor, but parallel exercises can empower the actor to maximize their time in training when they do get it.

This is where meditation, largely mindfulness, comes into the picture. During almost all of my time in Meisner training I heard the same argument: Meisner and meditation don't mix. In the next chapter we'll begin directly confronting this misconception, and throughout these pages you'll discover that not only do they mix but they share enough values that they can support one another. The right types of meditation can make your work better in the Meisner technique, and together both can nurture creating an efficient, rich process able to handle many variables of an ever-changing industry. Merging one approach to acting and another to living a fulfilled life can create perhaps the most important ingredient in the working actor's process: relevance to today's needs.

Alongside the Meisner exercises in each chapter, then, you'll also explore complimentary meditations. These are derived from mindfulness meditation and Zen. All of them are secular in nature, and none should ever step on the toes of any beliefs or traditions. These are geared solely towards answering the question, "How can the actor continue to thrive in today's industry?" The meditations themselves can all be practiced individually, for periods in between training or when no opportunities to train arise. As you'll see, the values of these specific meditations compliment the actor's journey in this training beautifully.

The examples of the Meisner exercises will largely feature multiple people, with enough guidance for you to set up your own practice group if you don't have access to established teachers or programs (additional online content is provided on the publisher's page for an expanded discussion on the topic of setting up your own practice group). Likewise, if you are already enrolled or have interest in a class, throughout these pages you'll get a sense of what to expect from quality Meisner training versus how to identify poor or misinformed approaches to the technique. Talking about how to teach this work in a book aimed at developing your acting might seem strange. To be blunt, there are a lot of problematic views found within the Meisner technique, especially when it comes to how to treat actors, so it's very important to look at examples of supportive ways of teaching this work as well as destructive approaches that, in my view, don't safeguard the actor's wellbeing. This is not done to trash all other Meisner teachers. There are many great practitioners of this technique in the industry, and having the means to identify them only strengthens your choice about whom you trust to mold and shape your technique.

My own background in both of these areas should hopefully help you navigate these waters clearly. As I said before I count myself extremely blessed to have worked with thousands of actors in varying countries across the globe, as well as having trained in numerous countries and styles, from Min Tanaka, Niki Flacks, Noh, and more. Meisner, however, is a special passion of mine. I trained in it for over a thousand hours myself as an actor under some of the most unique experts in the field, later becoming certified under one of them. The Meisner in this book is not the complete approach to the technique that I teach, but rather contains enough exercises and through-line to give you a strong overview of the work as well as the different areas in which meditation compliments it.

My background in meditation began where it does for so many people: from a personal need. I first found out about meditation when in the throes of recovering from a bad breakup. To be fair it was my first real breakup, and not understanding what to do with all those deep teenage emotions (i.e. hormones), I did what any self-respecting heartbroken person does: go straight to the self-help section of the local book store. Luckily for me, however, I came on an interesting book called *How to Expand Love* by the Dalai Lama. It seemed to offer what I was looking for, and the practical meditation exercises inside began to solidify what a technique of meditation actually looked like.

Soon after encountering this book I received a wonderful opportunity, which was to see the Dalai Lama in person at Stanford, where he would be conversing with various scientists about the role meditation could play in cognitive science. The back-and-forth dialogue between him and neuroscientists alone was breathtakingly eye-opening. It was my first insight about the many fields that could benefit from meditation. I began to wonder if acting could, in any specific way, utilize it. From there I encountered my first experience with mindfulness, practicing the late Thich Nhat Hanh's approach with a community in Colorado. Hanh was nominated by Martin Luther King, Jr., for the Nobel Peace Prize, and he even came during the time I was there to give a series of lectures. Seeing Thay, as he is warmly called by his students, speak and teach while on tour from Vietnam felt like being infused with a small touch of awakening. It was one of the only times I'd ever felt like I met a truly enlightened individual. In meditation I have been fortunate enough to learn different answers and perspectives from some wonderful teachers and mentors, including Reggie Ray, Al Kaszniak, Jerry Gardner, and others.

I'm not in any way a master of things, but together we can draw on the combined knowledge I have, as well as your own experiences as an actor trying to navigate the waters of today's industry, to create not only a modern expansion and rethinking of the Meisner technique but also a stronger personal technique that may offer you great help in the future.

Important Caveats

Before we begin it's important just to quickly cover two relevant points about this book that will help you navigate it. Firstly, the content is structured like a hybrid of both a meditation and a Meisner course. The big take-home there is that both sets of exercises are progressive and are going to build upon one another sequentially. It might be tempting to jump straight to a later chapter because it sounds like the ideal fit for your problem right now, but most likely you'll be dissatisfied with the results. Embedded in each chapter are values, terminology, and evolutions of exercises based on previous chapters. In the meditations, you'll be starting simple, gradually building a core discipline that continues to expand and take on new aspects. Whether by yourself or able to work with others, this book contains a heavy element of practice within it. It might require a little more time, but it's worth starting from the beginning on this journey; that way you'll gain the most from the content and will know if it is right for your needs.

Secondly, and most importantly, at the end of the day meditation is an exploration of the mind's relationship to reality. While this is fine for most people, it is often oversold in acting as fully benign and with no risks. It might surprise you to learn that many meditation apps and practices are under investigation by some good behavioral scientists. What they are exploring is the how mindfulness training can actually harm a very small subset of meditators, leaving certain people worse off. This is an emerging discovery, and no one is really happy about it to say the least. In an ever increasingly complicated reality human nature is desperate to have some things that can be seen in rose gold tones and as perfectly safe for everyone. Meditation, it seems, is beneficial for most, not effective for a few, and risky for a small minority. If this interests you, Willoughby Britton, Miguel Farias, and Jared Lindahl are just a few names currently working on unravelling this challenging situation.

What is this small minority of people for whom meditation can be harmful? Unfortunately, the characteristics of at-risk individuals are still being investigated, with answers slowly emerging, so for here it becomes helpful to introduce a caveat for you: not all acting techniques work for every actor. In the same vein mindfulness and meditation won't work for everyone.

As someone likely in the majority of people safe to practice, you're going to get benefits from these exercises. If, however, any of these meditations trigger something overwhelmingly dark, worsen an existing condition, or in any way leave you feeling unwell, stop practicing immediately and seek the necessary care. Nothing in this content is designed to elicit such a response, nor are these meditations intended to use or prod your past experiences. They are fundamentally concerned with your experience of *this* moment, nothing else. If your past experiences begin overriding this work in a negative way, that is a red flag.

To clarify this caution, experienced actors know that sometimes growth and breakthroughs are personally challenging. Shifts in our perspective can be uncomfortable. In both meditation and actor training, insights and awakenings can bring laughter as well as tears. If you have any of these growth experiences in this work, and the result is bittersweet, then know upfront you're not alone. We all live and learn. The salient thing to do in this case is congratulate yourself for moving forward, forgive yourself for any potential judgments about "lost time," and embrace your new knowledge and perspective. These examples, however, are a very different type of experience than one that leaves you feeling distressed, helpless, or at risk. Suffering through anything is counterproductive to the growth path in this work. If any of the content in this book elicits those states, it's worth saying again: this is not the intention of this training.

We've laid enough groundwork, and probably sown enough confusion and raised questions, that if we didn't do something practical now you'd probably chuck this book. Having covered our bases, as well as starting points, let's embark on what I expect will be a warm, joyous, and eye-opening journey. This work has taught me one thing I can guarantee: when the moment arrives, it is often far more profound than anything we could have anticipated. Let's begin.

2
This One Moment

Tidy Yard, Open Mind

It was a problem that seemed to have no answer. Kyogen had been up all night, combing through his various texts, sutras, and other manuscripts. For a student of many spiritual disciplines, it should have been a no-brainer. But the question posed to him by his new master earlier that day kept eluding him.

"Master," he had asked, "what is the ultimate truth?"

"To answer that," his master replied with a somber expression, "please tell me this: what was your original face?"

"My original face?"

"The one you had before you were born, before your parents were born, what did it look like?"

Kyogen couldn't think of anything on the spot but, sensing this to be an easy answer, he went back to his room and began confidently poring over and through his many documents on spiritual awakening. Seemingly nonsensical or paradoxical questions were no stranger to many spiritual disciplines, often having a clear, coded answer buried within them. He was confident his master had asked him one of the standard classics and, as such, the correct answer could be found with enough research. As the hours waned, however, he became increasingly distressed. It turns out that despite being the ninth-century equivalent of a living Wikipedia for spiritual questions, Kyogen couldn't find any suitable answer. The perfect student within him had been defeated. Finally, at sunrise, pale and filled with dread, he returned to his master.

"Well?" his master asked, noting the pained expression radiantly exploding across his student's face.

"I have no answer," Kyogen said shamefully. "Do you know the answer, master?"

Rather than being disappointed or smug, the master smiled warmly at this. "I do," he said, "but if I tell you it won't be the same as when you figure it out for yourself. You wouldn't forgive me."

"'But—"

'You'll thank me later, I promise.'

It was clear he was not going to get his answer and, despite his master's assurances, Kyogen could not be satisfied with his failures. He gave up his place as a student of Zen, left his spiritual pursuits behind, and took up life as a hermit and laborer. The world of spiritual discipline wasn't for him, he told himself, he was better off accepting his lot and trying again in another lifetime. He had asked for too much: the knowledge, enlightenment, and awakening were simply not for him. Brief side note to our story, you might recognize this mindset as a parallel with reasons some actors will give themselves when they mistakenly believe there is no hope for their career and it is time to leave the profession.

Some years later, having taken up the role of caring for a house, Kyogen was sweeping the yard which, on this morning, was an absolute mess. The night before a storm had torn through the area, casting debris and leaves everywhere. Some versions of this story cast a pebble as the star of this moment, others a piece of roof tile broken off during the storm, but regardless something small and hard was hidden amongst the leaves. Kyogen gave a particularly vigorous sweep, and the small shard went flying. Its dangerous speed was stopped by a nearby bamboo tree. Upon impact, it made a startlingly loud *knock!*

When he heard that knock, Kyogen stopped. The vibrancy of the world around him began to take hold. The sunlight was violently, beautifully bright. The singing of the birds was magnified a thousandfold, each sound filled with the richest texture. Colors, sensations, all jumped out with such magnificent definition, and yet everything blended into one whole experience. A smile began to spread across his face. His entire perception of life had, in an instant, shifted as the image of a kaleidoscope does when suddenly rotated.

Overwhelmed and slightly shaken by the experience, Kyogen rushed back to his room. He lit a stick of incense and bowed repeatedly in the direction of where his old master lived, hundreds of miles away.

"Thank you," he said through tears, "you were right. The answer is far better now that I have found it myself. Thank you."

Years away from temple and practice, living another life entirely it seemed, Kyogen had experienced a moment of true awakening. He had seen his original face and now understood his master's question.

The Two Halves of an Actor's Process

When I was in my final stretch with the Noh theatre in Tokyo, I decided to send out one last round of drama school applications. It was my fifth year applying, and I had told myself it would also be the last. I had begun to question whether formal training in a university was the path I needed. At the time, a wonderful school in Kerala was offering me a scholarship to study a traditional form of Indian theatre called Kathakali for at least one year, longer if I wanted. For once I had options so the thought of not getting in didn't distress me too much. It's often said that once you stop wanting something your chances of getting it increase exponentially, and it seems this was the case. After an interview with the Royal Central School of Speech and Drama I put aside any more thoughts about drama school. Several months later I opened my acceptance email.

The program at the time was, for me, the perfect one. Though the course was called Actor Training and Coaching the majority of it at the time looked far more like a structured actor training program. We would spend two days out of the week trying a new approach to acting, and the other two experimenting with teaching it. While it might seem this was the ideal for a teacher, in fact I found it a wonderful growth experience for me as an actor given that, alongside the exercises, we would also learn the reasons for doing them. This was a big shift for me. Particularly when it came to strands of acting more popular in the West, whether it was classical Stanislavski, the Method, or physical training, far too often in my classes I'd been given almost no explanation for why we were doing certain exercises. If I asked, and I'm not talking about a prolonged debate but a simple "Why are we doing this?", the common answer would be to stop overthinking things, that I was too much in my head and simply needed to focus on being in the moment. Which, if we're honest, to a confused actor this is about as helpful as asking them to consult a fortune cookie from the local takeout down the road.

Years later, reflecting on those experiences, I recognize that while it certainly is possible to be overly cerebral about something, in my experience generally actors get the message without much effort. If they are too much in their head they'll stop their questioning and go, "I'm just overthinking this." Intuitively most of us can sense fairly quickly when we are using the wrong set of tools to solve a problem. As a teacher having been on the receiving end of sometimes reasonable but difficult questions and requests for explanations, I also know it is far too easy to put the onus on the actor for a coach's inability to explain something. "You're overthinking this" is often code for "I don't really have a good answer for you, so bugger off."

The reason many actors usually have questions, sometimes a lot, about their training is fairly simple: most acting exercises involve some abstract or impressionistic components. In Michael Chekhov classes, for example, you'll often hear about techniques revolving around what is known as radiating. When it comes to being human, there's nothing inherently natural about radiating that also doesn't result in severe DNA damage, so it's reasonable for the actor to want to understand the concepts behind a tool as well as how to use it. Meisner is very much the same way, though it may not seem like it to some. The exercises on paper make little sense without the reasons and contexts for them, but a fair amount of Meisner teachers I've met and read about seem almost terrified to give explanations, concerned that too much theory will drive an actor deeper into their own head and that the optimal way to work is to "shut up and just do it." In my experience, very few Meisner-trained actors get adequate explanations, and counter to the fears of some this results in technical, not intellectual, problems.

If you've been a confused actor in a class, not just in Meisner but as well other approaches to acting, then you'll know how much an imbalance between doing something and understanding the ideas behind it can sabotage the portability of the exercises, tools, or skills to translate into practical results for your work. The benefit of this book, or any thorough book on this technique, is that it's going to show you what the balance of both looks like, the weaving of theory and practice. The small trade-off to approaching the work in this way is that, like Kyogen, you won't get all the answers up front. The process of discovering them in practice, and of seeing things fall into place, won't happen in the first few chapters, but gradually, and especially at the end, the whole picture will be in front of you. Most importantly, you'll be glad when they do come in their own time because you will own them both in understanding and in practice.

Three Deep Breaths

Here is the first of the meditation exercises. Though they may seem simple, they will build one on another, gradually deepening. There's also another reason for starting with small building blocks. In a guided class you don't have to remember anything, since the teacher or facilitator provides the instructions. In a book, unfortunately, you do. Given that the bulk of these meditations will be with closed eyes, there is a real risk of you having to open your eyes, look back at the page, and ask, "What was I supposed to be doing again?" thereby creating extra effort and defeating much of the real value in these experiences. It's better to begin with simple steps rather than too many that force you to continuously reference the book.

Exercise: Meditation 1

Instructions: Find a seated position that is comfortable. Adjust until the desired comfort level is achieved. Then return here. Begin when you are ready.

***

That's it. That was your meditation. Have a great day.

Hang on a second, you might be asking. That was it? How is any way is that a meditation? All I did was get comfortable sitting. That's not meditating! To which my response is, that's a great point. So let's use this exercise to talk about what meditation might and might not be. When you were just getting comfortable in your chair, were you meditating?

To answer this correctly, it might help to think about this first by examining what you *weren't* doing. I'll give examples of the most common pushback I've heard to this question. Even if yours isn't covered, I'm sure you can inject it to give reasonable support to the answer most give: obviously no, that was not meditation.

On the one hand, there's a lot of credit to be given for that answer. After all, to start with the basics, I didn't specify how you should sit or what you should sit on. When most of us think of meditators we often envision people sitting on their knees, back straight, chin slightly tucked, hands carefully placed in the lap. Or perhaps we see our meditator sitting cross-legged, either in the half lotus or full lotus position, planted firmly on their meditation cushion. Or maybe we see someone floating on a gigantic pink lotus, if my pack of Nag Champa is to be believed. We rarely imagine someone slouched in a La-Z-Boy, however comfortable they might be, as a prime example of an expert meditator. Even simply sitting in a chair is an image not normally synonymous with meditation. And yet, that's all I asked you to do, find a comfortable way to sit, any way you chose, in whatever position, and I had the audacity to imply this could be a meditation.

Looking at our expectations around the role even sitting plays in meditation tells us that what we are investigating is the *form* of meditation as we believe it should look. We often bring prejudgments to the table, cultivated either from our own practice, experiences, or pop-culture imagery. Differences in perspective can create great divides we aren't even aware of that may show up later in the work to haunt us. And the issue of form here runs deeper than just sitting. Consider the breath. Notice how there are no instructions there? Let's revisit the instructions and add one single line:

Instructions: Find a seated position that is comfortable. Adjust until the desired comfort level is achieved. Take three deep breaths. Then return here. Begin when you are ready.

Does this feel more like a meditation exercise than the first one? I would suspect that many of us would agree—some level of focus paid to the breath is a deeply intrinsic part of meditation. Entire practices revolve around the breath: counting it, labeling it, using it to direct emotion and energy. At the same time, before we consider lack of any attention to the breath as a slam dunk rebuttal, we have to ask if there are some early indicators this might not be the perfect answer. Consider in the newer version I asked you to take "deep" breaths. Must the breath always be deep in meditation? Are there other types of meditation in which breath is not the focal point of a practice at all?

Consider meditations built around visual imagery. Working with images that are highly evocative can be extremely rewarding for some meditators. Envisioning the medicine Buddha floating on a lotus might not do anything for some of us, but other people regard this to be the equivalent of physical medicine. On the flip side, rather than an image, meditating towards an intention is equally valid. Metta, an entire discipline, uses imagery to specifically target the expansion of loving kindness, even towards people you have not met yet. Breathwork might be a part of these meditations, but just as often it can be a small or non-existent element.

Breath is just one of many examples of our expectations regarding meditation. I didn't ask for any chanting either, or reciting special phrases or words known as mantras. Chanting and mantras are integral to several popular forms of meditation – take them away and you lose those practices entirely. We also haven't even touched on walking meditations found in Zen, mindfulness, and other formal practices. And what about meditative experiences?

Transcendent experiences, especially in nature, have been beautifully described by conservationist John Muir, who made communing with nature his practice (if you haven't read any of his works, they are magical). The lack of any seemingly formal practice or discipline in these scenarios broadens the possibilities in defining meditation to a near-infinite degree.

The definition of meditation, it seems, and more to the point the question of whether that was a meditation or not, is far more porous and slippery when we look closer at it. It shows a bit of time and care might be needed in this and the next few chapters to at times check in and make sure we're on the same page. It also makes me wonder if we have similar assumptions about acting that make it harder for us to ensure we were all on the same page as well.

So, we have an act of getting comfortable while seated. No breathwork, no closed eyes, no seating instructions, no seeming goals or intentions. Were you meditating or not? Well, let's visit a similarly challenging question that often begins most Meisner training sessions. In looking at how both of these questions are similar, the answers each might reveal a point of deep contact for you to begin your work using these two approaches. It also gives us a profound connection often lacking in many formal training programs that ensures we can work in the best way for your acting: a common point of agreement.

The World Around Us

Exercise: Present Moment Capture

Set-up: Wherever you are, find a seated position and get comfortable. Set a timer for 30 seconds, don't count the time in your head. If you find yourself in public, you may want to set your timer to vibrate rather than make a sound if it concerns you at all. During the exercise you can either close your eyes or keep them open with an easy gaze, in other words not searching for anything. The exercise will begin once you are settled and prepared, and start the timer.

Instructions: In these 30 seconds all I'm going to ask you to do then is listen. Just listen. As soon as your timer is up come back to this section for the next set of instructions. Go ahead, set yourself up, and begin when ready.

Second step: Having just finished, grab a paper and pen, or open a notepad, writing program, or app on your phone, tablet, laptop, etc. Write down what you heard, as many sounds as you can remember. The writing is a valuable aspect of this – don't try to keep all the examples in your head. You'll want to have a small list of answers you can reference. When you're finished, have a quick look over the following notes and examples and make any adjustments you feel relevant.

Notes/Examples: It can be easy to think that what you are being asked to do is a complicated writing exercise. There is certainly such a thing as too little information. It may be true you heard "stuff," or "noises," but the lack of any kind of specificity won't help you. There is, however, such a thing as information overkill. Writing, "The sparrow outside the window first began with a high-noted falsetto call which then descended into a guttural set of overtones which harmoniously bridged back into the falsetto, running for the entirety of the exercise," could fill David Attenborough with joy, but "birds singing" is just as good a capture of that moment. If you happen to know the type of bird, even better, but that's about the level of detail you need.

For my 30 seconds, here is my list of what I heard:

Creaking floorboards
The ice in my glass settling
My joints cracking
The neighbor's truck starting
The air conditioner coming on
Bird singing outside
Birds fluttering by my window
A plane overhead
The sound of the lights
My own breath

For me, what I have is a succinct list that captures fairly well what arose in the past 30 seconds. It's simple and accurate, everything we need for now. Some people I have worked with tend to treat this exercise more cerebrally, writing things like, "I heard sounds in my mind," or "I heard my own thoughts." In an exercise designed to capture the sounds around you, this is a little too much work for what we are after. While hearing does, in a scientific sense, happen in the brain, what you are looking for are actual sounds rather than imagined ones or distracting thoughts. If this happened to you, repeat it so you have a list similar to mine. It really is as simple and boring as just listing what you heard, with no extra value for cleverness or being creative.

So here's the question to begin bringing this into focus: when you were just sitting there, listening to what you heard and noticed, were you acting?

That's the question we want to start to get a handle on. That act of sitting and listening, was it acting?

Just as with the meditation exercise, let's first start with the obvious answer and the reasons I often hear to support it: no, that was certainly not acting. But why? The first common answer I hear is: where were the lines? True, no scripts were handed out, no dialogue or at least blocking to memorize. That rebuttal, however, tends to answer itself. Does an actor need a written script to be acting? The boom in devising, modern and ancient forms of improv, as well as the work of great filmmakers such as Ken Loach and Mike Leigh, suggests otherwise. Some of the finest moments in cinema history have stemmed from moments of complete improvisation. Sometimes a script is the plan to deviate *from* rather than stick to.

Even without lines, for others something major is lacking in the exercise: a character of any sort. No backstory, circumstances, or physical actions associated with a scripted individual. This is a much stronger objection, in my view. Most drama and comedy involves scripted characters, the majority of whom are vastly different from how you might see yourself. Many devising companies, including Complicite, Frantic Assembly, and Odin Teatret, incorporate characters into their storytelling even though much of the action is organically created by the ensemble. Many improvisers talk about sides of themselves to which they allow permission in their improvisations that wouldn't be expressed in the rest of their lives. Larry David, genius creator of both *Seinfeld* and *Curb Your Enthusiasm*, has spoken about how he views his improvisation to be a dramatization of himself, rather than how he actually behaves.

A persona, or granting permission to certain behaviors, doesn't cleanly fit the realm of fully scripted characters, but neither does it fit with the idea of acting without some degree of character either. It is very hard to find examples in acting in which there is no separation between the actor's everyday experience and what can be considered a character or shades similar to one. We also recognize, however, that powerful acting is a marriage between the character on the page and your authenticity. It is an extremely fluid concept, a far more negotiable variable when trying to determine whether something is acting or not. Given how flexible it is, character is not a cleanly reliable metric for answering the question of whether or not simply listening counts as acting.

The final argument against this question I often hear is a simple but valid one: there was no direction or audience. Yes, there's a task from a book, but that's hardly the same directing as actors encounter within the industry, which might focus on everything from blocking, to actioning, to delivery, and so on. The lack of an audience is an equal consideration. Theatre revolutionary Jerzy Grotowski remarked that what makes theatre so unique is its witnessing. Even on film sets, a high degree of observation is made of your acting work by the crew, director, and fellow actors. Certain actors experience this even more powerfully than when on stage, that moment when "Action!" is called and all eyes are scrutinizing different aspects of their work in extreme detail. Being witnessed is a crucial, perhaps key component of an actor's work, and it's missing here.

At the end of the day, there just isn't much similarity in this experience to what you might consider the art or craft of acting. There's no chance to utilize essential tools you value, from analysis to sense memory and so on, and though there was a time limit there was no real start or finish that made you feel like the job of acting was done for the time being. What the exercise lacked is what you depend on: a chance for you to utilize the process and abilities vital to creating character, excelling at delivering a quality performance, and securing more opportunities for yourself in the future.

Given that it seems like such an obviously easy question to answer, it might surprise you then to learn that, according to many of the values of the Meisner technique, you indeed were acting for one very crucial reason.

Changing Waves

Let's start with the most recent part of the discussion. When you were sitting there, just listening and taking note of what was around you, were you acting? The "no" answer is partially correct: you weren't doing the entire thing. There were no costumes, directions, scripts, objectives, and so on. These are all relevant aspects of an actor's process that must be taken into account, even if how much they are present might vary based on the project. What you were doing, however, is engaging with the foundation of acting in the Meisner technique. The phrase Meisner and my teacher Scott Williams used to describe this is 'investing in the reality of doing.'

To unpack this idea, let's return to the exercise itself. When you were listening, were you pretending to listen? If you were, unfortunately you've missed the point of the exercise, as well as the benefits it offers. The more likely answer, however, is no, there was no level of pretending. Nor was there any demonstrating of the listening. After all, did you put your hand to your ear, yelling, "Hark! What do I hear?" Probably not. For all intents and purposes, you were doing the real thing. That's what the second half of the phrase means, the reality of doing, or, in simpler terms, really doing something. Investing simply means giving your attention to something. As my teacher Larry would say in classes, you were giving your full attention to really doing the act of listening.

It may not seem like a big deal when we frame it this way. After all, you listen with varying degrees in your personal life. How's that special? Well, when it comes to your acting, it might help to look at it this way: in the exercise you were listening with total authenticity. The theory goes, had a camera been on you, or if you were on stage, your authentic listening would have made you look remarkably believable.

Authenticity is one of the biggest, and most complicated, questions for actors. We know that bringing a level of authenticity into your work is a prized skill, but it's often very hard to both identify and train it. Usually when you do get it, it feels more like a glimmer, something that appears mysteriously and then disappears, making its ability to be replicated questionable. Yet, here in this simple exercise you were able to bring total authenticity to what you were doing on command. And you don't need my assurance – you know full well you were being authentic in those moments. How do you know that's what happened? You wrote down what you heard. That is the evidence you were actually listening and not affecting or pretending. You really heard those sounds and captured that in your notes. Though we are in the early stages, the long-term implications this has for your acting and the shift to be made are fairly monumental.

In the Meisner technique, we call investing in the reality of doing the foundation of an actor's craft. Basing your entire process on this starting point marks a departure from many conventional ideas, tools, and entire systems. When I was an actor in training, and later meeting actors who had never done Meisner, I was shocked to continuously hear that many people consider acting to begin with something false. You, after all, are not the character on the page, and so from the get-go there is a degree of lying or imposter syndrome. In this mentality the metric of good acting, and the tools created to achieve it, becomes then to fool the audience that what they are seeing is actually real. Or at least real enough to convince them.

Though for many actors, the possibility of inhabiting another persona or walking in another's shoes sounds incredibly exciting, the Meisner technique makes a strong case that this is not the optimal perspective to root your acting in. Basing your technique on authenticity asks you to begin in a new way, and this change can be alarming for some. For one, it doesn't make your acting dependent on a level of fakery. Pretending or affecting convincingly might be considered an essential skill in the actor's craft, but as you'll see the fake-it-'til-you-make it approach often creates far more problems for the actor. Whether on camera or on stage, forcing a result is a surefire way to put across something you were not hoping for: the appearance of an actor forcing something inorganic to happen. Audiences are, by and large, intelligent viewers and listeners. They see your attempts to fool them. The beauty of an intelligent audience, however, is you can have it both ways: they'll spot your bullshit, but they'll also see when you are being authentic and basing your work on a high degree of authenticity.

Investing fully and authentically into whatever you are doing as an actor is a great skillset to develop and train. Every exercise in this technique will train that ability. It is also powerfully relevant to your needs today. If you look closely at some other approaches to acting you may have encountered you'll recognize that even systems that are based on imagination, pretending, or affecting do tackle the issue of authenticity. The popular viewpoint is the authenticity in an actor's work comes later, after character research, homework, imagination exercises, and so on. A simple question to ask here would be, "Why wait?" We've just shown it is possible that you can begin with the end-goal, starting where most techniques ask you to spend large amounts of time and effort to get to. If authenticity is where the work of an actor goes eventually why don't we just begin with it and train it from day one? Investing in the reality of doing is not the entire picture of what is asked of an actor, as we've recognized, but it is one major piece of the puzzle. The even more startling thing is you didn't need to think about doing it – you just did it.

Speaking of authenticity, however, how about that whole meditation thing? Let's revisit that and see how it connects into what you've just been exploring in the Meisner work.

A Flower Opens

At the end of the very first exercise in this chapter I asked: was this an act of meditation? Getting comfortable in a chair may not seem a great example of meditation. There's no counting breaths, specific postures, chanting, mantras, and so on. Yet, even in this simple act, we have the ingredient that unites all great meditation practices. In the same vein as investing in the reality of doing begins with an act of authentic attention, so too does this. To make yourself comfortable you first must become aware of two points of reference: your experience of yourself in the present, and then the trial-and-error of relating with the world around you to alter that experience. For example, if you were suffering with a particular injury, say a back strain or knee pain, the only way you are going to get comfortable is to first take note of how that is feeling in the moment. Though it happens largely unconsciously, the first step, this checking in with oneself, is rooted in a very powerful concept: experiencing the reality of now. You didn't have to imagine yourself any differently, or try to visualize or change your state. You were simply observing what was happening to you in this moment. That presence can't be scoffed at, particularly when combined with the level of awareness you had.

I mention awareness, but how do you know you had this awareness? The only way you could have become comfortable would be to have a keen sense of what was happening within this moment. The very act of getting comfortable in a chair actually reveals a level of engagement with the present moment. You sense your body, you move, and then you sense it again. Though the action may feel basic, this level of awareness and engagement is the seed nearly every strand of meditation practice depends on for its success, even if the latter stages may look entirely different from one another. This is an act of mindfulness.

Mindfulness meditation is seeing a surge of popularity unlike ever before. It has been documented to have numerous health benefits, from stress reduction to improvement of the cardiovascular system. It is an effective form of mental health treatment when combined with therapy and medication if necessary. Prolonged meditation practice has even been shown to benefit long-term neurological health, with entire changes occurring in brain patterns and functions. At the time of writing it is being investigated by numerous researchers as a complementary treatment for Alzheimer's, chronic pain, high blood pressure, smoking and addiction recovery, anxiety, immune health, depression, insomnia, and more. The interest in it is real.

Though it may feel like mindfulness has jumped onto the scene all of a sudden, its origins go back thousands of years, to strands of Buddhism primarily including Vipassana and Zen. Though the mindfulness explored in this book is entirely secular, and therefore compatible with any belief system, it is based on formal practices found in old-school approaches to meditation. Working in this way gives us a context of deep concepts and philosophy that can be applied to your acting in a meaningful way. Just about every time I've encountered a meditation technique oriented towards actors it almost always goes back to the same thing: general stress reduction. For the record, stress reduction is great, and more people could use it. Combating anxiety is certainly beneficial for your acting and mental health. At the same time, it's too nonspecific. Relaxation benefits just about everyone in nearly everything they do. There's nothing special about what it can do for your acting. We need to do better than that.

While you may feel at times reduction in your anxiety from the practices in these pages, reducing stress isn't the goal of classical mindfulness meditations. It may be a helpful byproduct, but we're after something much richer and more relevant, including overlapping results and values that can be found in the Meisner technique. This overlap is very exciting, because it implies it is possible that you can train elements of your craft both by yourself and when with other people. An at-home practice also suggests that when you do get the chance to work with other actors your experience will be more meaningful.

So, getting comfy in a chair: meditation or not? Certainly yes. An act of mindfulness, and training it, doesn't depend on complicated chants, rituals, postures, or so on. It simply asks one to be awake to this moment. That was your first of many meditations in this book that can be practiced just about anywhere. As you go on they will get deeper and more personal, but they will always remain grounded in simplicity and connecting with reality. That is a superb skill for any actor looking to make inhabiting the moment an element of their craft that can be replicated with confidence.

Common Ground

I keep alluding to values that unify both Meisner and mindfulness, but what are they? There are in fact many, but let's start with one by looking at these two exercises and asking what is the common denominator? What links your brief mindfulness session with investing in the reality of doing exercise?

That point of common ground where both the Meisner technique and mindfulness begin is attention. The act of paying attention fully to what one is doing is a key ingredient to beginning your work with authenticity. Attention's value in acting is rarely given the time it needs. I usually see it mentioned in beginning or foundational courses as something you *do*. "Pay attention to your senses, to your surroundings, to your cues." What is almost never explored is the idea that attention can be developed and trained like a muscle. Because most acting practitioners recognize it as a foundational element of one's craft, the mistake often made is the assumption that after awhile the actor has developed and trained their attention enough that the topic doesn't need to be mentioned anymore. Oddly enough, those same actors will then get to scripted scenes with a partner and be told mysterious things like, "You're not in the moment!", "There's no chemistry!", or "Be more present!"

It almost never matters whether the actor I am working with is a first-year university student or has been in the industry for decades: attention remains at the root of most actors' problems. When you are given obtuse and mystical-sounding feedback like, "You're not being in the moment," there is often a simple explanation at the heart of what feels like a complicated issue. As you will discover in practice, the ability to train your attention and give it to the important things will be of more long-term value to you than almost all of the character work, imagination exercises, actioning, visualizations, text analysis, physical work, and improvisations you can do. If it hasn't happened to you it's most likely happened to an actor you know: you think you've got a working process, built from months or years of doing strong, emotionally draining (sometimes damaging), and complicated exercises. Then the moment you hear a simple but profound criticism like, "You are not connecting with your partner," the whole thing begins to fall apart. Rationalizations begin to appear: they're not giving me what I need, the script is challenging, or though I don't know what, I must be doing *something* wrong.

In this scenario, just like Kyogen going through his texts to solve the puzzle of the original face you begin to realize you may not have the answer in your toolbox, no matter how much time and sweat you expended on it. At a loss for an answer, actors become overwhelmed and settle on the only seemingly valid conclusion: rather than the tools being a failure, it's you. You are somehow the one responsible for the crime of being given bad information. In my experience the actor is rarely at fault – we simply don't spend enough time on the priorities and make the critically problematic assumption that once attention has been trained a little it can be left alone. Unfortunately that idea leads to problems which compound over time.

Both Meisner and mindfulness meditation are keenly interested in training attention as a matter of technique. It's only possible to authentically do something as an actor once you give it your full attention. Investing in the reality of doing makes attention a core component – giving your attention entirely, without pretense, to what is asked of you. In the same way, even a basic mindfulness exercise like getting comfortable in a chair can only be done with a careful use of attention. Every exercise, then, in our work must sharpen this vital, essential, and far-too-often overlooked skill. Particularly when you are unable to work off any other person in the room, whether it is for a self-tape or a virtual audition or performance even, a well-trained use of attention is going to confer a defining advantage upon your work.

What's Behind the Answers?

Most likely I've already made, and will continue to make, blanket statements that may be jarring compared to how you are used to working. While most actors are generally comfortable with statements that may challenge their tools, in some this can unfortunately ignite a stand-off mentality wherein the actor perceives that I'm demanding them to give up something within their process they hold dear. I just want to be clear that I'm not, in any way, insisting you abandon views, tools, or perspectives you believe in. Those choices will fall to you in the end. Yes, the concepts you will engage with in both the meditations and the Meisner technique will ask you to change your views on certain things in the hopes that they improve your work. What you need, and what I hope to supply, is *evidence* for that decision.

Evidence is one of the things I am most adamant about when an actor comes to either a new approach or a new take on one they are familiar with. Every tool has potential consequences, sometimes improving your work while at other times setting it back. As an actor you are right to be cautious about changing or abandoning tools you believe work for you. I am sure you've had the experience where went to a new teacher or training system and had your brain completely scrambled as your process was turned upside down. For some that can result in months or even years of confusion. New perspectives ask for a major overhaul of our views and process. Every teacher and coach believes their way is the one best for actors and, while that level of confidence may be good for the teacher, you're the one who is going to be putting these skills to the test in the job arena.

The trap most teachers fall into is believing that a result in the classroom will be the same as one in the work environment. In the rare event a student tells them something didn't work in the field, the teacher finds reasons to justify why the system is fine but the actor must have done something wrong. This is a larger conversation not meant for these pages, but my blanket view for an actor is never believe that something works without evidence. In this training you'll be given what I believe to be strong evidence for not only the claims I'm making but why they will make your life far easier in an already challenging profession. The decision for whether they actually work ultimately falls to you ensuring they succeed where you need them the most.

It seems like we're off on the right start: make investing your attention authentically the core foundation of your technique, and train that level of investment both with other people and at home. Sounds good, right? Well, as with all seemingly good ideas, a challenge from reality rides out to meet you head-on. Now it becomes vital to identify and offer solutions for a problem that has plagued actors since time immemorial.

Summary

Both meditation practice and acting exercises each have their own set of priorities. For actors, the benefits of meditation are often too general and not specific enough to their unique needs. In the same way, some approaches to acting root themselves in the idea that good acting involves pretend and convincing the audience of the reality of an illusion. The Meisner technique's starting principle of investing in the reality of doing places its emphasis on authenticity, thereby addressing not only the demands of multiple mediums today but also the pressures technology has placed on an ever-changing industry landscape. Both Meisner and mindfulness meditation offer an evidence-based mechanism to train the actor's attention, a key component essential to success in any approach to acting. It is this question of attention, and its relevance to an actor's process in cultivating authenticity, that we must continue to expand upon in future sessions.

3
An Audience Within

To Be Seen

In the previous chapter we began to tease out some interesting possibilities which may have profound implications for your process. Rather than basing your acting technique on pretending to be something you are not, or that your job is to become as "convincing" as possible to an audience, we introduced the idea that it is better to root your technique in being authentic to whatever you are asked to do. The meaning of this will continue to unfold as the training progresses, but it begins with an act of attention. Attention is the backbone of the Meisner technique as well as certain strands of meditation practice. Mindfulness can become a complimentary practice for training by yourself.

Starting with this chapter, you are going to begin seeing partner exercises. These hypothetical examples will complement the independent work you can do alone. They provide a good sense of the structure of the Meisner technique as well as the values being trained. You are also going to begin encountering examples of both good and harmful ways to teach this work. We touched on this a bit in the introduction when I wrote that the Meisner technique has a history of problematic teaching, and that being able to recognize that keeps you protected when seeking training in this work. In addition, there's a further benefit to the value of you knowing how these exercises are meant to be structured, as well as the healthiest ways to teach them. By the end of this book, if you don't have access to Meisner training in your area, you'll now know how to set up some informal sessions with your colleagues. There are ways to facilitate this work in order to ensure it can be done with no "teacher" present. All it needs is a basic understanding of both the exercises and the principles behind them. Lastly, if you are an actor looking to teach this material as well as use it in your own practice, these explorations will be quite nourishing.

One brief note I would like to make here about the example exercises are the presence of pronouns that respect multiple gender expressions. Every example in this book is based off of a real experience I've seen in my teaching, with all names and at times some details changed to respect privacy of course. The majority of actors I've worked with have identified as either male or female, but on occasion I have worked with an actor who preferred they/them pronouns. The bulk of examples in this book will use the conventional he-she pronouns only due to my staying true to the experiences and individuals I've encountered. The lessons in all of these examples, however, apply regardless of one's pronouns and preferred expressions.

Exercise: Meditation 2

Set-up: Find a place to sit and get comfortable. For most people this is a chair with your feet on the floor. No need to sit on the floor in any classic meditation pose, though if that is what you prefer you are welcome to. Generally practitioners find that lying down is not as effective as sitting, tiredness being one of the main distractions. You can experiment with what you prefer but, for the most part, sitting in a chair works great when in doubt.

Instructions: When you are as comfortable as can be, close your eyes. You are going to count backwards from 15. The counting happens on the exhale. Breathe in, and on the exhale silently say to yourself, "15." Then breathe in again, and on that exhale silently say, "14." And so on until you reach 0. When you're finished, come back here for a discussion. Begin whenever you are ready.

***

For most people, this exercise seems very simple but ends up being extremely challenging. What makes it hard isn't the physical experience. Spending a minute or two sitting comfortably in a chair is fairly easy for most of us. The real challenge is the mental aspect. As you might have just discovered, even a simple act such as counting often brings up major obstacles. You may have started off strong but two breaths in that *one thing* you have to remember to get from the store might have come up. You might have had thoughts like, "This is stupid. It doesn't make any sense." You could have experienced a pang of anxiety related to your acting that seemed to come out of nowhere. Maybe you're beginning this book in the midst of career turmoil and that feeling hangs over you like a perpetual cloud now.

We could slot in ten thousand hypotheticals which all continuously point to the same issue: your thoughts are a distraction to your intention. Even more so, they seem to pop up out of nowhere. It's not like you can just leave a message for them to harangue you later. If you finished the exercise and thought, "I was a bit distracted, maybe I wasn't in the right headspace for this," you're not only not alone, but you experienced something of real self-teaching value. Any mindfulness practice that is dependent on a singular state of mind or experience is not one worth your time. Yes, it's easier to meditate when we are relaxed and able to focus, just in the same way it's easier to weightlift on days we are feeling strong and confident, but a mindfulness practice must be just as valid whether you are calm, anxious, focused, distracted with fifty things, feeling blissful, uneasy, and so on. It needs to be portable across your experiences, not easily halted when things get difficult or inconvenient.

The possibility that mindfulness is just as valid regardless of what you are feeling clears up one of the biggest misconceptions about it. Early in my practice, when I used to hear about mindfulness I tended to think of it as a stress-relieving tool. We go to a mindfulness class to feel more calm, at ease, able to better handle the challenges of our day. There are entire classes and schools of contemporary mindfulness who also agree with this idea. Nearly everything in these sessions, from repeating phrases to counting breaths, has relaxation in mind. It's what I later heard referred to as the "California cool" approach, and it happens to be the one recommended by organizations such as the NHS for health benefits (though the phrase probably hasn't caught on with them yet). Unfortunately this approach is neither practical nor helpful for your acting.

After finishing a meditation exercise you might feel a variety of things. You could be relaxed, at ease, totally blissed out, and that's great. You might also finish feeling distracted, restless, unwell, a little anxious – again, so long as nothing major is triggered that could be problematic to your mental health, those experiences are equally fine too. Stress-relief might be a byproduct of this work, and that can be helpful for your acting, but it isn't the goal. We are after something much more profound and rich for your acting technique.

Mindfulness trains your attention. It's a superb vehicle for doing that. It also opens the doors to other types of exercises from practices such as Zen that can do even more impressive things for you. What you've just discovered in practice, however, is that distractions can derail the experience. What do we do about that? Mindfulness is deeply rooted in reality, of which your thoughts are a part. If we make distractions the enemy to training your attention, we end up working against the reality of your experience. Persistent thoughts are a challenge to any meditation practice, so how do you start handling them?

To help answer this question, let's check in on the Meisner side of things and see if actors encounter a similar set of problems and questions early on in their training. If they do, perhaps these shared challenges can offer a common solution that continues to develop and forward your growth in this training.

Public Enemy

Let's take this concept of investing in the reality of doing forward into its next stage. Ideally this exercise should be done with several people, rather than just by yourself. It can, however, be done alone, which will still provide a taste of the experience. If you are alone, however, still read the examples and discussion to get a sense of how this exercise teases out one of the biggest challenges to an actor.

Exercise: Investing in the Reality of Doing

Set-up/Instructions: Within a group, everyone takes turns doing the exercise one at a time. The key factor here is that it is witnessed. You'll each bring something *to do*. I mean this in the most basic sense: a simple, physically engaging task that has only a minimal cerebral component or none at all. The task itself should be quite un-extraordinary. Let's see a few examples of this.

Example 1: Scott pulls up a seat in front of us. Having brought some polish in he begins to paint his nails, doing his best to ensure he does a superb job. If he knows his way around this activity he might finish the entire thing. If not, after two or three minutes, he'll stop.

Example 2: Reza takes off a single shoe and unlaces it completely. They then relace it, being careful to ensure it is even on both sides, until they put the shoe back on and re-tie it.

Example 3: In this hypothetical training session we are in a room with some exposed brickwork. Kate gets up and begins counting them. If there are many bricks she might choose only a section, or if it's just a single wall or patch she might do them all. Let's say the entire length of one wall is brickwork. She counts them all to herself and at the end gives us a number.

We've got three examples from Scott, Reza, and Kate. Let's explore each one a little and see if it can start to illustrate why this is superb training for your acting.

Beginning with Scott's experience, this exercise reveals how our Meisner training is gradually evolving while staying true to its valuing of authenticity. Scott's example is a perfect demonstration of our priorities. He brought in real nail polish and the necessary components to accomplish his task. Rather than pretending or miming the actions he invested his attention fully into what he was doing. There were plenty of opportunities for him to bring in imaginary elements, but rather than engaging with things not there, this exercise places the value on engaging with what happens in the moment. This can also be seen by the possibility of him not finishing. Let's say Scott is familiar with painting his nails, and completing the exercise within a reasonable amount of time is possible. Great. Likewise, however, if he has never done this before, then this becomes an equally good activity. The activity will force him to give his attention to getting something right while also juggling that it happens to be totally new to him. This tells us something vital: you don't need to do things you are skilled at to get the benefits of this exercise. It can be your first or fiftieth time, but a perfect outcome is not the goal. It's what you are doing with your attention that matters.

You'll also notice the length of these examples rarely goes beyond two or three minutes. While they can go longer, generally in the beginning this is a good time length because it doesn't push your concentration to the point where you become stuck in your head trying to work out whether you are doing the exercise correctly. The same golden window can be found in Reza's example when they were unlacing, lacing, and then retying their shoe. Reza was perhaps the most tactile and least cerebral of the examples. We like that because it minimizes the risk of checking in with yourself asking, "Am I doing this right?" Self-judgment and criticism can be a major hindrance. Reza minimized the risk of becoming trapped in any pattern of thoughts by having a deeply simple but clearly identifiable end result: when the shoe is laced, the activity is done.

For actors less likely to feel the pressure of self-judgment, Kate's exercise is the most cerebral but still tactile of the three. It's also the classic model example of this exercise. For a large portion of his teaching career Sanford Meisner taught at the Neighborhood Playhouse. The exposed brickwork there has taken on a near cult status, since counting bricks was so part-and-parcel to the experience of doing this exercise. Posterity aside, Kate's experience also reveals the biggest challenge to basing your technique on authenticity. Let's expand on her example more. I'll also interject myself as a coach and, along the way, start to introduce some perspectives on the right atmosphere for a training session. The example you're about to read is based on most actors' experiences in this exercise.

The Power of Being Witnessed

Kate volunteers to work. One of the walls in the room is made of gorgeous old brickwork.

"What about counting the bricks?" I ask.

Kate begins to do so. She uses her finger to keep track of the bricks, at times quietly mumbling a number to herself. Rather quickly she gives us a number.

"72," she says.

"Love it. How did you get that number?"

"I just counted the first row, which was 8, then multiplied by the top number of bricks, which was 9. 72."

It's a great answer she gives, partially because there is major potential learning value within it. The first question asked to the larger group is, "How was her investing in the reality of doing?" This type of a question is important because it frames how we are going to talk about each other's work in the future. So, before any answers can be given, I lay out the rules: if you want to talk about another actor's work, you need evidence to support your claim. Not your impressions or opinions, but specific, concrete evidence. As the coach I'll continue to monitor the early sessions to ensure we stick to this brief. In relatively short time, this fixes one of the most problematic aspects of working with actors, which is the desire to say about a colleague, "I didn't like it because it's not how I would have done it."

In my experience, this is a common habit most actors find themselves adopting. By and large they have been taught to think about their acting in terms of what they would do if they were in a similar situation. It's the type of self-visualization work that is applied to everything from carrying out one's objectives and tasks to how to handle an audition. Why do I want to silence this popular position and way of solving problems? The short answer is that it doesn't help the actor. In the moments when a colleague is working that will never be you. This is another actor working on their own process with their own unique challenges. Visualizing how you would do it doesn't help for one simple reason: you're never going to be able to have that experience. Even if you do the exact scene with the same lines, the moments will be different for you. When you apply the metric of how you would do something better than another actor you are envisioning a scenario that will never happen. That's not only a great way to drive yourself mad with frustration but it also doesn't do much for your own growth.

If you've ever been in an acting class wherein fellow actors are allowed to judge you based solely on their own opinions you'll notice how distracting it is, as well as how hard it becomes to remain open and available. If you're constantly secretly watching over your shoulder, waiting for an opinionated comment, you'll become more protective of yourself and your emotional wellbeing. To be clear, this is a healthy response, but it comes at a cost. You will be more in your head, stiff in your work, and less able to connect. Being evaluated by a teacher is hard enough; being judged by many gives rise to an instinctual natural response to safeguard yourself. Far too often actors are told their lack of openness is the problem rather than the circumstances around them encouraging them to close off. In any training session, if it feels as though your fellow actors have all become directors freely giving you suggestions about what you could have done better, it's going to become far too easy for things to feel personal in a non-productive way.

The far healthier way of observing the work of other actors is to put your own experience aside and try to closely watch what is arising for that artist. That way you'll have a better sense of what may or may not come up for you. Watching them encounter a problem, and then work to solve it, also gives you equally valuable tools. The hunger essential to any successful training session in my view is not the one that prioritizes your desire to know the future but to see clearly what is happening now. Hence, why we want specific, concrete pieces of evidence to support your theory on another actor's work.

Which brings us back to the question I asked the hypothetical group we are working in: how was Kate's investing in the reality of doing?

"I thought it was really good," one person says.

"Why?"

"When she was counting it didn't seem like she was doing it for us, to 'show' us she was counting."

"What gave you that impression?"

"The way her hands were so engaged, those small almost micro-gestures that didn't seem performative. She also went back a couple of times to double check her work."

This is what I mean by concrete evidence: looking at the behavior and actions of the actor to try to get at what was happening. Your opinion is still an element of that, but now it is based on evidence rather than general, nonspecific feelings. That's ground we can use to agree or disagree while keeping the actor protected. Another way I ensure the safety of the actor working is to keep checking in with them. It's minimizing to talk about another's experience while they are in the room and never offer a chance to clarify if our interpretation makes any sense.

"What do you think, Kate? Do you normally use your hands when you count?"

"Definitely. I'm a very tactile person, I need to have my hands engaged constantly."

"Perfect."

Another actor says, "Plus the mumbling, I couldn't hear what she was saying, it looked like it was more for her than trying to perform for us."

"Lots of people talk to themselves without realizing it," I agree. "Do you also do this?"

"Far too much," Kate replies, and we all laugh. Though it may be hard to feel on the page when a discussion is being carefully monitored the warmth in the room increases. Humor, even if jokes are cheesy and poorly timed, lets the actors know they can have a genuine two-way conversation about their experiences and process. It's a small thing but I've seen it work wonders, and sadly I've also seen what happens when the room becomes lost to hostility due to a teacher's lack of willingness to consider the actor's experience. It's very hard to move forward into the deeper waters if laughter is at the very least not possible.

That said, however, I also have a suspicion about a challenge Kate may have encountered. Though I've rarely taught in a space that could be considered pretty, by chance I've been fortunate to always be in a room with some brickwork. This has allowed me to see the counting exercise many times, and nearly always the actor tries to quicken the process by multiplying. Sometimes there may be a clue buried within that.

"I think there was ample evidence that you were investing in the reality of doing, and that the counting was authentic. But I do have one question, and it has to do with the multiplication."

"Okay . . ." Kate asks, a nervous tone in her voice. I'm well familiar with this tone. This is the tone that comes from the actor who was given a set of instructions, did them well, and then the teacher pulled the rug out from under their feet by saying, "But did you think of *this*?" The "this" refers to an outcome they wanted to see but failed to ask for. When a teacher asks you to go up and do something, and doesn't tell you some secret step to the puzzle, there's very little learning value in it for the actor. In fact, all I've ever seen it do is put actors in their head and make them paranoid about what they are doing. Scenarios like this are sadly a very common occurrence in how the Meisner technique is taught. What hopefully is clear, which will be confirmed by many examples in future chapters, is that the success of this work *depends* on the actor's input about their own experience. Teachers are not mind-readers, and to the extent we try to be, all that it communicates to actors is that there are people playing god over their autonomy. The experience of the actor is what guides the feedback in this work, almost never the other way around.

"I'll be happy with either answer," I say, doing my best to ensure she knows this isn't one of those trick questions, "but why did you multiply instead of just counting them one by one?"

"Well, that would have taken forever."

"To be clear you did absolutely nothing wrong by multiplying; if I wanted you to count a certain way I should have told you in advance. But, and tell me if I'm on the right track, I wonder if you had a fear of boring us."

"I think so. I mean 72 bricks would have taken a *long* time to count."

"That's true. But I wonder, what's wrong with boring us?"

"Well, you are the audience."

"And it's bad to bore the audience?"

"Absolutely."

"Is it okay to say then that the pressure of being observed is what led to you multiplying instead of counting one-by-one? That there was an audience and boring us has disastrous consequences? Either answer is perfectly valid."

"Yes, that's fair to say."

It must be said, I have seen actors be completely undeterred by doing something while being watched. It's very rare, and the entire point in exercises such as these is to bring out the feelings of pressure from the audience. Even if this is not the actor's experience, the conversation continues as normal. We simply talk about it in terms of what most actors experience, rather than that individual. Even if they didn't feel the pressure from the audience this time it certainly doesn't mean they won't in the future, so discussions about the pressure to perform and not be boring are always worthwhile.

Kate's experience reveals the essential challenge to the idea that you can base your acting technique on being purely authentic to the moment. The pressure of the audience, and to perform well, roots us in being concerned firstly with what we perceive are the needs of the audience. That can change everything we do, including how the lines come out and which behaviors, both large and small, arise in the moment. What we fail to remember, however, is that there is often a difference between what we perceive the audience to want and what they actually need. Audiences are by and large very smart, in that they can detect insincerity just as easily as authenticity. Furthermore, rather than being there to see *you* they are there to see people living out a set of circumstances – in other words, characters within the world of a story. If you are constantly trying to tend to them, all they will see is an actor not connected to what is happening around them, and the audience's attention will not be on the right elements. Your good intentions will bury your performance.

The often severe anxiety that drives an actor to be habitually concerned about the audience comes from a core belief more than a few actors hold about the profession: your job prospects, both the projects you take on now and future ones, are intricately linked to how happy you can make the audience. Unhappy audiences can quickly lead to a lack of opportunities doing what you love most. Feeding this anxiety further is also the definition of the audience. A working actor's audience is not only the people who come to see you perform on stage or in the cinema, but also your agent, manager, casting directors, teachers, directors, and anyone else who may have a hand in when your next opportunity comes along. How many times have you either gone to or thought of attending a workshop with a name casting director in the hopes that your presence alone might land you a role or connection? The ingrained mentality that you must be constantly taking care of others and "giving" in your performances can lead to you feeling like a circus monkey stuck on a perpetual loop. This is not healthy for your technique. Is it any wonder even well-known established professionals suffer from such severe anxiety when it comes to being observed by others?

Rooting your craft in being authentic to your own experience is a bold move, and it departs from many of the pressures the crowd-pleaser mentality places on you. In a few chapters we'll revisit the issue of the audience once you've done some more practical work. For now what we need to focus on is this obstacle the audience presents to your authenticity. What is the one thing that can interfere with your attention the most? The audience. The very same people who pay you to not give them attention are the ones who will unconsciously keep drawing your attention. That's a brutal irony if there ever was one. Let's take a look at the tools and strategies some of the more popular approaches to acting have come up with to transcend the hurdle of the audience.

Sorry, You Want How Many Walls?

The most popular approach hails from the grand-daddy of 'em all: Konstantin Stanislavski. Despite the many different ways to spell his name, the conclusion on him is fairly uniform: Stanislavski, by and large, did immense good for acting today, with an impact so vast it is nearly unimaginable. Despite living his latter years through one of the most horrendous purges on record and losing the man he considered his son and heir to his legacy, Stanislavski's work birthed and contributed to numerous stands of contemporary acting techniques still in use: from the imaginative prowess of Uta Hagen to the affective realism of Lee Strasberg to the devising techniques embodied by companies such as Odin Teatret (though rooted deeply in Grotowski's way, Eugenio Barba on many occasions told us that the company began where most fledging amateurs do: with the books of Stanislavski), and yes, even the Meisner technique is considered a branch of the Stanislavski system. Sanford Meisner himself was one of the founding members of the infamous Group Theatre, a hub of visionaries including Meisner and Strasberg but also Stella Adler, Harold Clurman, Elia Kazan, and others.

The question of the audience and how it impacted actors did not escape Stanislavski. Nor was the idea of what is known as a fourth wall his invention. Its earliest roots lie in the works of philosopher Diderot and later playwright Moliere, but it came to fruition in the 1800s during a movement in the theatre called naturalism. The naturalism plays of the times shifted from large-scale stories to domestic dramas and comedies, which demanded a new level of intimacy. While I'm sure scholars would pick me on the finer details, here is in my view the working actor's definition of the classic fourth wall: life, particularly drama, often happens within four walls. Since the audience needs to see the play, however, we should probably cut one of the walls away. For the purposes of the action onstage, however, that wall still exists. All the performers pretend that wall is still up and ignore the audience because, in line with the theory, they aren't really there.

This is how the fourth wall is often understood. While largely a technique taught to actors for stage I have on occasion seen it be used in screen acting training by replacing the audience in seats with the crew, director, and camera. Some acting teachers will even extend the idea of the fourth wall. What do you do, after all, when acting in a play in which the actor has to look out into the audience? Some theories suggest planting imaginary characters or images in place of the audience, thereby expanding the imaginary component essential for the fourth wall technique to work. Sticking with the general concept of the fourth wall, let's ask if, for the modern actor, this helps solve their problems. Does pretending the audience doesn't exist actually work?

From the thousands of actors I have met, taught, or worked with in my own years of training, the very brief answer is, no, it does not seem to help much, if at all. It goes against human nature itself, given how primed we are to be uniquely attuned to our environment. One piece of evidence that supports this is the Hawthorne Effect, which comes from the field of perceptual psychology. Its impact has been studied in various forms since as early as 1920, making it one of the oldest theories in contemporary psychology. What it implies for your acting work and using the fourth wall as a valid strategy might be deeply eye-opening.

In the late 1970s, researchers were trying to understand whether or not a potential treatment for cerebral palsy could improve the devastating effects the disease has on a person's motor skills. A treatment like that could make major strides in restoring quality of life. And great news – after some time on the medication, all of the patients reported their symptoms had improved. When the researchers looked at test results other than testimonies, however, the results weren't as thrilling: it turns out none of the patients had significantly improved. Not a single one. It had been a collective illusion on their part. Despite all of them believing otherwise, the experimental treatment had done nothing to improve motor skill function.

What was going on in the study that created such a divide between the patient's perceptions of what was happening versus the reality of the situation? The researchers did some digging and it turns out that all the extra attention the patients were receiving from staff, researchers, doctors, testers, and so on had done wonders for their psyches. The self-knowledge that they were being observed and were important improved their mental health, leading to the belief there had actually been physical changes. While we certainly like the mental health benefits component, it also shows how much the power of being observed can alter your perception of reality and the behaviors that arise from it. Nobody from the study was aware of how much their behavior was being changed just by the recurring fact that they knew they were being observed, but it did change. Our perceptual systems are very smart: they detect minute changes in our environment and adjust before we are even aware.

No matter how strong you believe your imaginative powers to be, you can't turn off your knowledge that you are being watched. The more you try to not let it get to you the more it's going to end up driving your acting performance. Turn it around 180 degrees from the audience's perspective. Rather than seeing you immersed in the action on stage they are going to be seeing you working to keep up the illusion and facade, denying what is actually happening around you in. That means you are going to be more immersed with your own experience instead of connecting with those around you. The same problems happen in a film take. The more you try and ignore the crew, director, and camera, the more attention it is going to drain from your ability to live in the reality of that moment. From the get-go the fourth wall has been a flawed concept, not in line with how human perception and its evolutionary roots work, and it has brought many actors, possibly yourself included, a fair amount of unnecessary stress and suffering. It turns out your instincts were right all along: denying reality is not a helpful way to support your quest for organic, dynamic acting in the moment.

If blocking out elements of reality is not going to be of benefit to you, even when alone or working only with other actors on a screen, we have to ask: is there a theory that can aid you in attempting to deal with the issue of the audience and the challenges it poses to your authenticity? The evidence is already stacking up that rooting your technique in pretending or attempting to fool the audience isn't going to work in your favor. Let's explore a concept you can make a part of your technique that favors being true to yourself in the moment and supports you in acting while knowing you are being watched.

Don't Leave Konstantin Alone in Public

Our hunt brings us back to the big trout of the acting world: Konstantin Stanislavski. While he was a proponent of elements of the fourth wall, he also came up with a unique and fairly novel strategy to incorporate into an actor's process. Recognizing the problems that imagining things not actually there creates for actors, Sanford Meisner further expanded on it. It is his version of what is known as public solitude that we can introduce as a possible solution for your relationship to the audience.

Public solitude has one major thing going for it: no matter how complicated your circumstances are, how unique your character is, or how nuanced or chaotic the staging is, it is always rooted in what is directly happening. Because of this, it fully supports your ability to base your technique on authenticity and giving yourself entirely to what is being asked of you without denying the unique variables of the moment. The giveaway understanding of it is rooted in its name: public solitude, to quote Stanislavski, can be best understood as the act of "being alone while in public."

One of the most helpful ways to make this more concrete is that, reflecting back on your life, you have already engaged in thousands of acts of public solitude. Perhaps recently you were on a train or public transport, your headphones on, listening to some music or a podcast. Were you actively working to pretend the people around you weren't there? No, more likely you were passively "tuning them out," or, in other words, absorbed in what you were doing without including those around you. Or maybe while driving and stopped at a red light you turned and noticed someone putting on makeup in their car. Are they imagining there is no one else around them? Of course not. They know they are temporarily stopped in traffic, that in a matter of moments the light will change and they will have to shift their attention onto the new elements of that moment. For the time they are putting on or adjusting their makeup, however, the rest of us simply aren't a part of their investing fully in the reality of applying makeup.

Reaching back even further, childhood is often a wonderful collection of public solitude examples. You're building the most magnificent castle created, a place so daring, imposing, and beautiful that nobody will ever find you there unless you wish to be found. As you carefully assemble the pillows in the living room, Mom or Dad comes in and says, "Dinner's ready." You say, "Just a moment," and then quickly finish your castle before going to eat. In that moment you were completely absorbed in what you were doing, fully authentic to yourself, and then just as easily you were able to exit that to deal with your parents, and then just as easily returned to complete your task. Public solitude allows you to handle unique, unpredictable variables of the moment as they arise, and to fully absorb yourself in each experience. In my own training my teacher Scott Williams would say it best: "Public solitude is a sliding-scale relationship with the audience. Sometimes they are a part of the experience, sometimes they are not."

Public solitude is about giving your attention to what has *relevance*. Getting better at identifying relevant elements is a major aspect of any good acting training, and moving forward cultivating that skillset is going to be at the heart of your experiences. In the moment, we in the audience might not be relevant to your putting on makeup, making a pillow fortress, or counting bricks. When you are working on camera or on stage, rather than trying to imagine observers are not there, which can create a horrible schism between how you are experiencing reality versus us in the audience, the other choice is to embrace it. We *are* there, you *are* being watched. We're simply not relevant to what is happening. If that changes for whatever reason, you won't be caught off guard.

One of the biggest areas I see actors continuously struggle with is auditioning. I've both been on panels and at one time was myself one of the so many actors coming into the room, asked to prepare a solo piece of text or music, or to read lines to a mark on the wall. As soon as I felt that pressure of being watched I immediately started working against the feeling. My defense mechanisms would engage and here would come either the hot flushing or equally annoying cold hands. The nerves and self-consciousness continued to rise, and soon I'd dug myself into a perpetually panicked hole that I would start bringing into future auditions. I don't think I'm alone there. Walk into the waiting room of any audition and you can feel the collective conditioned fear.

If this has been your experience, and you've begun saying to yourself, "I just don't know what's wrong with my auditioning." the answer is nothing is wrong with it. Even more luckily, you don't need years of training to fix it. More often than not the key to most actors' problems when it comes to auditioning is how they handle the issue of attention. If you've had the experience of auditioning for the same casting director several times, you may have noticed your nerves start to calm a bit when you see them. If you've had the opposite reaction, don't worry, this happens too. In the event you've experienced this slight relaxation, you may want to reflect that all that has changed is your relationship to them watching you. It might still send the nerves racing, but not as much. To put things in terms of public solitude, you've begun to be comfortable with not worrying about them, of letting them watch and do their thing because now you've accepted into your body that their observing you isn't relevant to you speaking your lines, delivering text, or performing your prepared piece.

Where we come to now is recognizing that it is possible to move past the first great challenge posed to the idea of authentically investing in everything you do. The mentality of public solitude empowers you to remain authentic while being observed. Mindfulness practice can equally aid in this by beginning to train attention without imposing the conventional conditions of having to always relax or calm the actor. Beyond just understanding it theoretically, if you can train your skill of public solitude, broaden your range of authenticity, and sharpen your attention to a new level, you open up a very exciting set of dynamic possibilities for your acting. It's time to begin putting those ideas into practice and training them, not just as concepts but living technique. And in the meantime, in the next chapter we are going to solve one of the biggest and puzzling challenges that has plagued thousands of actors for centuries.

Summary

The current question the Meisner technique has raised is this: how does the actor handle the pressures and implications of being watched? Large amounts of research in psychology show how an awareness of being observed can change a person's behavior dramatically. Conventional fourth wall strategies no longer seem to stand up well when stacked against the data, because it takes far more work to imagine an audience is not there, oftentimes at the expense of the actor's performance. The tool of public solitude involves choosing which elements to give your attention to without denying the existence of others, and may prove to be the strongest strategy for contemporary needs, particularly as actors attempt to juggle more work digitally where the optimal "conditions" for acting may no longer be present. While slightly in the background for now, meditation practice is going to become increasingly more valuable in supporting the transition of these tools from theory to working technique.

4
Miru Me, or The Eyes that See

Unwinding Threads

Whether you've practiced meditation for decades or have only heard about it in passing, a common theme across different approaches is the self. Though it may not be clear yet, both Meisner and meditation are intimately concerned with questions about the self and what to do with it. While nobody is under the illusion that the industry is an easy one to work in, it is also true that sometimes the thing that trips us up most is ourselves. Actors find themselves pitted against particularly difficult forms of self-doubt and questioning. One of the best actors I've ever met, and had the pleasure to train with, once asked me for a bit of coaching. She was feeling somewhat stuck in her career and wanted help identifying her biggest issues as well what she could do to improve on them. This was in London, not exactly a small town with no industry ties. She was in the heart of one of the world's busiest hubs, a place where an actor needs to be on their A-game.

The session took place in a friend's flat (for us Yanks that's an apartment), after the two of them had done a bit of scene practice. Her friend went to put the kettle on while we started to talk.

"So, Royce."

"Nadine," I said, getting out my notepad. Most of the time I don't use notes during a coaching session, since what is organically coming up in the moment is often more than enough to occupy the time. When it comes to career planning or solving more complex problems, however, I find them to be helpful. And was that ever the case here. "Can you put the problem into words, or is it not at that stage yet?" I asked.

"Oh, I can easily put it into words: I'm not doing enough for my career."

Nadine's comment was received with great familiarity. It seems that in any city I teach or train in, regardless of where in the world, one common theme disturbs working actors: they're not getting where they want to be, and the conclusion they come to is they aren't doing enough for their careers. The problem lies with them.

"Well, the good news is this gives us a place to start," I said. "Let me ask some questions to try and understand what you currently are doing, and then we can see if there are any gaps. Does that work for you?"

"Sounds good."

"How many hours a week are you working?"

"About 35."

"Acting or non-acting work?"

"No acting work right now. I'm working at a pub about twenty hours, and I substitute teach to make up the rest of the hours I need."

This type of information is also extremely helpful, because the strategies and advice that can stem from being busy with either acting work versus non-acting work are unique to one another. Believe it or not, there are plenty of actors working full-time acting gigs, forty hours a week or more, that aren't satisfied. One colleague of mine was regularly getting small roles in West End musicals and couldn't have been more miserable. Yes, it was acting work but not the kind he wanted. Had Nadine had a similar issue we would have focused on different elements of her career, but in this case she was working full-time with no acting work coming in. That's not a great place for any actor to find themselves in and, unfortunately, it's what happens to the majority.

"Have you got an agent?"

"Yes. He doesn't get me much work."

"Do you try and stay in touch?"

"He never returns my calls. Ever."

Unfortunately, this is also not uncommon. Half the time I wonder why actors ever keep the agents they have, but I would never say that out loud. As a coach my priority is to work with the version of reality you've built for yourself, not sit in judgment of the elements you deem important even if our views might differ.

"So you've got to find your own work?"

"Yes."

"How's that going?"

"Well, I thought I was doing what I needed to. I spend a few hours every week searching for jobs, following up with my contacts, and writing to casting directors and directors about any upcoming opportunities."

That already caught me slightly off guard. Generally when an actor could be doing more, this is one of the major areas I find can be shored up. Seeking acting work is a highly active, rather than passive, process, and a fair amount of work opportunities, some of them quite good, will come through your initiative to try to open a door for yourself. Most will be closed, but on occasion you'll get an unexpected bit of interest or, hold the grail high, a job you actually like doing. But Nadine was already working one of the major channels. Two or three hours on top of highly active full-time jobs can already be a major ask.

"How often do you see other actors?" I asked.

"Like socially or for work?"

"The two can be linked, but I'd place the emphasis on work."

"No less than three times a week."

"Okay, and what are those meetings like?"

"Two days I'm part of a scene practice group, and then I do my best to attend a networking event once a week."

"And that's a busy week for you?"

"No, usually in a busier week I'll be performing at one of the open monologue nights, or taking a class."

"Right. And how many hours a week, on average, would you say this takes up?"

"At least nine."

As I stared at my pad, basic math began to make me twitch. At 35 hours a week, plus let's round it up to 12 for her research, outreach, and activities with other actors, she was at 47 and counting.

"How about shows, do you get a chance to get to the cinema or theatre at all?"

"Always once a week."

Though some people might not consider this a valid use of time for a working actor, as a coach I always encourage actors to be actively seeing things, whether watching something or attending a live performance. The best insights into the industry, and the niches you may want to work in, come from looking at what is getting greenlit and reviewed, and what trends are emerging in the marketplace. For Nadine, however, this was another time commitment on top of some already heavy scheduling. I sensed a bigger issue was looming.

"How much are you sleeping?" I asked.

"Four . . . six hours a night."

"And how's that been feeling?"

"Not well, I'm . . . to be honest I'm exhausted."

As she should have been. Actors are essentially their own start-up businesses. Nadine was in the spot most working actors find themselves in: working full time, and desperately trying to stay busy in a relevant way on top of that. Burnout is a very real problem for actors, and spring 2020 onwards up until now has compounded the severity of it. Nadine is an extremely gifted actor. She was at the time and still is one of the best I've seen at work. Yet here she was, burning herself out, and the only rationalization she could use to explain her exhaustion was somehow, despite working full time and busily engaging in the industry at the expense of her health, she was the issue.

That mentality is what eventually led her to leave the industry. There were no red flags, no major areas she was wasting her time. She was engaging with professionals, working with them regularly, fearlessly (to the world, at least) and continuously putting herself out there. Even when we looked at the specifics, how the scene study classes were structured, the names of the casting agents she was reaching out to, if the monologue venues were good ones for exposure, and so on, after investigating all of that thoroughly, there was nothing I could see that jumped out to me as a major deficit in what she was doing. My biggest fear for her was her health, and I suspect her fatigue started to have a negative impact on her work, leading to a vicious cycle wherein she couldn't let go of the thought that somehow she was the problem. Eventually she began to wonder if she were cut out for it at all. She left the industry, returning a couple of years later for some small work, and has stayed on the periphery ever since.

How does that happen? How does one of the most gifted actors lose touch with reality? It was so clearly just a matter of time until her career continued to build and eventually caught fire. This is not an uncommon attribute of gifted actors: oftentimes they decide the industry is done with them long before it actually is.

Nadine's example tells us some things about this idea of self, or more to the point, what we could think of as the dark side of the self. Negative self-talk. A lack of self-confidence. Of course the self isn't all bad. A healthy abundance of self-confidence and self-assuredness is a marker of strength. One of the things that makes the self so confusing to talk about is that the word is used in so many different contexts. As we go through these pages we'll start to get a better understanding of the self by looking at parts of it that are both helpful and challenging for your acting. Let's see if we can start to identify one now.

Exercise: Meditation 3

Set-up: In all future exercises, this section will now simply read, "Set up your practice." This is because the set-up of your meditations will largely be similar unless noted otherwise. The set-up is the same from the previous chapter. If you ever are unsure about what this entails, come back here for that information. Here are the suggested steps for setting up a meditation practice: find a place to sit and get comfortable. For most people this is a chair with your feet on the floor. No need to sit on the floor in any classic meditation pose, though if that is what you prefer you are welcome to. Generally practitioners find that lying down is not as effective as sitting, tiredness being one of the main reasons. You can experiment with what you prefer but, for the most part, sitting in a chair works great when in doubt.

Step one instructions: **For this session you'll be doing 10 minutes of meditation. In this first part set a timer for 5 minutes. In this meditation you are simply going to be paying attention to a single point of the breath. While you're reading this, with your eyes open, take a slow breath through the nose (the mouth is perfectly fine if you have difficulty breathing through your nose). Notice that there are several places you can feel the breath: tip of the nose, back of the throat, the chest, the expansion in your stomach, and so on. Don't pick the spot ahead of time, trust that in the meditation you'll find it naturally. Once you begin the meditation just choose one point to pay attention to. When you are finished return back here for the second part of the meditation. Whenever you are ready, start your timer, close your eyes, and begin.**

Step one notes/questions: There are two points to reflect on before doing the next 5 minutes. Firstly, did you find yourself intentionally taking deeper breaths or guiding the breath in any way? If so, this is a common experience. It can be tempting to think that paying attention means directing the breath, but even in these few seconds of reading this section you've probably begun to breathe unconsciously again. For your meditations, you can begin with taking a few deep breaths, but then leave the breath alone. It's been taking care of you before you were even aware of it, it can handle itself for five minutes while you just notice it.

The second point is this: during those five minutes did you find yourself struggling to pay attention to that singular point? If you found yourself distracted by thoughts, this might start to feel like old territory: in just the previous chapter you struggled to count backwards from 15 to 0. Distracting thoughts, what in Zen is sometimes referred to as "monkey mind," is very much a part of the meditation experience. Some people who take up a meditation practice begin to find themselves only wanting to do it on days they feel more focused. It feels harder to meditate when scatter-brained, especially if you find you are judging yourself. What's that, actors being unnecessarily hard on themselves? You don't say! So, in this next part, and in all future meditations, if you begin judging yourself remind yourself of this: judgment is just another thought, and then come back to the breath.

Step two instructions: Set up your practice again if necessary. Set a timer for 5 minutes. Continue to pay attention to a single point of the breath. It doesn't have to be the same one as before. When you begin, you can take a few deep breaths to root into the sensations of breathing, but then let the breath come and go naturally. If you find yourself struggling, or being hard on yourself, simply notice that and come back to the breath. Whenever you are ready, start your timer, close your eyes, and begin.

Step two notes/questions: There's an immense power in simply noticing a thought, or feeling, without needing to give too much emphasis to it. Not only judgments but thoughts of all random types and sorts will arise during meditation: shopping lists, memories, things you are worried about. Just as denying the existence of the audience won't help your acting, denying your own thoughts won't help your meditation practice. They are there. The idea of simply noticing a thought is much healthier for your practice. Noticing a thought might be auditory, as in hearing the content of it, or visual as in seeing it, or just a sensation. What you'll also notice, however, is generally once you recognize you were distracted, the thought itself tends to disappear. Putting self-judgments in this category is a wonderful thing to do and yields large benefits over time. You don't need to tackle them head on and engage in mighty thought battles. Most likely you've already tried that and, if you're like most of us, you lost badly. All those epic struggles tend to do is reinforce how powerful those judgments are in the first place. Let's try a new approach, then, which is using the principle of public solitude to disarm them gradually: they are there, but they simply aren't a part of the task at hand, which for this exercise was paying attention to a single point of the breath.

The Power of Embodied Thoughts

Working with your relationship to thoughts, and how to contextualize them, is at the heart of mindfulness training. The goal is not to be totally undistracted. That will not happen. One's mind is present on day one and does not leave the practice, so incorporating it, rather than running away from it, is embracing the reality of being a human engaged in doing something. There is a similar problem in our acting when we find ourselves unable to handle distracting thoughts. Most actors I've worked with are trapped by the challenges of negative thinking. Self-doubt, judgment, and overly harsh criticism often hinder the career of an actor, particularly the need to keep going when things are difficult. Jobs dry up, and new safety protocols make it even more challenging for you to do your best work. It's easy to tell another actor that the industry is ever changing and periods of no work can be followed by ones of abundant projects and opportunities, but far harder to apply the same simple truism to yourself. It's often said an actor has to be their own hardest critic, and this might be true when it comes to learning from what is a clear mistake. Make it a general rule, however, and soon your inner critic takes a flamethrower to everything you do, making it nearly impossible to differentiate between when things are going well and when genuine improvement is needed.

To be clear, though this veers towards the topic of mental health, I want to ensure I don't overstep my own boundaries by stating upfront that I don't wish to change the way you think about yourself and your life. That is beyond my skillset and is inappropriate for a coach to step directly into what is best covered between a client and a compassionate, gifted therapist. What I do hope to provide is evidence that thoughts like this form a major technical problem for the actor: it's the nature of distracting, normally judgmental thoughts, that keeps you in your head and out of the moment. The roots of this in my experience stem from conclusions that arise during both training and working on the job: actors become convinced they must be constantly monitoring themselves. Whether it is ensuring that you are achieving your objectives, executing your tactics, getting your actioning right, or even more basic components like saying a line the way you believe it should sound, over time actors are turned into mini-directors. The belief that you must be constantly watching what you are doing leads to a deeper pattern, what can be called an automatic habit. After enough self-monitoring and censoring has occurred, the kneejerk response is to always be vigilant of yourself. With the attention constantly on you, it makes it very hard to openly give it to more important elements in the project, such as the other actors.

If constantly watching and judging your work means you are stuck in your head, and to many actors it does, then this is a challenge we have to address. Public solitude might have handled your being distracted by an audience, but it doesn't say much about what to do when you are trapped in your head, no longer able to break the cycle of constant self-monitoring after years or decades of habitual conditioning. The idea of "being in your head" might be a mystical, nonsensical phrase, but it remains such a challenging, monolithic criticism for an actor. You know how powerful it is when an actor is in the moment, and you also know how precarious it is when you aren't. Audiences can turn on a performer in an instant when they sense that individual is no longer richly connected to their experiences in the present. It's a fear that is everywhere for an actor, and yet very few of us actually, if we dig a bit, know what it really means.

Let's start with a very simple exercise and see if we can find a technical way to deal with the challenge of being in your head and not being in the moment. Such an exercise gives you the means to get out of your own way and continue to build on the authenticity in your work we are after.

Exercise: Three Moment Exercise, Version I

Set-up: Two actors sit in chairs facing each other. The distance between them ideally should be knees are close to one another but not touching. What this gives is the dynamic of no starting contact but being very much "in each other's space."

I'm going to list the instructions later, because a scripted class session can help clarify this exercise. In our hypothetical group class, Chris and Stefania are going to be working.

"This is called the three moment exercise," I say. "It's named that because there are only three moments in the entire exercise. So, it's pretty short.

We'll have you both doing it many times but just to state the obvious again: this is only three moments in time. Chris, let's have you begin."

"Okay."

"I want you to look at Stefania and notice something about her. What you notice has to be a fact. It can't be an opinion, question, or a speculation of any kind. You'll say what you see, and that's moment 1."

"Just say what I see?"

"Yes."

"Black hair."

"What about it?"

"She has black hair."

"Who does?"

"Stefania."

"Great. So, how about making it specific to her? Why not say, 'You have black hair?'"

Making an observation specific to the person being observed is an important component that yields deep riches. Consider the exercise when you sat in a chair, listened to the sounds around you, and made a list. If you had just written down "I heard some sounds," it might have been vaguely true, but there wouldn't have been anything unique to the moment. Making an observation specific to your partner makes it far more concrete and relevant to the moment at hand.

"You have black hair," Chris says.

"Perfect, that's moment 1. Making an observation of your partner. Well done."

Normally at this time the actors start to get worried. I'm saying to them well done for stating the obvious? Yes, and the value in that is only going to become clearer.

"Stefania," I ask.

"Yes?"

"Since Chris began the exercise moment 1 was his. Now moment 2 is yours. He just made a truthful observation about your hair. All you're going to do is repeat what you heard."

"Word for word?"

"Yes, but from your perspective."

"What do you mean?"

"Does Chris have black hair?"

"No."

"But you do."

"Yes."

"So if he says, 'You've got black hair,' you would say . . ."

"I've got black hair."

"Perfect. Chris, can you make the observation again and let's see both moments?"

"You've got black hair."

"I've got black hair."

"Two moments down! Now, since you began the exercise the final moment is yours, Chris. In moment 3, you're going to say what you saw in moment 2."

Here is often where I see some eyes glaze over.

"What?" Chris asks, unsure of what I mean.

"When you made an observation about Stefania's hair, she repeated it. While she was repeating, was there nothing happening?"

"I mean, she was talking."

"Just talking?"

"I'm not sure."

"How about we do it again and this time look at what she is doing."

"Should I do anything different?" Stefania asks.

"Of course not. Just repeat word for word what you hear. You don't need to help him with anything."

They begin again.

"You've got black hair."

"I've got black hair."

While Stefania is saying this the corners of her mouth rise in a nervous smile. This time, Chris catches it.

"You smiled."

"Perfect!"

Before continuing, let's take a step back to start to start exploring how this is a valuable exercise for your acting. Though it's a simple exercise, there is quite a lot to unpack. Each moment in this example was rooted in reality. That's the value of asking the participants not to worry about opinions, questions, or speculations when observing one another. Keeping the exercise in line with reality keeps you uniquely attuned to what is actually happening right now. Let's, for example, see another version of the same exercise in which Chris uses an opinion as an observation. To start getting us familiar with the structure of the exercises, I'm going to label the moments, as well as the behavior in moment 2 that prompts the new observation.

> (Moment 1) **Chris:** You've got black hair.
> (Moment 2) **Stefania: (crinkles her face):** I've got black hair.
> (Moment 3) **Chris:** You didn't like that.

It could be true: maybe Stefania didn't like that comment. At the same time, maybe she did and Chris misinterpreted her expression. If an arising sneeze caused her to scrunch up her face then Chris's observation would lose all accuracy to the moment. In fact there are many things that can obscure our attempts to read other people's minds. Someone might be sick or having a case of minor allergies, and we interpret the wetness in their eyes or redness in their face as emotion. In the same vein, when we are in a particular state ourselves, whether anxious, agitated, or overly joyful, emotion easily clouds our abilities to identify what is happening with other people. This ability to see things outside yourself clearly is starting to reveal something deeply inherent about this exercise: one mark of its success is based on accurate observations. Even if you made the most elaborate, opinionated observation in the history of your language it could still turn out to be wrong in terms of what is happening in the moment. Being accurate to the moment is a clue that starts to give us a sense of where this is going. Let's see a few more examples to begin solidifying the concept.

This time, Stefania begins. Chris has on a clean white button shirt.

"You're wearing white," she says, smiling.

"I'm wearing white," Chris repeats, nodding his head.

"You nodded."

Another great exercise. Now that they've both done one, the cycle resets and Chris begins again.

"Your nail polish is chipped," is his first moment observation.

"My nail polish is chipped?!" Stefania exclaims in the second moment, looking down.

"You looked down."

These two new example exercises are equally loaded with opportunities to be opinionated. Stefania could have said Chris was wearing a "nice shirt," and he could have observed her nails as messy or unkept. While these might have made the exercise feel more juicy, it would have come at the expense of the accuracy to the moment. Strangely enough, however, notice what Stefania did when Chris observed her nail polish was chipped. It caught her off guard to the point that she checked without thinking about it. It seems, then, that even simple observations have the power to be provocative and elicit bigger reactions than you may have thought possible. Now let's see a common mistake in this exercise and explore how it reveals early indications of the core value of the Meisner technique.

Stefania begins this one.

"You're wearing black boots," she says.

"I'm wearing black boots," Chris says, scrunching his lips.

"You moved your mouth,"' Stefania says.

"I moved my mouth," Chris says, accidentally breaking the pattern of the exercise by creating a fourth moment. He slaps his forehead when he realizes he's added an extra moment where there shouldn't be.

"Great," I say, "so we've just discovered something about the exercise. Even though 1–2–3 might feel like a simple set of steps, it can be easy to take the simplicity for granted and lose the structure when we get distracted."

"Yes, I think that's what happened," Chris nods.

"Luckily there's a very easy way to solve that. Notice that there's nothing in the instructions about speed. So, since we're not committed to a particular pace, there's a real value in slowing things down. To help you better keep track, in between each exercise take a nice, long moment to settle yourselves before starting the next one."

They both take the idea, as well as a deep breath, onboard. Chris starts the next exercise.

"You're wearing earrings," he says, pointing.

"I'm wearing earrings," Stefania says, touching her ear.

"You touched your ear."

They settle, breathe, and now it is Stefania's turn to begin.

"You're wearing a necklace," she says.

"I'm wearing a necklace," Chris repeats, smiling in spite of himself.

"You smiled."

Looking at the numerous examples we have here, a few ideas might be slowly emerging. Firstly, let's look at the structure of the exercise. Rather than Chris or Stefania, I'm going to temporarily label the two people in the exercise as A and B. It doesn't matter who begins the exercise, but whoever starts becomes partner A. Here then is the layout of the exercise:

> Moment 1: A makes an observation about B.
> Moment 2: B repeats the observation.
> Moment 3: A says what they saw in moment 2.

After a pause happens, the same exercise begins only now with partner B starting. Once they are finished, it's A's turn again. It's a simple, cyclical exercise, and the pause in between rounds encourages everyone to not make a race out of it and memorize the structure. But what is the richer, deeper value on offer in this exercise?

Let's revisit the concept of being in the moment. How does an actor know when they are in the moment? Some would say it's something that just happens organically. While acting you suddenly might feel more connected, in tune with your fellow actors, receptive to the sights, sounds, and feelings around you. The feedback you receive? "You were so connected, you just flowed! How did you do that?" Either you admit you don't really know, or you believe you do know and when you try to replicate it the result is disappointing: the next time you still give it your best, but now it feels like more effort. That flow and ease is gone. Even worse, this can compound: having touched an experience in which everything just fell into place, you become increasingly more anxious about it *not* happening again. Trying to retrieve it drives you deeper into your head. This can lead to consequences in your performance on either stage or screen, potentially resulting in fewer opportunities for you.

This is why "being in the moment" is a pointless exercise in semantics. Everyone seems to be able to recognize it and yet almost no one is able to talk about it in replicable terms. It's needlessly become the holy grail of anxiety in acting: to be in the moment, fully alive, or completely screwed when not. The way most of us talk about the actor in the moment is totally unsustainable for making it a part of your acting toolbox, and yet we have to recognize that when people use this phrase it points to a genuine problem. Fewer things are a bigger challenge to your authenticity than the inability to connect fully with the present and what is happening around you.

The three moment exercise solves this problem for you completely. Even harder to believe, you don't need to do it for months or years on end to learn to be consistently in the moment. Once it falls into place for you, as it does for nearly every actor who does this, you'll find yourself being surprised at how overly complicated other people make the issue of the moment.

Let's approach it with a simple question: when you are on stage or on camera, trapped in your head, being nagged by judgmental, distracting, or critical thoughts, are you being in the moment? Most of us would say no, but hang on – aren't you still in the moment? You just happen to be stuck in your head in this moment, but you haven't exited time itself. What's the big deal, then? Many of us would rightfully groan at this and say that's not what we mean when we are worried about being in the moment. At the same time, however, this tells something unique, which is that there is a clear example of what being in the moment *doesn't* look like. Excluding being stuck in your head as a valid example gives us a clue for what being in the moment should look like.

Let's break down the three moment exercise down and notice something new. We'll use an example from Chris and Stefania.

> (Moment 1) **Chris:** You've got black hair.
> (Moment 2) **Stefania:** I've got black hair. (smiles)
> (Moment 3) **Chris:** You smiled.

In this example, what's special about the observation in moment 1? It's a fact rooted in reality, so that's great, but beyond that not much. In fact, when compared to moment 3, something about it seems to lose steam. But why? Consider that so far the moment 1 examples aren't unique to any moment in time. The probability of Stefania's hair color changing during their session is extremely low. It's a great observation because it is anchored in something true, but Chris could in theory make that his starting observation 15 times. What about her smile, however? Now that was special to this experience. It arose in the moment she was repeating, and then was gone the next. How was Chris able to catch that? Only by being fully in the moment with her.

This is the takeaway of the three moment exercise. It offers a way to capture the moment by design. How did Chris know he was in the moment? He observed something that was unique to moment 2. He only could have done that by being present in the moment with Stefania. He wasn't in his head but richly with her. You can go back over every example and find evidence of this. It sounds simple, but the moment itself has never been a complicated experience – only the fretting, anxiety, and fuss we make over it. Let's see a few more. I'm going to script them similarly to the previous ones so we can keep getting comfortable with the technical structure.

> (Moment 1) **Stefania:** You're wearing a wedding ring.
> (Moment 2) **Chris:** I'm wearing a wedding ring. (laughs)
> (Moment 3) **Stefania:** You laughed.

Pause

> (Moment 1) **Chris:** Your shirt is red.
> (Moment 2) **Stefania:** My shirt is red. (blinks)
> (Moment 3) **Chris:** You blinked.

Pause

> (Moment 1) **Stefania:** You're wearing jeans.
> (Moment 2) **Chris:** I'm wearing jeans. (adjusts in his chair)
> (Moment 3) **Stefania:** You moved in your chair.

Each time, these actors are saying what they see. It doesn't matter if it's simple, that can be built upon. What matters is how intimately and clearly they captured the moment. This is a technical means to train yourself to isolate the moment each time you do this exercise. What's more, it reveals that in acting there is a way to think about being in the moment that you can take with you into any arena, and that is paying attention to what is relevant. When you are stuck in your head, thinking about what you're going to do next, your attention is focused on something irrelevant. The audience isn't there to see you try to work out something intellectually. They want you to live out the story and character you're playing, and the first way to do that is to ensure you are giving your attention to what matters. Your fellow actors are filled with rich, temporary behaviors that you'll miss if you don't pay attention to them. These little momentary behaviors are what root you into *this* performance, or *this* take. This is why when most actors try to be their own director, they end up trapped, their habits blinding them from connecting with the simple but profound variables that make up each performance. In this exercise, not only are you sharpening your ability to cleanly observe what matters, but you are also working on rooting yourself into the moment each time. That is a habit that will serve you well and, should you ever find your ability to connect waning, you now have the exercise that can replicate those results each time.

There's a lot of material to cover in the three moment exercise, and so we'll break here. In the next chapter we'll not only continue to develop your observations but also identify new challenges that come up against your process, building towards an even more profound experience of interconnected acting. We've solved one of the biggest challenges actors grapple with, and now it's time to take the journey into even deeper, more exciting possibilities for your tools and artistic process.

Summary

The self is perhaps one of the most challenging aspects of meditation. There are numerous ways to talk about it; so many in fact that it can lose meaning. One way to begin understanding the idea of self for you as an actor is to identify which elements of it can cause problems. Self-judgment, doubts, and over-monitoring are just a trio of numerous challenges created by our self and identity. Mindfulness allows an actor to begin investigating the self, as well as providing a means to recontextualize the power of judgment, criticisms, and distracting thoughts. This points the way to the challenges of not being in the moment as well as being trapped in one's head, two of an actor's biggest concerns. An actor's thoughts and distractions often become a force of habit, nearly impossible to break without a return to the meaning of the moment. A version of Meisner's three moment exercise developed by the Impulse Company offers actors a clean way to orient themselves into the moment each time, solving the problem of being trapped in one's head and making the question of the moment a matter of replicable technique rather than unsolvable mystery.

5
The Ounce You've Been Waiting For

Expanded Presence

Sometimes, though not always, people have some misconceptions about what it means to go deeper into the experience of meditation. One might believe they'll descend into some sort of esoteric, ethereal mindset where they are constantly on a cloud of enlightenment. Unfortunately, or fortunately depending on your perspective, meditation isn't an exit from the world. Rather it's a re-entry into it, a way to rediscover certain aspects of life that roots you more firmly into an experience that feels more aware, or awake. When it comes to your acting, constant distractions can be a major source of suffering. From self-judgments to anxieties about your career path, the common denominator is almost always the same: a disconnect from the present moment. Learning how to reclaim your attention and give it to the immediate variables around you won't solve your problems; those will still be there and they need to be dealt with. What that skill will do, however, is empower you to handle things in proportion rather than being swept away by a tide of concerns, worries, and distractions that grow so large they paralyze your ability to take action or do anything about them.

A major element of meditation practice is exploring your own consciousness. Your perception of reality is inseparable from how you experience it, and so discovering yourself in relation to the world around you is a key component in understanding how it impacts you and your behaviors. This is the seemingly paradoxical nature of practice: though you can never disconnect from yourself, you can begin to loosen the grip your perception holds over things. Piercing your daily experiences with moments of mindfulness, wherein you might suddenly catch yourself having been lost in thought, softens the perceived difference between yourself and the rest of the world. This isn't the same as losing yourself – rather, it's losing the need you hold over yourself to be constantly unique and different. It's that pressure that can cloud you from the present moment, the very same moment you are being asked to inhabit as an actor.

Exercise: Meditation 4

Set-up: Set up your practice.

Step one instructions: For this session you'll be doing 10 minutes of meditation. Set a timer for 5 minutes. In this meditation begin with a single point of the breath, but now if other sensations in the body arise notice them. The feelings of the breath aren't the only ones that arise from the body. Notice what else comes up. If you find your attention getting too distracted simply come back to the breath. You're slowly going to begin expanding your field of awareness. When you are finished return here for the second part of the meditation. Start your timer, close your eyes, and begin when ready.

Step one notes/questions: During those 5 minutes, did you find yourself at times distracted by thoughts? If you did, try simply noticing the thought. You may find that as soon as you pay attention to it, it goes away. Paying attention to a thought doesn't necessarily mean following or fixating on it. If you're making dinner for a friend this evening and are anxious about the recipe, telling yourself "I'll just quickly think through it and then get back to meditating" won't help. You might have noticed by now that distractions never stop, and so attempting to barter with them isn't the optimal strategy. Noticing a thought, either by saying to yourself, "I was thinking about the recipe," or seeing it visually and clearly, is often enough for it to disappear. If more thoughts arise in your next 5 minutes, experiment with this and see if it helps. Once a thought disappears, return to the breath.

Step two instructions: Set up your practice again if necessary. Set a timer for 5 minutes. In this meditation continue to pay attention to sensations that arise within your experience. It might be feelings of pressure from your body in the chair or the cushion, or your feet on the floor. Maybe there is tingling, pain, or tension. If the room is cold, or hot, where do you feel that on your body? Note here that the goal isn't to scatter your attention and document everything as it is happening. Start with the breath, and then notice what arises. When you begin, you can take a few deep breaths to root into the sensations of breathing, but then let the breath come and go naturally. Start your timer, close your eyes, and begin when ready.

Step two notes/questions: Though it might sound controversial, there's nothing particularly special about the breath. It's an automatic function we aren't aware of 99% of the time. That we can become aware of it, however, makes it a superb refuge if your attention is being thrown around the place. It doesn't need a mystical infusion to be valuable. Its power is that it is a reliable anchor point and will always be with you. This makes it a convenient reference point if you ever find yourself constantly distracted.

It can be easy to judge yourself for being scatter-brained, giving rise to that doubting voice that suggests this isn't the right time to practice. The rationalization that a meditation practice isn't for you because it doesn't always feel good is a convenience trap. Most of the time we don't feel good. That doesn't mean we feel bad, but the majority of our daily experience tends to be spent somewhere in the middle, just trying to get through the day. Is your mind going all over the place and giving you trouble? That is your meditation for the session, then. Notice the distractions for what they are and then come back to the breath. If they bother you again, pay attention again. There's nothing glamorous about a practice some days. Meditate while calm, and meditate while absolutely distracted. Rinse-and-repeat is where it counts.

On the other hand, you might have also begun to discover glimmers of physical vibrancy. The human body is a brilliant repository of momentary sensations. Oftentimes we dull these. We have to get to work, and so try to ignore if we are feeling more anxious or calm on a given day. Maybe cold is affecting you more, or there's a minor pain in your arm because you were good and got your vaccine. Little details such as these often reveal the unique nuances of the moment. What's more, without our awareness they come and go. Training your attention to notice your own experience is a strong way to keep connecting with the relevant variables of the moment. True, sensations in your body are inside you versus outside, but the habit of attuning to what is happening around you begins first with understanding where you are in any given moment. A practice that openly deals with distracting thoughts and judgments can help you better connect with the world around you. By placing them within a context of being part of, rather than dominating, your experience, you begin to slowly wake up to other present elements of your life.

Exercise: Three Moment Exercise Version I, Continued

When last we left the three moment exercise, we were onto some very exciting possibilities, starting with its potential to solve one of the biggest challenges actors face: the moment itself. Through the simple act of consistently isolating single moments in time you begin the process of training yourself to think of the moment not as some ethereal concept but as something technical, rooted firmly in attention being directed outside yourself. The exercise, however, also began to imply there was far more depth on offer, and this is where we are picking up. This earliest version of the three moment exercise carries within it a lot of content and ideas; breaking it up helps to simplify the work and isolate one major variable at a time. Where this drill is leading, however, is solving another daunting challenge for you.

As a refresher, let's look at the structure of how a three moment exercise goes with partners A and B.

A begins by making a truthful observation of partner B. This is moment 1.

B repeats the observation as they hear it from their point of view. This is moment 2.

A says what they saw in moment 2. This is moment 3, and the end of the exercise.

A and B take a moment to reset, and now it is B's turn to begin the exercise.

Pausing in between each exercise helps everyone keep track of the order. At the same time, however, we have to start asking: can we begin to mine more quality out of the experience? It's true that we don't know what the moment is going to be until it arrives. If you and your partner plan what behaviors to feed each other in your moment 2's, you've lost all the value of the exercise. Your partner doesn't know what you are going to observe, and you don't know what they are going to do when they repeat. The only way to know the moment is to wait until it arrives.

The key to any moment, however, is observation. Clear observation is the only way you can identify what is happening in a given moment. How then can you begin sharpening your attention to detail, thereby ensuring you get the most out of each moment with your fellow actor? Let's see if the three moment exercise offers any possibilities for how you can improve your ability to observe and clearly identify each moment as it arises even better than you already have been.

So far across all the examples, we have seen two types of observations that can be cleanly categorized. The first is the type of observation that begins each exercise, and that is simple facts. Noticing that your partner has black hair, is wearing jeans, or is sporting a wedding band are some of the observations we saw from Chris and Stefania in the previous exercise. These types of observations are rooted in basic facts, or as we'll call them, basic observations (sometimes I use the word "call" in place of "observation," but it means the same thing). In this work we love basic observations. They are a bread-and-butter call you can always revert back to if you find yourself stuck in your head. They may be true across many moments, and so not as specific to any one in particular, but basic facts remain extremely valuable calls. When you are working on the job and for whatever reason find yourself distracted, unsure, or feeling unwell about your work, see if you can notice something basic about another actor or the person reading lines. Are they wearing jeans? Do they have any rips or unique styles? If a blouse, are there buttons, strings, etc.? How about jewelry of any sort? Starting with something simple and true might be all that you need to reorient yourself in the moment.

For the Meisner technique, basic facts form the bottom of a hierarchy of observations. My Meisner teacher Scott called it "the hierarchy of calls," and I've heard other Meisner teachers use similar terms. To begin finding our way into this hierarchy, let's ask if a basic call is at the bottom, what is one step above? In this session, we'll have Savannah and Noel work, and maybe their exercises will start to reveal the answers.

Savannah begins. She and Noel both take a moment to settle themselves before starting.

"Your socks are brown," she says, noticing the line of them peaking over Noel's high tops.

"My socks are brown," Noel repeats, scrunching her nose.

"You crinkled your nose."

The observation made in moment 1 is superb. Savannah called what jumped out to her and that it was a fine detail added a lovely layer to the experience. This reveals two important attributes of the exercise. Firstly, you don't need to search for what to observe – almost always it will jump out at you in the moment. If Savannah had looked Noel over and decided the socks were the most interesting thing to name, she would have been layering on more than what was present in the moment. Bringing your own interpretive powers to the moment, as we have been seeing, is a great way to end up trapped in your own head. Rather than assessing the moment, this exercise asks you to simply observe it. Second, though the socks were a small detail, size doesn't matter when it comes to an observation. If Noel had been wearing a large, oversized shirt then that would have been just as good. What matters is that the socks caught Savannah's attention and she said what she saw.

Though the observation made in the first moment was strong, do you notice something more prominent about the observation in the third moment? Let's say I ask the two actors the same question.

"Qualitatively, does it feel different than moment 1?"

"Yes," Savannah says, and this is often the answer given.

"How so?"

"There's something much more . . . 'in-the-moment' about it."

"Because?"

"Well, she didn't crinkle her nose before she said that, and she stopped afterwards."

"It felt more personal," Noel adds in.

"It seemed that way," I agree. "In the third moment of every exercise, what are you observing in your partner?"

"What they do?" Noel asks.

"Yes, and what are some of those things that you've seen already?"

"Facial expressions . . . body language," Savannah says.

"Movements," Noel chimes in.

"Perfect," I say, and I mean it – though they may not realize it yet, we're moving towards something profound for their acting. "What's a word that describes all of those things?"

"Behavior?" Noel asks.

Bingo. Looking at the examples here and in the previous chapter, we can see that first moments often begin with a simple, basic observation, while third moments almost always end with an observation of behavior. To be clear, this isn't a hard and fast rule of the exercise. The instruction for moment 3 is to "say what you saw," not "observe only your partner's behavior." If as your partner is repeating in the second moment you suddenly notice their shirt is torn, you very well could observe, "You've got a rip in your shirt!" These are, however, exceptions. More often than not behavior is what is going to be observed. But what is so special about behavior when it comes to your acting? What makes it not an equal but a better thing to observe in your fellow actor?

To start getting a handle on this, let's ask what makes a basic observation less valuable. Consider the brown socks. Most likely, unless a dramatic sock change occurs, that observation is going to be true for the entire training session. True is good, but that it can be true in every moment lets a little air out of the momentary nature of acting. There isn't as much immediacy to it. Behavior, on the other hand, is entirely momentary. It arises and, if you miss it, it will be gone before you knew it was there. At the Impulse Company Scott Williams would often say, "Behavior is the currency actors spend and receive in a performance," and Meisner himself even had a quintessential phrase associated with his training: "An ounce of behavior is worth a pound of words."

The ability to clearly observe behavior is a doorway into the moment. It's very true that when you are trapped in your head, distracted by your own anxiety or self-monitoring, you're still in the moment. You can't exit the space-time continuum, no matter how many sense memory exercises you do. As we've also covered, however, audiences don't seem exactly warm to actors who are constantly observing themselves, almost always at the expense of the connections, chemistry, and unique variables around them. The moment as it relates to your acting is very specific – it is about what is happening outside you. Behavior is the perfect phenomenon to train yourself to begin catching. Perhaps you notice that tonight your colleague in a scene is frowning a lot. She didn't do that the performance or take before, and why she is frowning is beyond you. You don't need to interpret her behavior to observe it.

To drive the value of behavior home, let's have Savannah and Noel start with one three moment exercise as we have been doing it, and then for curiosity's sake let's see what happens if they start the following one with a behavioral observation.

"You're wearing a bracelet," Noel observes, beginning the exercise.

"I'm wearing a bracelet," Savannah repeats, sighing.

"You took a deep breath," Noel observes.

The two take a moment to pause before Savannah begins the next round.

"Your eyes are moving," she observes.

"My eyes are moving," Noel repeats, laughing.

"You laughed," Savannah says, finishing the round.

Let's say I ask the actors if there were any difference between the first and second exercise, specifically with regard to moment 1.

"The second exercise felt much more specific," Savannah comments.

"I agree. Was there a difference in intensity?"

"I wouldn't say it was more intense but it felt more connected," Noel says.

"When she began with behavior?"

"Yes."

Noel's response echoes what most actors will discover. Since behavior is of such value to you in your work, beginning with it as a starting observation deepens the experience within the three moment exercise significantly. Again, there's nothing wrong with a basic call. "Brown socks" is just as valid as "your eyes are moving," but there's a rich qualitative difference between them. Adopting this difference translates into bringing far more specificity into your acting work. The cardinal value Sanford Meisner would often insist actors live by? Be specific.

In the case of observations, specificity and depth are synonymous. By sharpening your ability to clearly see another actor, you bring in more intimacy, connection, and chemistry. It also amplifies your public solitude dramatically. When you are wrapped up in another actor, hungry for what the moment brings next, suddenly the concern about the audience diminishes. Incorporating behavior into the hierarchy of observation gives you a better starting point, always knowing you can fall back on basic observations if ever needed. Let's see a few examples. Just to keep track of the pacing, I'm going to script these to keep attention on the structure. It may seem obvious, but a change is coming that will make you happy you had the structure memorized.

> (Moment 1) **Noel:** You're sitting on your hands.
> (Moment 2) **Savannah:** I'm sitting on my hands. (raises eyebrows)
> (Moment 3) **Noel:** You raised your eyebrows.

Pause.

> (Moment 1) **Savannah:** You're moving your legs.
> (Moment 2) **Noel:** I'm moving my legs. (looks down)
> (Moment 3) **Savannah:** You looked down.

Pause.

> (Moment 1) **Noel:** You're not moving.
> (Moment 2) **Savannah:** I'm not moving. (stops speaking)
> (Moment 3) **Noel:** You closed your mouth.

This is a trio of great three moment exercises, both in technical strength and also the opportunities on offer to keep refining observational powers. Let's now consider two possible outcomes that are often present in the repeating of the second moment. The first is that the partner repeating feels the need to "do" something with the observation, to feed their partner a behavior or be performative based on what was observed. Intentionally playfully raising the eyebrows or looking down at one's legs to indicate the observation has been heard are two examples. It's worth being clear that there's no value to approaching the exercise with this mentality. You'll notice there are absolutely no instructions to make something happen when you are repeating. The observation made in the first moment isn't an offer as in improv. It's just what it sounds like: a simple observation of you. You don't need to deny anything organic repeating that observation brings up, but the important point here is you don't need to intentionally create anything either.

The desire to be performative at this stage is natural, often arising from conditioned habits. Behavior is far juicier than a basic observation, and it's much easier to want to play with being told "you raised your eyebrows" than "you are wearing brown socks." But remember the exercise from a few chapters ago when you simply listened without any indicating, pretending, or fakery. You traded the automatic habit of being performative for a far more impressive skill: being authentic to the moment. Moment 2 here offers a similar split in the road. Sure, you could interject a lot of indicating and performing that is inorganic to the moment, or you can open yourself to another set of possibilities, and this is what brings us to the second possible outcome.

Look over each of these second moment examples again. The other potential outcome is that these could all be impulsive reactions to an observation. If you happen to be fidgety and someone observes this, it might elicit a response in which your eyebrows organically go up. Likewise, you may have the impulse to look down if you've been unaware of moving your legs. For many reasons some observations will elicit an impulsive and unexpected reaction from us. More and more you're going to begin encountering moments when you are caught off guard, surprised at a call or what it does to you, and this is worth moving towards. These are waters where you end up surprising yourself, a very good place for an actor to work and train. Exercises in which so many variables are known don't prepare you for the many complexities you will face on the job. Training with structure but also unexpected surprises aligns more strongly with what you will face outside a classroom.

There's a beauty to working this way. Over time it removes the pressure you place on yourself to always be performing, to be what in marketing terms is called the "purple cow." Your authentic reaction as it arises in the moment is enough, and the evidence for that will keep compounding in future chapters. It can be frightening that you don't know what will arise in the moment, to simply trust that it is powerful enough to take care of things. That is a lot of control to give up, so start small. If you find yourself in a three moment exercises being performative or trying to help the other actor in the second moment, just drop back and see what it feels like when you trust in the moment to take over and put the responsibility for the success of the exercise on your partner's shoulders. Leave the moment alone and see what happens.

What this begins to tease at is a concept we will continue to revisit as this training evolves, which is the difference between ideas and impulses. We're already beginning to see how your desire to do something with the moment is more of an idea, while a response organically generated by your partner is an impulse. Let's look at the third example of Savannah and Noel's exercises to see if this concept points the way to an even richer, more nuanced observation you can make of another person. Consider when Noel observed that Savannah wasn't moving. Is that a good call or not? On one hand it is rooted in truth: Savannah was literally not moving, but she also wasn't tap dancing, turning into a Martian, or drinking a cup of gin. There are many things Savannah is not. As a tool for your acting, it doesn't seem this type of observation will be of great value. There are many things the moment will not be. Your task as the actor is to deal with what comes up rather than things not there. It's why we place such an emphasis on concrete, easily identifiable elements over imaginative ones. As you plug more into the world around you the less you will need imagination as a tool. You are enough, and reality is enough. Or, as Douglas Adams beautifully put it, "Isn't it enough to see that a garden is beautiful without having to believe that there are fairies at the bottom of it too?"

Let's say I ask Noel what was going on with that observation.

"Something in her behavior was jumping out at you," I say.

"Her not moving just kept bugging me."

"That's a powerful effect."

"Definitely."

"But not moving doesn't really capture it, does it?"

"No . . . she was just being so still."

"How about that?"

"What?"

"Stillness. Could you have observed 'you're still'?"

"Hmmm . . . I could have."

"Would that have been a fair description of what you saw?"

"Yes."

In the Meisner technique we like stillness. Stillness tells us so much about what is happening inside a person. In daily life it's quite a striking behavior. It can be an expression of ultimate compassion or can equally inflict just as much pain. The stillness that arises from the indifference of a loved one during an argument can cut worse than most hurtful phrases. Its meaning depends on the moment, but stillness is, by and large, a powerhouse quality. Noel's saying she was bugged by it isn't a problem with Noel, it highlights how immense an impact stillness can have. It also points the way to the next type of observation, one even more nuanced and powerful than behavioral calls.

Consider that when Savannah's stillness was screaming out to Noel, it's possible there were other behaviors on offer. She may have been blinking, or moving her foot a little, but it was the stillness that called out to Noel. She didn't need to reach for it, it was in her face before she knew it. Let's say Savannah had also blinked. Would observing that be a bad call? Of course not, but missing the stillness, so profound Noel had trouble wording it, would have meant missing out on a piece of behavior so unique to that moment. The stillness was telling Noel more about Savannah than any other piece of behavior in that moment. It was an essential behavior.

Behavior is Enough

Essential observations of behavior are the next call in the hierarchy of observations. These behaviors tell us something about what the other person is going through in a given moment. We don't know what it is, and that is perfectly fine. Simply naming an essential behavior is far better for staying accurate to the moment than trying to interpret what it means. Let's see another example of a common essential call of behavior, one that was a particular favorite of Meisner's.

>**Savannah:** You're smiling.
>**Noel:** I'm smiling. (goes red)
>**Savannah:** You blushed.

What a powerful moment to observe, as well as to be caught in. When someone calls an essential behavior of yours it feels like a hot spotlight is suddenly shown on you. Meisner would praise the blush so highly for one simple reason: "You can't fake a blush." The blush has become so iconic because of the weight that single piece of behavior carries in the moment. Entire elements of makeup have been created across centuries just to imitate it. At the same time, however, there are many reasons somebody might go red in the face. They could be angry, joyful, aroused, irritated, about to sneeze, suffering from an illness, and so on. The reasons are vast, and when it comes to making these observations you've already begun to get a small hint the Meisner technique is going to continue to drop: you cannot be in the minds of other people. Your attempts to interpret a moment, to psychoanalyze the actors around you, are just going to keep landing you in hot water.

There's a broader element here worth briefly introducing, and that is the reason simply observing can be so hard for many actors. In some training approaches you are often taught to try to get at what's behind a particular behavior, and this starts when you're encouraged to dig into your and each other's personal histories. While it's rarely stated, oftentimes the darker the experience being called up, the better. Several professional colleagues of mine have gone to various training sessions, with name teachers, where the focus was on using your personal history to generate raw, real emotion. From three different people who didn't know one another, and went to three separate schools, do you want to know the phrase I kept hearing when I asked how it went? "Everyone had such horror stories about their past. When they were sharing, I almost felt ashamed I didn't have more trauma or abuse in my life." In future chapters you'll give be given evidence for why this way of working is not only counterproductive but can be explicitly harmful to your technique. For now, conditioned habits like this lead actors to try to interpret behavior when they come to this training, or to seek intense justifications for why their partner did something.

Acting is not the place to try to interpret behavior in the moment. There's no opportunity for you to be continuously exiting the scene and checking to see if your interpretation is on the right track. Learning to observe by guessing often comes at a cost, especially when the task at hand is to be living out the circumstances rather than questioning yourself and those around you. Unfortunately, many approaches to Meisner are filled with guesses about states of mind. Observations such as, "That pissed you off," "You're sad," and "You liked that," are often justified under the pretense that you are simply expressing your point of view. To this we have to ask, what's so great about that? Your point of view is often what lands you in your head, insisting a good actor must be both mind-reader and miniature director. Interpretation has a place but, when it comes to making specific, and more to the point, accurate observations of the moment, it has much less value here. Rather than speculate about a behavior's origins it is much healthier to observe and work off it.

Leaving your interpretations at the door is how you get the benefit of observing something as profound as a blush without risking losing the accuracy. Why is it happening? Who knows. All you know is that it is profound in the moment, a superb observation that gives you a lot to work off of. When it comes to reading the minds of others, our best bet is to embrace the advice stoic philosopher Epictetus gave more than two thousand years ago: to read the mind of another is a gift fit for only a god. Leave the gifts of the gods to the gods. Trying to do otherwise will only bring you grief.

Subtle Moments Equal Powerful Technique

The essential call of behavior marks a profound turning point in your observational skills. You'll always be able to clearly identify basic facts, but more often than not behaviors are what will root you into the moment. On occasion a behavior will manifest that is so impressive it demands to be observed. That's the beauty of the essential behavior – you don't have to reach for it. The key is to be able to train yourself enough to see it clearly as it is manifesting.

Introducing essential behaviors like stillness or blushing brings up a subtle but important technical question: how do you accommodate profound observations that occur across several moments rather than just one? Let's look at an example of that happening.

> **Noel:** You're still.
> **Savannah:** I'm still. (remains still)
> **Noel:** (laughs) You're still . . . still!

Noel's frustrated laugh indicates the difficulty of observations like this. The behavior commanding our attention can occur for a single moment or many moments. It's important then to keep the moments unique to one another. All that requires is just avoiding words or phrases like, "You're still doing that," "You keep moving," "You can't stop," and so on. It gets slightly messy when we start blending moments together, a generic paintbrush technique that dampens the benefits of specificity. Moments, rather than patterns, are your greatest asset in acting.

The technical adjustment then would be:

> **Noel:** You're still.
> **Savannah:** I'm still. (remains still)
> **Noel:** (laughs) You're still!

Essential behaviors reveal there is a vast and deeply rich experience outside yourself on offer. This experience is filled with subtle moments, some of which can be profound, but all of which yield a guiding anchor as you make being in the moment a consistent, replicable part of your technique. Depending on the moment any behavior can be an essential pointer about what is happening within your partner. A trembling hand, moving agitatedly side to side, crossing your arms, scratching your face – the list is endless. All you have to do is be there to observe them, and the sharp attention to detail you're developing in both these exercises and your mindfulness practice will be a valuable aid.

Observing stillness in particular reveals one final benefit worth mentioning before closing the chapter on it. Consider this scenario: have you ever been acting across from somebody who was giving you nothing? Maybe they seemed deeply preoccupied with seemingly everything except for being connected with you. Or maybe the lights just weren't on in general. Either way, it feels like acting with a block of wood. That's a painful situation most actors at one point or another will find themselves in. Working with somebody who is just not committing in the same way you are impacts your relationship, the scene, or the project in general. It can be an infuriating experience. So what do you to solve this issue? Classic strategy number one suggests you talk to your fellow actor about it. Trying to keep it polite at first, you ask things like, "Hey, can you do something different on that line? I'm just not getting what I need to give me the motivation to say my line or do my action." Though the other actor might agree, you've just created a recipe for a potentially disastrous scenario.

Ask yourself this: do you enjoy it when a colleague takes on the role of a manager to give you advice about your job and how you should be doing it? Probably not. You don't want to be rude but, if you comply, you give somebody else power that is not clearly defined by your contract or job description. That's exactly what is happening when you ask your fellow actor to change things up in order to make your life easier. What might begin with good intentions from you can quickly lead to a toxic relationship. If you're somebody who doesn't appreciate when you receive criticisms or advice unsolicited then what's to say your colleague is going to be happy to? That actor may do what you want for a take, or a rehearsal or two, but they might also start to resent you after a while.

Classic strategy two suggests that when you have a problem with another actor you take it to your director. This is the very preferable approach. It also helps maintain the homeostasis of the job roles. While the idea of ensemble or a collaborative spirit might sound sexy, in any successful collaborative organization there is still a clear delineation of power and responsibilities. There's a lot of value in doing your part to maintain the integrity of a hierarchy. Trying to solve interpersonal problems when it isn't your job is only going to bring you more trouble and will rarely have the outcomes you hope for. At the same time, however, it's worth asking if there is a way you can solve the issue of working with a non-responsive actor that doesn't involve you having to negotiate with them or asking the director to step in to mediate.

Stillness offers that opportunity. Making stillness a part of your observational technique means you've made it something valid to respond to. It doesn't matter that the actor isn't giving you what you want. After all, we do need to turn this around and recognize it's not your job to get the outcome you like in another people. Human beings are going to do what they will, and you can either get upset about not getting what you want, thereby putting you constantly at the mercy of the whims of others, or you can respond to it. Why is the disconnected actor bugging you? Not because they're not giving you anything. They're giving you stillness. Rather than acting on that impulse coming up you're instead turning back to the old habit of judging, deciding you don't like their stillness and can't work well with it. In this way you quickly turn an opportunity into an issue.

Allowing stillness to be part of your observations means you will never be without something to work off of. Incredibly moved to tears by your partner's stillness in a scene? That's your response. Irritated as hell? Equally good. It's a response that is arising because of clearly observing the moment. Working in this way takes the pressure off of you trying to handle not only your own performance but everyone else's. It also has the added benefit of allowing you to shine even if the other actor is not. If your partner isn't present and not giving their attention, the audience will clearly sense it. They'll also be able to see you working off of that in a rich, organic way. If an actor has decided for whatever reason to phone it in, or isn't capable of doing any better, it isn't your job to save their performance and sacrifice your own as a consequence. That's the road the ability to observe and not be threatened by stillness offers: a means to protect your own performance and keep the pressure off of yourself.

We've debunked the mystery around the moment, continuing to build on the authentic foundations that began with investing in the reality of doing and public solitude. We've also begun to orient more towards specific, accurate observations as a means to support that authenticity. Now we have to begin seeing what that authenticity itself looks by introducing a change to the three moment exercise that will increase the intensity and spontaneity to a major degree.

Summary

Mindfulness meditation practice is an experience in making contact with the moment. Through each practice, particularly as you encounter and re-contextualize the power of your thoughts, you'll be able to continuously identify new elements within your awareness as they arise. Likewise, in the three moment exercise the power of the moment becomes more magnified as the actor sharpens their technique. The common denominator to success in both is observation, specifically the actor's ability to clearly see what is happening within the moment as it arises. From simple, basic observations such as articles of clothing to intricate – and sometimes essential – behaviors, the three moment exercise can take the actor far in their quest to uncover the mysteries of making the moment an object of replicable technique. A forthcoming change to the exercise, however, reveals that observation is only half of the mechanisms by which the Meisner technique operates, and creates an opportunity for further growth and development of one's process.

6
There's Wisdom in Forgetting Your Head

Where There is Space

Even though the likelihood is we've never met, I think we can agree on one thing: you have a head.

Before this seemingly obvious statement begins to alarm you, let's take a moment to consider this. As you've encountered it thus far, meditation offers a means to explore your own conscious experience of the world. It asks questions of you such as: how do I connect with the present moment, what do I notice within it, and what distracts me from observing it clearly? Most people don't think of mindfulness in this way. They see its ultimate function as a means to take the edge off, reducing anxiety and stress. While this can be a helpful byproduct, the possibilities run far deeper. Practicing while stressed, anxious, angry, or joyful are all examples of how broad the scope of your attention can go. The more you incorporate a practice into your daily experience, whatever the emotional tone may be, the more you begin to become familiar with consciousness itself.

At its core, this is valuable. You cannot separate reality from your conscious experience of it. Every desire, sensation, thought, and experience is a byproduct of consciousness. If you had no brain, or a physically damaged one, you wouldn't be able to experience the world as you do now. Since consciousness isn't going away, exploring it in your mindfulness practices can lead to experiences that feel distinctly richer and clearer than others. For example, after a session you may feel yourself a little less separate from the world. Stimuli, what you hear, see, and sense, could appear more blended. If you haven't had this experience don't worry, it can take a while, and these moments are usually subtle. If you have encountered this, one aspect you

DOI: 10.4324/9781003255321-6

may be curious about is how in moments when you feel more connected to what is around you, the vibrancy and uniqueness of life doesn't diminish. In some ways it becomes more intense.

It may sound strange to be talking about these types of experiences in a book for acting, but exploring these possibilities offers a helpful means for you to begin touching some key insights in practice. When mindfulness is used solely as a tool to reduce anxiety it makes dulling experience its primary goal. Before we judge this, let's be candid and say this can be a good thing. My friends and loved ones who suffer from panic attacks, for example, could use a little more dulling of certain experiences, and would never claim that having less severe panic attacks would dampen their experience of life. Similar examples aside, however, any tool that blunts your experience of reality, or tries to narrow it to exclude less pleasant experiences, is not a helpful one for your acting. Rather than picking and choosing which experience in the moment we like the best, a strong meditation practice opens you up to a range of moments, asking you to be prepared for what will arise rather than thinking you can control it. This is also a value of the Meisner technique, and it brings us back to the issue of your head.

Being trapped in your head is, for many actors, a criticism that feels like a death sentence for their hopes of succeeding. We've taken that phrase and stripped it of much of its mystery, now making the act of being in the moment and not getting trapped in your head part of the same tangible experience. But what if we could continue to expand further on this idea of removing your head from the equation, rooting you more clearly into what is happening around you as a result? What if, as a matter of technique, you could lose your head altogether?

Exercise: Meditation 5

Set-up: Set up your practice.

Instructions: For this exercise, we're going to temporarily pause the mindfulness work you were doing and see if we can flesh out something new. To accomplish this, you'll engage in an exercise that starts with pointing and asking questions.

Hold your hand in front of you, all fingers open, so that you can see the back of your hand. If unclear, you can reference this image.

Keeping your hand in front of you, curl all the fingers into a fist except your index finger, which should be now raised in a pointing gesture. Here is an image to help.

Actually using your index finger, point to an object in the room. Notice its shape, size, and color. Notice it as an object. Go ahead, and return here when done; there's no time limit on this but it should only take a few moments.

Now point to your foot. Notice if it has a shoe or sock on. Notice its shape and color. Return here when finished.

Point now to your abdomen. Notice its shape, color, and any movements. Return here when finished.

Now point to any object straight in front of you. Then rotate your hand 180 degrees, so that your pointer now faces you. Hold that, and then return here for some questions.

There's Wisdom in Forgetting Your Head

Ask yourself about what you see here. Do you see a shape, color, or movement? Or, where your head should be, do you instead see largely empty space? Stay with this exploration a few moments longer, and then return here.

Discussion/Notes: Depending on your experience, it may feel as if there's either a lot or not much to unpack about this exercise. Both are true. First, a little background and clarification might help create some context. The pointing exercise as it is known comes from Zen, first from Douglas Harding and later Richard Lang, whose verbiage I've used here. Contrary to how it might feel to some, the pointer exercise isn't a cerebral, overly complicated thought exercise. It is, true to the simplicity we keep discovering from exercises within both mindfulness and Meisner, a way for you to connect with an element of your experience. That element, of course, is the realization that you have no head.

We've all agreed to the obvious: yes, you certainly do have a physical head. It exists, and as any of my friends who suffer from chronic migraines can confirm, it can be a real pain some days. At the same time, however, we have to ask: is what objective science tells you the same as your experience of life? In the pointing exercise, you may have come upon a unique discrepancy. Science and other people can confirm you have a head, but in your perceptual experience there's no such thing where it should be. Some people might say they can see the ridges of their nose, but look at yours and then look at anyone else's. Do they appear even remotely similar? Most people have an average nose, it doesn't stick out like Pinocchio's, it's proportional to the size of a face. From my perspective, the things I see in the corner of my eyes look like massive bumpy ridges. They look nothing like the nose I see on other people. The same is true with lips. Some people might be able to puff out their lips, but again what you see resembles nothing of the size and scale of lips you observe on other people. If you wear glasses, you may see some lines and even some structure in the corners, but this still doesn't look like any pair of glasses I've seen on anyone else. Objective science tells you you have a head. Your conscious experience, however, doesn't confirm that. Oddly enough, it implies the opposite.

There are more extreme ways people have tried to demonstrate the existence of their face. One way is to use a mirror. So, if there's one close to you, look into it. Now, point to your head. The instinctual response of many when asked this is to point somewhere to their face in the mirror, but this isn't your head, it's an image of it. So, they point to their actual head, and their reflection shows a finger pointing to a face. It exists for as long as they keep the mirror there. As soon as the mirror is gone, it vanishes. How many other people do you know whose existence of a head depends on a mirror constantly being nearby? From your perspective, you are looking at another object in the world, but you still can't see your actual face. Even if you went to the extreme and either pinched or slapped your cheek, or asked someone to do it for you, how would that prove anything? You would feel sensations, tingling, and texture, but again, how does this, from your own experience of the world, confirm you have a head? Instead what seems to exist is a unique type of empty space, a space that requires no thought to experience and in which you let in everything within your visual field.

Your acting stems from your personal, conscious experience of the world. As we've just barely started to uncover, mindfulness practice can be a way to explore your experience of reality, not as anyone tells you it must be but as you uniquely encounter it. Encountering your own headlessness offers a means to begin recognizing your unique personal experience of your life. Like all of the exercises you've been doing, there's nothing esoteric and mystical about it, but instead it is grounded in a simple, almost too obvious, experience. Solving the issue of being in your head seems too good to be true. From your experience since birth, you never had one to worry about in the first place.

Rather than suggesting your experience of reality is the only one in existence, it's entirely reasonable to assume we are all having our own experience of the world in which everyone has a head except for us. This places each of us in a unique position: we are all living in a headless experience of reality, but I have no idea about the unique elements of your own. Undoubtedly you keep hearing in your acting classes it's important to focus on your unique qualities, what makes you *you*. The moment you are called into a waiting for a casting, however, and see a dozen other actors eerily identical to you, each with the same hair, a similar height, and so on, it's going to call that into question. What your intimidation fails to remind you of is that you have an experience of reality in that situation nobody else does. They may be having their own but, from your point of view, you are the only one who is experiencing reality in such a unique vivid way, existing not as the talking head others see you as but instead open space. You don't need me to confirm it – you just need to point at that space to remind you of your actual experience of life.

If at this point this exercise feels vague, baffling, or even too simple, know that this is a perfectly valid response. There's a range of reactions people have when encountering their own headlessness: wondering, bemused, confused, irritated, joyful, unimpressed, and so on. Each response is valid, and all that needs to be said here is this is an early stage in the practice. For now, rather than a concept, it helps to think of it as an experience, an experiencing of something unique only to your point of view. Consider that if we sat facing one another, having a conversation, from my point of view I would see your head, but from your own, there is only space in which the world floods in. What's odd here is that many of us rarely connect with our own actual experience of reality in this way. We become conditioned to believe that we experience the world the same as everybody else and so ignore the glaringly obvious difference right in front of us.

Headlessness builds on the authenticity this technique is rooted in, and so incorporating it alongside Meisner training yields great value. It is, in many ways, the ultimate essential behavior you can observe of yourself. It is as true an experience of life as you can ever have.

Threaded Moments

When last we left the three moment exercise, we had begun to tease out a series of possibilities. Not only does it solve the problem of being in the moment by making it far more technical and concrete than is often understood, but it also provides a means to train your observational skills. Making your observations specific to the moment, ensuring as high a degree of accuracy as possible, leads to new questions. What, after all, is the most important thing to observe? The lights? The wrinkles in your trousers? The answer is the other person.

Most acting takes place in concert with at least one other human being. Here someone inevitably says, "But what about one-person shows?" to which the easy answer is, how many of those do you plan to do in your career? I have had the occasion to work with a few people who mainly do one-person shows, but it may surprise you to know that they never ask this question.

Why? Because they've figured out in practice that working with the energy and dynamics of an audience has a striking resemblance to the excitement of working off another actor. They give you energy and you give it back. The human element outside you is the common denominator in acting, not an exception to the rule.

Since human dynamics are a large part of the actor's experience, we also have to ask if your partner is the key to handling other challenges you may encounter. Take the issue of acting in the moment, for example. Each moment is unique, and yet it gets hard to keep attention sharp if your focus is constantly on things like the lights, sets, props, your own lines, and so on. Those variables come with a level of constancy – unless something major happens they are going to be mostly the same every night. The same can't be said of your co-actors. Though their lines might be constant, their behaviors certainly may not be. An unexpected tremor in your partner's voice can open up an entire range of responses in you. If they seem distracted or, as we explored before, aren't giving you "much," that stillness can lead to huge organic responses within you. Being able to observe and catch these behaviors is a clean, reliable way to continuously ensure you are in the moment. Even if that's not the whole equation, it's a major part of the puzzle that has been solved.

We seem to keep circling around this idea that other people can bring out responses in you. When we say that, however, what exactly are we talking about? Consider that a response that comes from you can be largely premeditated or thought out. You have an idea about how to say a line, execute some blocking, create a bit between you and another actor, and so you respond based on your intention. This is so common to the actor's process it might be strange to hear me spell it out, but it might be equally surprising to explore the possibility that there can be problems with this approach. Ideas, after all, are only as good as reality will let them be. If you've ever had the perfect execution in your mind, only for it to be clunky, awkward, and generally a misfire when you actually tried it, you'll know what that discrepancy is like. Responses that come solely from you run a risk of hitting the rocks of reality. We have to consider they may not be the optimal thing to base your technique on.

A response brought out by another person, however, carries within it an element of surprise. This is due to the very nature of that experience. It always carries within it something unique to the moment. The moment when you are suddenly startled by another person, for example, can elicit huge and unexpected responses from you, bringing a range of emotions. You'll notice we haven't talked much about emotions yet, despite many conventional approaches to acting being intensely interested in the idea of emotion and how you can generate it. What we are beginning to explore instead is an alternative possibility: what if other people can largely take care of the emotional aspect of acting for you? Surely that would be a large amount of weight off your shoulders. No more need to worry about emotional recall, affective memories, or constantly digging into your past for material. It would be a great shift to no longer have to ask that of yourself. And yet if you look to life there are indeed examples of when other people took over the job of our responses, whether through actions or saying things that brought out reactions completely surprising in us. In fact, if we look more broadly, a great deal of life seems to be spent trying to deal with the responses the world brings out of you rather than you constantly trying to generate emotion on the spot. That's more true to the human experience. Why can't the same possibilities exist in your acting?

If you boil down the Meisner technique to a single phrase, this is what you would come up with: what happens to you as an actor doesn't depend on you but on what the other person is doing to you. In the context of many other approaches, that is fairly radical, but today we are going to begin seeing the first pieces of evidence to support this idea. The more as a matter of technique you make your work dependent, not on the responses you want to have, but on those elicited by your fellow actors, the more you are going to be in sync with the unique variables of the moment. By proxy, that means you are richly connected to the moment. As a result your behavior becomes attuned to the moment, making it more unpredictable. It's this set of ideas on which the Meisner technique has staked its entire body of training. Again, it bears repeating: what you are going to do as an actor doesn't have to depend on you. It can instead depend on what the other person is doing to you and, as a result, what they are making you do. The actor who works by that line of thinking is a different beast entirely.

Why the other person matters so much in this work has to do with this idea of responses generated outside you. By nature, a response that you weren't expecting has a uniquely unpredictable edge. It is tied in completely to the moment and, as such, keeps you rooted in the immediacy of the present. To an audience, this translates to some big-ticket values: authenticity, immediacy, gravitas, fearlessness, and courage. Those last two might surprise you, but it's intimidating to accept that a large part of your acting could be spent not knowing what you are going to do next. You will know some things: your lines, blocking, costumes, and so on, but how the lines come out, if there's a unique expression of that same blocking, all of that becomes surrendered to the unknown when you make your technique dependent on what is outside you. As my Meisner teacher Scott would say, however, the potential pay-off is immense: it's only when you don't know what you're going to do next that the audience won't. That's an exciting attribute to ascribe to your acting.

As we've agreed on, and to quote Carl Sagan, "Extraordinary claims require extraordinary evidence." Let's start testing some of this in practice with a new extension of the three moment exercise.

Exercise: Three Moment Exercise, Version II

Set-up: Two actors sit in chairs facing each other. The distance between them ideally should be knees close but not touching. What this gives is the dynamic of no contact but very much "in each other's space."

As before, exploring the exercise will be a back-and-forth between hypothetical examples and us stepping back to examine the values in these scenarios. So let's see actors Jay and Ellie do a couple of three moment exercises to re-establish themselves technically.

> **Jay:** You're still.
> **Ellie:** I'm still. (laughs)
> **Jay:** You laughed.

Pause.

> **Ellie:** Your eyes are moving.
> **Jay:** My eyes are moving. (raises eyebrows)
> **Ellie:** You raised your eyebrows.

Two great examples of a three moment exercise. Moment 1 begins with a clean observation, which can either be a basic observation, behavioral, or, if present, an essential behavior. Nothing needs to be determined in advance.

At the same time, however, we do have to recognize a design flaw in the exercise. While necessary at first to keep the structure, that pause has essentially created a staccato experience. Unless you are in some particularly unique, most likely devised, play, speaking in patterns of 1–2–3 with a pause isn't going to clearly mimic the flow of speech in acting. It's true that great acting happens in the moment, but have you also heard that the best acting happens moment *to* moment? That's what we've sacrificed temporarily to get comfortable with the structure – the moment-to-moment flow of acting. This chapter's version of the three moment exercise is going to fix that, introducing a new change that will facilitate your powers of observation working in a moment-to-moment way. It can also shed more light on this very unique idea that your best acting might be determined not by you but by the other person.

The change is simple, but you'll be glad you're familiar with the 1–2–3 structure. Simply put, we are going to eliminate the pause. Let's see how Jay and Ellie navigate these waters.

"Ellie," I ask.

"Yes?"

"Let's say Jay begins. He makes an observation about you. Then what?"

"I repeat it."

"Yes. And then?"

"He makes a new observation?"

"Perfect, and then?"

"We pause and I start the new exercise."

"And the new round starts with?"

"My making an observation?"

"You got it. What happens, however, if we tweak that slightly. What if instead of the pause you just make your observation?"

"Okay . . . how?"

"What if, as Jay is making his observation in the third moment, you watch him? Maybe you'll see the material for starting your new observation right there. Let's try and see what happens."

Jay begins his observation. He notices Ellie is smiling nervously at my new directions.

"Your smile is tight," he says.

"My smile is tight," she repeats, nodding.

"You nodded," Jay observes, smiling and laughing.

"Now," I ask, "when Jay said 'you nodded,' what did you see?"

"Well, he was laughing at my nerves," she says, giving Jay a playful punch in the arm.

"Sorry," Jay says, chuckling.

"Actors can be cruel," I agree jokingly. "Well, what if instead of pausing that had been your new first moment?"

"Straight to it?"

"Sure, the behavior was already there."

"So I would have made the observation, . . ."

"And Jay would have repeated what he heard, and then you would have made a new third moment observation."

"Hmmm . . ."

"Let's try a full round like this and see what happens. I won't interrupt you. Jay, start us off with a new exercise."

Jay begins: "You're looking at me," he says.

"I'm looking at you," Ellie repeats and, as she does, she sits on her hands.

"You sat on your hands," Jay observes, moving in.

"You moved in," Ellie observes.

"I moved in," Jay repeats, smiling.

"You smiled," Ellie observes, narrowing her eyes.

This is an example of a perfectly executed pair of three moment exercises, the only difference being that now the pause has been removed and the two have been linked. The structure you worked hard to memorize over the last two chapters is there and is now serving you well. The moments, and the observations within them, are starting to flow. To clearly break it down let's look at this example in terms of structure.

    (Moment 1) **Jay:** You're looking at me.
    (Moment 2) **Ellie:** I'm looking at you. (sits on hands)
    (Moment 3) **Jay:** You sat on your hands. (moves in)
    (Moment 1) **Ellie:** You moved in.
    (Moment 2) **Jay:** I moved in. (smiles)
    (Moment 3) **Ellie:** You're smiling. (narrows her eyes)

As you can see here, structurally nothing has changed. What has happened however is the observations are now connected to the moments in real time. During the pause, plenty of moments were rushing by. We were just conveniently ignoring them since our priorities were in a different place. Now, however, since we've recognized that great acting happens moment to moment, we have to be honest that ignoring moments is probably not a wise strategy to keep in your technique. Ditching that, we maintain the integrity of the exercise but now allow for flow in the experience. And though I've normally been listing only pairs of exercises, the three moment exercise can carry on for a long time. Look at the example above. In the final observation Ellie narrows her eyes. That would become Jay's first moment observation in the new exercise. Let's watch a few more and see if that reveals another big value of the Meisner technique. To keep track of the structure, I'll lay it out in a similar format as before.

(Moment 1) **Ellie:** You shook your head.
(Moment 2) **Jay:** I shook my head. (lifts chin)
(Moment 3) **Ellie:** You lifted your chin. (frowns)
(Moment 1) **Jay:** You frowned.
(Moment 2) **Ellie:** I frowned. (goes red)
(Moment 3) **Jay:** You blushed. (points)
(Moment 1) **Ellie:** You're pointing at me.
(Moment 2) **Jay:** I'm pointing at you. (opens hands)
(Moment 3) **Ellie:** You opened your hands. (raises voice as she says this)
(Moment 1) **Jay:** You raised your voice.
(Moment 2) **Ellie:** I raised my voice. (screams)
(Moment 3) **Jay:** You shouted. (moves chair back)

Now this is an interesting exercise. What is going on here? It seems like both of them hit moments of annoyance with one another, Ellie especially taking some umbrage at what Jay was doing. But what happens if I ask them about the cause of each other's behavior?

"Lots of emotion came up in this experience, it got charged very quickly," I say.

"Yes," both agree.

"Ellie, what happened there?"

"I'm not sure. He just kept pissing me off!"

We laugh, making sure that even though the emotions that arose were genuine, the actors know the exercise is now over and nothing needs to be taken personally.

"Were you trying to get angry at him?"

"No, that's what was weird about it. It just . . ."

"Happened?"

"Yes!"

This type of experience is common in the technique. It doesn't only happen with anger but can also occur with joy, frustration, intimacy, sadness . . . you name it. Emotions seem to arise organically, and what catches actors off guard about them is the lack of premeditation seen as so essential in other approaches to acting. Ellie wasn't trying to get angry. She didn't think to herself she would juice the exercise by trying to provoke Jay. In fact quite the opposite seems to have occurred: in carefully observing Jay's behavior, a response of authentic irritation arose. Something in his behavior kept needling her, and she expressed it magnificently. This is but one of many examples of something you do being determined by the other person.

What's unsettling, however, is the degree of it. Ellie certainly wasn't on the verge of losing control or seeing red. If I had sensed that, the exercise would have been stopped before we hit that point. There's little value to any actor training when emotions become so dominant they override the experience entirely. There's almost no place in the acting industry for jobs that demand you lose your sense of self and awareness of the space and go completely ballistic. As such, in training there's no benefit to pushing yourself to emotional extremes of that degree. That's also the point where things can become dangerous, both for you and those around you. So, let's just be clear that this example of Ellie's anger wasn't unsettling for those reasons. It simply caught her off guard because in acting rarely do we feel the heat of authentic emotions as we do in life. So much of actor training is spent fretting about how to create emotions. This technique is different. In life our emotions are often brought out of us by outside stimuli, and that reality is mirrored in this training. Given the authenticity these experiences have we have to ask then is it okay Ellie became spontaneously angry at Jay? Even though I never specified anything about emotions, are future expressions like this acceptable, provided they come from the other person and not your own intentions to deliberately flex your emotional muscles?

Let Me Get That for You

When we ask this question, the central issue we are circling is not an acting one, but a cultural one. The topic at the core of asking about the limits of authentic expression is politeness. We all understand, for example, that anger in an acting class generated intentionally, through prodding our memories, imagining scenarios, and so on, is generally acceptable if that is what is called for. It's a little different when it arises spontaneously with seemingly no obvious context. Jay, after all, wasn't deliberately trying to needle Ellie. Something in his behavior just irked her, and she let it out without asking for his permission. That's, at the end of the day, a very impolite thing to do. Most of us have been raised to moderate our emotions in one way or another. We were taught from early on that suddenly becoming irritated with another person is inappropriate. Even if they deserve it, the wiser thing to do is turn the other cheek, bite your lip, be the better person, and so on. Anger is a more relatable example but politeness limits more than just frustration and rage. Even when you are in a great mood, brimming with joy to the point of bursting over some good news, it does feel generally impolite to dump that onto other people. What if they are having a bad day and your bubbliness would inflict more pain?

The impact of politeness doesn't extend just to emotions but is also seen in your observational work. What if while working you happened to notice a giant mustard stain on your partner's shirt? Politeness dictates you do not bring it up. What if they hadn't blown their nose properly and a little leftover was hanging out of one nostril? Certainly don't bring that up, or very discreetly mention it so they can correct it immediately. Politeness also suggests you don't point, make rude gestures, and so on. For a technique based on what happens to you depending on the other person, this poses a unique dilemma. The self-censoring nature of politeness seems to run counter to both the core value of the Meisner technique as well as the authenticity you are building on. It impacts your ability both to observe and to respond to the world around you. What do you do about this then?

The answer is, as all things are in this work, simple. To quote Meisner, your new motto shall henceforth be: "Fuck polite." Yes, that's really what he said. Now, before we just assume everyone knows what a charged statement like that means, it's important to emphasize how much it's actually quite a loaded one, filled with specific meanings as well as dos and don'ts. For one, "fuck polite" is not a command for everyone in training to be deliberately rude to one another. That would be you bringing into the work an agenda to be rude, which would be in total violation of the heart of the technique. Any idea that comes from you is often less interesting, surprising, and unpredictable than an impulse brought out spontaneously by those around you. Being intentionally confrontational or provocative in this work is technically a very weak strategy. It also trains habits that, when tested in the job market, are going to come back to bite you hard. This is not what it means to make "fuck polite" an active part of your acting process.

What "fuck polite" does mean, however, is that you have full permission to say what you see. If your colleague has that floater hanging out of their nose, observe that and work with it. When it comes to your observational powers, "fuck polite" can best be understood as not deliberately obscuring yourself from certain parts of reality that aren't societally acceptable, or have very strict rules around them. Likewise, since you are observing clearly, those observations will also bring up responses. You might have the impulse to laugh, help, or run away in disgust. These responses aren't ideas coming from you but are impulses generated by what you see, and so are directly in line with the Meisner technique's values. Every response is fair game so long as it comes from the other person. As an actor, "fuck polite" will train in you these two extremely valuable habits: to be honest about what you see, and to respond to it without shame.

You may recall that in the past chapter I kept alluding to two mechanisms that make the Meisner technique run. The first half, which you have been working on so diligently, is observation. The second, which you will now begin encountering in much more depth from this chapter onwards, is response. The two are directly connected and entirely dependent on one another. "Fuck polite" frames your ability to observe clearly and respond fully in a very meaningful way.

While this all sounds fine and good, I can hear the nervous skeptics saying this goes against certain cultural norms and rules that have been ingrained for decades. Am I suggesting politeness in general is a bad thing? The answer is absolutely not. Politeness is, at its core, a series of social agreements about how we all need to behave to get along. This is extremely important for our day-to-day existence. If society lived by the rules of "fuck polite," the world outside would be far more volatile. Politeness is a great attribute outside your acting. Amiable people are generally easier to get along and work with. In life, don't point, help your neighbors with nose floaters, and sometimes be kind even when you want revenge. Even in other elements of your acting, such as networking, interacting with other actors or industry members, waiting in between takes or scenes, "fuck polite" is not very advantageous. Unless there is a specific reason to respond otherwise, politeness is your best default mode.

In your acting, however, whether in rehearsals or during a take or performance, bringing in an agreement of fearlessness you have made with yourself is a powerhouse virtue. The actor who comes in and puts their attention on their fellow actors without fear of what they will observe is already extremely exciting to work with. There are fewer things more powerful than the feeling of being truly "seen." Likewise, the actor who allows responses to come up and expresses them without fear of consequences is equally unpredictable and attuned to the needs of the moment. The lines that accompany those interactions will take on those qualities of spontaneity, aliveness, and honesty. Aren't those values that we see in the greatest acting? A philosophy I live by that guided my decisions is the belief that an actor should pick the training approach that makes them the actor they would want to watch. If technique is what you train, "fuck polite" is the key you carry within you to unlock your skills across a variety of situations.

The fear that you will lose your ability to be agreeable if you shift your perspective when it comes to your acting is a concern stemming from ingrained habits. You're not going to lose your ability to be polite. You are simply recognizing that your priorities are different when it comes to the demands of an acting job. Great drama is rarely about politeness unless in an ironic way. Learning to shed the skin of your polite façade and replace it with something far more authentic is an excellent attribute to bring into your acting.

Safety in Danger

There are a few remaining qualifiers that can help hem this concept into a working tool for you. The first has to do with the very rare set of impulses you do not want to express in this work. Yes, I did say earlier all responses are fair game in this technique provided they are generated by your observations of the other actor. This is still true. At the same time, however, there are a small minority you won't allow yourself to express, and those have to do with anything that may compromise physical safety. Take anger, for example. Allowing genuine authentic anger to arise spontaneously carries within it the chance it will manifest physically. The impulse to hit, for example, can arise on occasion. Before you become concerned this is somehow only unique to Meisner, I would argue that we experience the impulse to be violent on a fair number of occasions in our daily lives. Ever been on public transport and someone either carelessly shoved you, banged into you with their backpack, or stepped on your foot? Did you have the impulse to hug them?

We'll delve into this more deeply in future chapters but, for now, while we want to welcome the anger, it is perfectly fine to sit on the impulse to hit, or to channel it into something else, like kicking the chair. This certainly does not mean to never make contact with your fellow actor. The impulse to touch is immensely powerful, especially when it arises spontaneously. This could be a shove, caress, kiss, or a number of other behaviors arising from a moment of true connection. It simply means that as you become better at recognizing your own impulses as they manifest, inhibiting the very small percentage that can compromise your or anyone else's safety is fine. There's no technical value in getting hurt, and this ensures everyone can go to rich, deep, and intense places while remaining safe.

If you just looked at the previous paragraph and thought, "Hang on. Hitting? Kissing? Did I miss something? Is the work meant to be that intense?" the answer is no, responses are not meant to be anything other than what is brought out by the other person. It's also highly unlikely you'll see those degrees of responses arising at this early stage. We're having the conversation well in advance so if those impulses do arise in later exercises there will already be some important groundwork laid for how to handle them. These are not the types of impulses you want to play catch-up with, trust me. Having an early understanding of boundaries encourages fearlessness. Don't pressure yourself to do anything other than what you have been doing. The size of the responses doesn't matter. All that matters is that they are truthful, arising from clear observations of the moment. Everything can be built upon that, including larger powerhouse experiences.

The final qualifier around "fuck polite" has to do with the issue of justification. In acting training sometimes you will be asked to justify your behavior. For example, if I were interested in the reasons behind Ellie's outburst, I may ask something along the lines of:

> "I noticed you got very angry with him, Ellie. Why?"
>
> "I don't know, there was just something in his behavior that was irritating me."
>
> "Interesting. Did it remind you of anything in your past?"
>
> "Well, my dad used to do something like that when he was being dismissive."
>
> "I bet that really bothered you."
>
> "Oh, yes."

After asking for more details about incidents with her father, I might make a suggestion like, "That's great you got so personal. Next time use that in your acting."

Another version of that scenario could also occur between Ellie and Jay, after the exercise.

> "Hey," Jay asks, "when you got angry at me, did I do something wrong?"
>
> "Not really. You were just annoying me."
>
> "Wow, I wasn't trying to. What was up with that? It seemed to come out of nowhere."

Though scenarios like this may feel familiar, neither usually leads to a good outcome. Teachers, especially acting teachers, have no business prodding your past like a tabloid magazine for the hot gossip on your childhood issues and traumas. They aren't qualified therapists, and so in the event a can of worms is opened, the decompression skills needed to talk someone out of a traumatic memory and help them process it are non-existent in that coach's arsenal. An acting teacher veering into this territory is more likely to leave you stuck in your head, mulling over pain and experiences you had done your best to not let intrude on your life. If the trigger is especially severe, you might be told "helpful" things like you simply need to develop a thicker skin, or that feeling things so raw is what a great actor does. At the end of the day, these are justifications for a coach or teacher overstepping their competence and capabilities to a major degree.

In the second scenario, wherein fellow actors seek the justification, the possibilities run just as wide for causing major issues. Every rehearsal, reading, or preparation session you walk into will be composed of power dynamics. In healthy work environments these dynamics protect everyone. In toxic ones, boundaries become so blurred that what is and is not permissible becomes an unknown. An actor seeking justification for why you did something might be genuinely innocent curiosity, but it's not their business. Even in casual conversation, this line of questioning blurs the relationship as colleagues. Whether in training sessions or on the job, from a colleague or director, if you encounter this type of questioning the healthiest thing to do is politely decline to answer. If you like to be direct, you can say, "Sorry, that's my business." If you prefer a more indirect route, play naïve and keep saying, "I have no idea, it just happened!"

In the way of working you are learning here, there's no need to dig into the past, nor to ask actors to justify in the context of their personal history why they did something in an exercise. All we care about is the context of the moment. Did your response come from your observation of your partner, or did it come from you wanting to do something to make the exercise more "interesting"? That's where the value lies, and it's how we keep actors in this work emotionally safeguarded. In the Impulse Company we would say, "What happens in the exercise stays in the exercise." That's a great agreement to go by and I would argue it's the only way to make "fuck polite" a sustainable tool. It's only if you don't have to worry about your observations and responses being psychoanalyzed that you can feel the freedom to observe honestly and respond deeply. It's how you can go to rich, deep, dark or light places and know you are safe coming out of the exercise. Your past will never be on trial. Outside the exercise, you can be your polite self who interacts with your colleagues in whatever way you believe best. Inside the exercises you turn on your acting skills and go wherever the moment leads. What happens in the exercise stays in the exercise.

Temporarily Complete, Largely Incomplete

As we finish off the three moment exercise for now, a few components remain that will be of much use to your journey through it and the rest of the training. In previous chapters we introduced and developed the concept of a hierarchy of observations, the underlying idea being that while all truthful observations are good, some can be, depending on the moment, better than others. At the bottom rests your observations of basic facts, and this might include clothing, hair color, jewelry, and so on. One step up is behavior which, even though it can occur in multiple moments, has a higher likelihood of changing and therefore is a much better thing to observe for the actor working to be consistently linked to the moment. Behaviors range the gamut from tones of voice to posture, facial expressions, and body language. Our exploration of behavior led us to a new type of observation, called the essential behavior. Essential behaviors are the behaviors that tell us something about what is at the heart of your partner's experience in any particular moment. What they may manifest as depends entirely on the moment, so giving an example without a context is challenging (though there are examples in the previous chapter if you ever need a refresher). Searching for essential behaviors defeats their value: if present, they will jump out and demand your attention.

This brings our current hierarchy to something that looks like this:

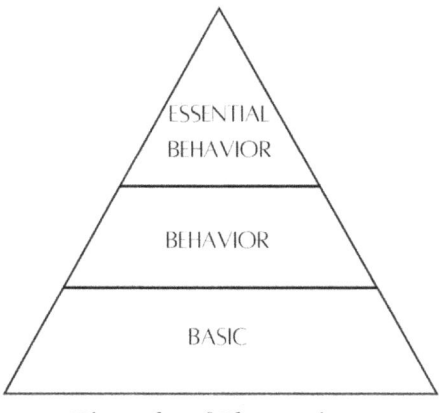

Hierarchy of Observations

In the beginning, the three moment exercise was skewed heavily in favor of observation rather than response, and this was by design. The constant regulating of the experience through pauses sharpened your powers of observation. In this version, however, the responses are becoming more intense. The connected, moment-to-moment nature of the exercise has bigger effects on people. One unexpected consequence is that your partner's behavior might become more difficult to observe. Let's see an example of that:

> **Ellie:** You smiled.
> **Jay:** I smiled. (laughs)
> **Ellie:** You laughed. (pokes Jay)
> **Jay:** You poked me!
> **Ellie:** I poked you. (blushes)
> **Jay:** You've gone red. (moves in closer)
> **Ellie:** You moved in.
> **Jay:** I moved in. (voice drops)
> **Ellie:** You're quiet. (touches Jay's face)
> **Jay:** You're touching my face.
> **Ellie:** I'm touching your face. (suddenly laughs, moves chair back, and hides face)
> **Jay:** Uh . . .

Firstly, before we address the moment Jay is rightfully stuck on, it's worth noting the wonderful moments of "fuck polite" present throughout the exercise. From intimacy, to playfulness, and even physical contact, everything is arising spontaneously because they have their attention on one another rather than their own intentions. It takes courage to express these authentic impulses. Ellie's explosion at the end is a prime example. Why, in a tender moment between them, she suddenly expressed so much is unknown to us. Even better, her motivation doesn't matter. The behaviors expressed are so rich and without self-consciousness that it's given Jay a lot to observe. But has it given him too much?

In this exercise the responses will be generally larger than ever. Whereas before we had our hands full with identifying a single behavior or essential behavior, what happens when you're staring at several all at once? Each one of those behaviors Ellie expressed could be considered an essential behavior, since they were all stemming from something major happening within her in that moment. What to do when this happens? Do you make a laundry list of behaviors and list every single one you see? You could, but this runs the risk of deflating the immediacy of the exercise. The exercise is not about listing as many observations as possible but rather identifying the one key to a given moment. It's about strengthening observational skills, true, but the observational skills also facilitate a rich interpersonal exchange. Long, complicated observations run the risk of the call drawing attention to itself rather than staying with your partner.

Instead, the helpful thing to do might be to make use of an impressionistic observation. Impressionistic calls are just what they sound to be: made up words or nonsensical phrases. This may raise some questions for you, so let's see an example of one to start unpacking not only why this call might be a superb option but also how it fits with the values of this work.

> **Jay:** You're touching my face.
> **Ellie:** I'm touching your face. (suddenly laughs, moves chair back, and hides face)
> **Jay:** You kablammed! (laughs)

Kablammed? What the hell is that? Well, it is a made-up word, and the only person who is ever going to know what it means is Jay. There's no linguistic value to it, and as far as accuracy to the moment goes, that depends on several factors. The primary one has to do with what is happening inside Jay. If he sees Ellie's massive response and thinks, "That was pretty big, I need to find a clever way of capturing that!" that is the wrong set of values to impose on the exercise. Trying to be clever or creative misses the whole point of the experience: it's not about you needing to do something with it. Injecting your own flair or interpretation means you're placing responsibility for the experience back onto yourself and, as we keep seeing, that only adds pressure and sabotages your technique. This is where the impressionistic observation runs into a far greater chance for misuse than any of the other calls introduced thus far.

If, however, Jay sees Ellie's behavior, and all that comes to him spontaneously is the single word "kablam!" then if he were to deny that and instead search for a more clinical observation, he would be losing the immediacy and uniqueness of that moment. Generally, most moments make sense and are readable. Some, however, won't be. Sometimes you see something so large, big, or unique that all you can do is express whatever sound or word comes to mind. An impressionistic call may not have the technical cleanness or sharpness of a behavioral observation. It does, however, have the benefit of solving an observational problem as it arises as well as keeping the attention where it counts, which is outside you.

These types of observations are, by and large, rare. Behavioral, and at times basic, observations will still form the bread and butter of your observational skills. For their ability to capture elements of the moment in profound ways and solve technical problems, however, impressionistic calls rank even higher on the hierarchy, though they will appear only every now and then if used properly.

The Rose is Not the Thing

For now there is one additional category of observation in the hierarchy that is worth mentioning. It is the rarest of the calls, but due to its power to completely and often ideally capture a moment, it ranks near the top. It is simply known as the metaphorical observation of behavior.

Let's see a moment in question between Jay and Ellie to get a sense of what a metaphorical observation of behavior could look like. We'll see a few rounds of three moment exercises for context.

> **Ellie:** You're blinking.
> **Jay:** I'm blinking. (scratches nose)
> **Ellie:** You scratched your nose. (sighs)
> **Jay:** You sighed.
> **Ellie:** I sighed. (shakes head, puts face in hands, rests elbow on knee)
> **Jay:** You're Hamlet!

Hamlet, huh? The old Danish prince returns for a spot of Meisner it seems. Hamlet, however, is a good example of a metaphorical call since the ideal Hamlet is rooted in personal experience. Some of us in a similar set of moments, for example, might have seen nothing in Ellie's behavior that reminded us of Hamlet. The beautiful thing, however, is that the value of this exercise isn't based on how creative or poetic an observation is, only that it captures the moment for the person making the observation. Metaphors have the unique power of being able to reconcile several essential behaviors into one meaningful whole. In just one word Jay was able to take the entire constellation of Ellie's behaviors and condense them into one observation. It doesn't matter whether we would agree with him or not. All that matters is that the observation is true for Jay.

In a technique that places so much emphasis on being accurate to the moment, alongside letting what happens to you be determined by the other person, metaphors can be risky things. If an impressionistic call runs the risk of turning into a clever experiment, metaphors put that danger on steroids. If Jay had reached for that observation, thinking to himself, "I'm going to call those behaviors 'Hamlet', and they'll love my creativity!" that would be a suboptimal strategy to take. If it's the difference between a clever call you came up with versus a basic call that won't change for the duration of the exercise, the basic call wins out every time. Staying rooted in reality, rather than your interpretation of it, is where the value lies. So how does a metaphor then fit with our work? Impressionistic calls have a certain logic to them; they are a unique way to solve the problem of not knowing how to label a behavior in the moment. By default, metaphors feel literary in nature, markedly different from any type of observation we use, and not necessarily in a helpful way.

To be clear, metaphors are controversial, and so if an actor decides not to make them part of their observational toolbox I back them up. At the same time, however, one way to help understand their value is to look at a close cousin, exposed through a minor tweak in our newest example.

> **Jay:** You sighed.
> **Ellie:** I sighed. (shakes head, puts face in hands, rests elbow on knee)
> **Jay:** You're like Hamlet!

Similes are a helpful contrast to metaphors. In seeking likeness, they compare and connect two different points. The process happens quickly but can be broken down as this: you observe your partner's behavior, search for what it reminds you of, and then observe the *likeness*. Your partner, however, can be like many things. Comparing them to something not present in the room, or non-existent, isn't necessarily a great way to be specific to your experience of the moment. In fact, it almost blurs it by asking you to bring your opinion into it. The extension of Jay's observation would be, "In my opinion, you're like Hamlet."

Similes don't occupy a place on the hierarchy for one very simple reason: they don't bring accuracy to your observation of this moment, but instead blend the present with your experiences in the past. Metaphors, on the other hand, are statements about your experience of something. They may not be true in a literal sense, but they are truthful to an individual's experience. For Jay, Ellie wasn't *like* Hamlet, she didn't need to be compared. In that moment, she simply *was* Hamlet. We in the audience can sit back and judge the quality of Jay's observation in terms of how much we agree with it, but alongside accuracy, observational skills are also about being true to your experience of the moment. If Jay had attempted to be clever or creative then his priorities would be in the wrong place. If he had tried to somehow blend all of her behaviors into one whole and come up with the most succinct observation he still would have too much attention on himself. If, on the other hand, in that moment all that comes to Jay is Hamlet, then if he didn't say it he wouldn't be truthful to the reality of that moment. The moment determines the call that is needed, and metaphors are no exception.

Bringing metaphors into your observational skills is a delicate rope to walk. It can be challenging to think of the metaphor in terms of still being generated by what is outside you. Of course the observation comes from you, but the inspiration for it will still be from your partner. Being wary of the temptation to be inventive and spice up your observations is paramount. Within that, fewer things are more powerful than a well-placed use of the metaphorical call of behavior. For now, this completes the hierarchy of observations. There will be one additional call to come much later in the process, but for the majority of this training this is what the observational tools available to you look like:

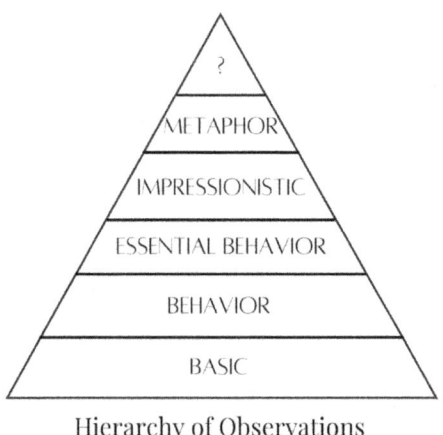

Hierarchy of Observations

The three moment exercise solves many problems for actors. It reorients their priorities and allows them to reclaim the use of the moment and acting moment to moment. That alone is incredibly powerful, and its values pair well with many other approaches to acting. Relating it to meditation, it's a wonderful way to experience headlessness in practice, when self-identity dissolves into the holistic experience of being interconnected with your partner. What we need to do now, however, is continue weaving the values of the three moment exercise further into your acting process. To do that we are going to put the exercise aside for a few chapters, returning to it later but in a new form. Now, however, it's time to visit a classic staple of the Meisner technique, and see what it can offer in terms of continuing to develop this process into a complete acting technique.

Summary

At its core, mindfulness is an exploration of consciousness. This investigation of your own experience is complimented by a powerful series of exercises in Zen that focus on reconnecting with your headless experience of reality. Rather than being cerebral, at its core this is an attempt to observe clearly your own experience. In its original form the three moment exercise develops razor-fine observational skills and helps redefine the concept of the moment into one that is practical and applicable to any situation an actor finds themselves in. What its structure prevents, however, is an engagement with the moment-to-moment nature of acting. In modifying the exercise to introduce flow, the three moment exercise becomes a journey in observe-and-respond, as well as an immersive way to discover headlessness in practice. As you begin experiencing powerful responses generated by observations of your partner, it becomes an ideal time to introduce the phrase that encapsulates the Meisner technique in its entirety: what happens to you as an actor does not depend on you, but on what the other person is doing to you. The fuel that fires great acting in the Meisner technique? Observe and respond.

7
Riding the Non-Wave

Matters of Distance

Headlessness is confusing, wondrous, bizarre, and relevant all at the same time. It suggests that as a concept your head can be dissolved, burned away from your experience of the world. In its place is emptiness, but not a darkness or void. Rather, what we see from is an open space. Objective science tells you you have a head and that is never going to change. Your own private, intimate experience of the world, however, says something quite different. Richard Lang, who took on the mantle of these teachings after their originator, Douglas Harding, passed away, has said we see the world from what can be known as "zero distance." Those who see your head see it from a distance, while from your perspective, you observe the world from zero distance, where there is no head to be found. We often fret about doing something profound with our lives and careers, forgetting that you live within an already profound experience that nobody else (from your point of view at least) has access to. That's not only exciting but, for your artistic process, it's relevant.

In your acting, particularly as far as training goes, you will continue to encounter moments when you seem to disappear entirely. You will still very much be present, filled with vibrant, dynamic responses and emotions, but it will feel like riding a majestic wave in an ocean of experience, and what drives the waters the entire time is your partner. If you haven't run into this, fret not, it can take time to become apparent. On the other hand, you might have discovered this on day one, or even first touched it in the previous session on the new three moment exercise. This immersion is part of the flow experience essential to great acting. The sharper your attention becomes in meditation, the more you begin to discover your actual experience of the

DOI: 10.4324/9781003255321-7

world. Headlessness is not an outgrowth of mindfulness so much as a part of the discovery process. Let's get to know it even better.

In this chapter we are going to do three meditation exercises. Budgeting about 20 minutes for them should give you sufficient time to explore and engage with each. If you are pressed for time, however, feel free to do meditations 6 and 7 together, and then 8 later.

Exercise: Meditation 6

Set-up: Set up your practice.

Instructions: In this exercise you're going to further explore your own experience of headlessness. While everyone will tell you that you have a head, you are going investigate what is true for your own experience of reality. Do these steps, and then continue reading at the end for some questions and considerations about your experience.

1. Hold a hand in front of your eyeline, palm facing towards you.
2. Begin slowly moving your hand towards where you believe your head is until you touch the top of your head.
3. Keeping your hand here, ask yourself a few questions. What do you feel? What do you see? Are you touching your head or, from your perspective, does part or all of your hand disappear and what follows are merely sensations?

Notes/Discussion: I only have two things to base my understanding of exercises like this on. The first is what other people have written or told me about their own experience. Beyond that, I only have what my own experience tells me. From my own experience my hand does disappear. I can see it at first, as it nears it gets disproportionately larger, and then once it is past my sightline I begin to feel sensations. Those sensations are a real part of my experience, I don't need to second-guess their validity. At the same time, they don't actually confirm to me that I have a head. They are just, at the end of the day, vivid and bright feelings. They certainly don't reflect how I feel or what I experience when I look at anyone else's face or head. From my experience, and the experiences of those who do this exercise, it continues to confirm with more senses, in this case sight and touch, that my experience of the world is vastly different from anybody else I encounter. From your point of view, this exercise most likely confirms the exact same thing. It's a powerful thing to realize you are having an experience of the world that nobody else has access to.

Exercise: Meditation 7

Set-up: Set up your practice.

Part one instructions: Building on this exercise, you're now going to try what Richard Lang calls the "single eye" experiment. Begin with these steps and then return to part two for the next set of instructions.

1. Hold both hands in front of your eyeline, palms facing outwards.
2. Joining your index and thumb fingers, put both of your hands together so you make what looks like a pair of glasses, like so:

3. Looking at your glasses, ask yourself if their shape implies you see out of one eye or two. Release your hands. Now, venture to part two below, but remember what it looks like to make your "glasses."

Part two instructions: In a moment you're going to put your glasses on. Put them on slowly, starting from a distance. As they get nearer observe what happens. Ask yourself, from your experience, do you still believe you see out of two eyes? Take a moment to explore this question from your point of view, and then come back to the discussion.

Notes/Discussion: Perhaps one of the defining qualities that makes us believe we have a head is the ability to see through our two eyes. Investigating this, however, reveals another aspect of our experience we take for granted simply based on the assessments of other people. Rather than seeing out of two separate viewpoints we experience life by seeing out of a single space. If you've ever been exploring, entered a cave, and turned at the entrance to look out at the world, this is what the experience might be more like. From our perspective we see out of a single empty space. The glasses experiment reveals that our sight might have boundaries and borders, but even these are hard to identify, and the nearer the frames get it becomes harder to keep identifying two separate eyeholes. It's interesting to explore your unique experience of the world, not as a matter of cerebral intellect but through simple curiosity. What is it like to wake up as you? Are you the identity the world tells you you are or is there far more space there than how others experience you? If we were to meet on the street I would most likely be speaking to your face, locked onto your eyes or looking at something around us. I would see your nose, head, neck, and so on. From the other end, however, what would you see of yourself? From the chest up, not much. In fact, all that you experience is empty, open space for the world.

Uncomplicated meditations such as these ask you to confront what in mindfulness is known as "the looker." When you look, who is really seeing? As we've explored, answering this question intellectually doesn't do much. Obviously, it's you: you are the one seeing the world and observing it. It's easy to reduce a vibrant, dynamic experience to a few simple clinical understandings and leave it there. Great acting, however, doesn't concern itself with your ability to intellectually understand a set of circumstances but rather how you live them out in front of an audience or camera. If you investigate the looker from your own experiences, you might begin to become familiar with this powerful, open space you exist from. A space not defined by other's perceptions of you but how you inhabit this world. That is the experience you will act from, and it's made all the more powerful by your increasingly sharpened ability to observe both yourself and the world around you. Let's build on this with another mindfulness exercise.

Exercise: Meditation 8

Set-up: Set up your practice.

Instructions: For this session you'll be doing 10 minutes of meditation. Set a timer for 5 minutes. In this meditation begin with noticing sensations in the body, whether it is your breath, feelings of tingling, pain, anything that arises. If you find your attention getting too diffused, come back to the breath but now you can expand your practice to include senses in the body. Notice if any sounds arise during your practice. You can incorporate these as well if they garner your attention. When you are finished return here for the second part of the meditation. Start your timer, close your eyes, and begin.

Part one observations/questions: During practice it can be easy to try to "do something" with your attention. You might have read the instructions about allowing sounds and thought, "When do I do that? Do I look for sounds or just stay with what is happening? Do I ignore one over the other?" to which the easy answer is: you don't need to ask those questions, and you don't need to do anything with your attention. The moment is going to handle what matters for you. Those might be feelings in the body, sounds around you, or both. The only technical thing to remember is that there is a difference between paying attention and getting bounced around from distraction to distraction. If you find yourself getting too distracted with different things rapidly grabbing your attention, then returning to the breath is a great way to orient yourself. If thoughts are distracting you, notice the thought, and then return to expanding your attention from the breath outwards.

Part two instructions: Set up your practice again if necessary. Set a timer for 5 minutes. Continue to pay attention to sensations that arise within your experience, as well as sounds. If no distracting thoughts arise then don't worry about this next part, but, if they do, practice looking for the looker. Notice the thought, and then for a moment or two actively look for who is thinking them before you return to the breath. This isn't a cerebral thought experiment but an actual act of becoming curious. Let's see what happens if you investigate your experience in this way when you notice yourself becoming distracted. Start your timer, close your eyes, and begin.

Part two observations/questions: In acting it is easy to get trapped in our head. We find ourselves constantly nagged by a distraction about something that is happening, or something that should have happened but did not. When this happens it might feel like no amount of deep breathing or self-talk can bring us out of this rabbit hole. Breaking down your relationship to moments like these can go a long way in aiding you in your work. Consider first that you aren't literally becoming trapped in your head. It can certainly feel that way, especially if the thoughts are loud and relentless, but in terms of practice, all that is happening is you are having thoughts and your attention keeps coming back to them. That recognition alone may not be enough to pull you out of one of these spirals if they are particularly strong, but they can give you a starting point to begin evening things in your favor. There's nothing to be done about being "trapped in your head." Nobody can reach in and pull you out, and in those moments you probably don't feel you have an escape key. Your attention being directed towards irrelevant things, however, is a lot more manageable and is something you can train yourself to get better at handling. It may sound silly but how we contextualize something really does make a difference, especially when it is a problem that needs to be solved.

When you look for who is thinking, you likely won't find anything. You can't turn your vision onto yourself. Within this seeming paradox, however, is a helping key. Ask how powerful is a thought if you keep looking for what produces it and keep finding nothing. You might even sense that as soon as you notice a thought, it begins to disappear. Seeking the thinker is an extension of that same phenomenon. This doesn't mean that our thoughts aren't powerful, but if they aren't tangible, monolithic things in reality, surely that can help move the dial in dissolving some of the perceived power your problems hold over you. This isn't the same as just telling yourself regarding a thought, "It's nothing, stop worrying about it." How well does that strategy work for you? Often telling ourselves an experience is nothing reinforces how strong it is over us. But taking a moment or two to actively look for who is producing the thoughts, to find the thinker, can be enough to start weakening the grip habitual thought patterns hold, or at least your relationship to how you think about things.

This possibility is just a starting point. It helps to know that there is practical benefit in what might seem like challenging, paradoxical exercises. It's easy to ask yourself about some of these meditations, "What can I do with this? What tools is it going to give me?" "Doing" implies these skills are for actions and problem solving. They aren't. What they instead do is realign your relationship to certain experiences and views, preventing problems from arising in the first place. Their deeper value serves as problem-preventers, not as problem-solvers. This, of course, is a long-term benefit. In the short term, however, continuing to train your attention and soften the grip of distracting thoughts will yield practical results. You may find yourself becoming less distracted or, if you are, able to put your attention back onto what matters with more ease. Or you might find moments of mindfulness starting to punctuate your day. While before you could spend hours distracted or lost in thought cycles, you suddenly find yourself paying attention here or there for a moment with a clarity not normally present. These are small starting points that will add up in a rich way with more practice and time. They certainly will also enrich your Meisner training.

So for now, continue to notice thoughts when they arise and become curious about what happens when you recognize you were lost in thought. On occasion, ask yourself, "Who is thinking these thoughts?" and actually try to look. If nobody is there, then notice that. The attention is the key, not the analysis we wish to bring to understand the moment. Perhaps one of the best early lessons this work offers is that you don't need to analyze something in order to embrace it.

Questionable Moments

Your work in the three moment exercise has yielded a series of tangible benefits, and hopefully by now a few things are becoming more clear. One example is the reasons for how the exercise is structured. The 1–2–3 nature keeps it simple, and each moment has unique value in terms of that structure. Well, all but one, whose contribution still remains unclear. That moment is moment 2.

Up until now, not much attention has been paid to the repeat in each three moment exercise. It was simply taken for granted. Looking at it now, however, we need to ask, for an exercise in a technique that prizes efficiency, what's the contribution of this middle moment? Looking closer, it almost seems out of place. The three moment exercise exists to develop a range of specificity in your observations of the moment. Moment 2 contributes nothing to this value. It's true that in moment 2 you find the observation for moment 3, but couldn't we just cut that step out? Let's use this chapter's participants, Kate and Susan, to illustrate this. First, they'll begin with a traditional three moment exercise:

Kate: You're smiling.
Susan: I'm smiling. (shows teeth playfully)
Kate: You showed me your teeth.

Susan's repetition yielded a great essential observation for Kate. After all, baring teeth, even in a gesture of play, can be quite profound to the moment. But what if we simply cut this moment out and made it a two moment exercise in which the partners just observe each other? That might look something like this:

Susan: You're still. (nods)
Kate: You nodded. (points)
Susan: You pointed. (moves hands)
Kate: You moved your hands. (nods)
Susan: You nodded. (blinks)
Kate: You blinked. (leans back)

Et cetera.

In one sense, there seems to be something cleaner about this version of the exercise. It is purely made of observations, and what better way to train your observations than by simply making a list of what you see? It also is much easier to remember this order. The journey to learn those three simple steps in this exercise can be a major struggle for some people. It's easy to lose your place in the exercise, get confused about the order, or disrupt the flow by either forgetting to repeat or repeating when you shouldn't. This change fixes all of those issues entirely. So what's the value of that single repetition, that seemingly odd third wheel in this equation? The answer, it turns out, is quite a lot.

Let's take the example just given, when the exercise becomes essentially a game of naming behaviors. In this sort of drill, what is the value of your partner's observation? Not much. You know they are going to make one, but so what? As soon as they finish, it becomes your turn. Is there even a value then to listening or, as soon as they begin talking, do you instantly start looking for your next observation, tuning them out? The exercise takes on the latter quality, in which you both work on your observation skills while ignoring one another. Tuning out your partner's observation in this type of scenario isn't you being catty but prioritizing what becomes valuable. It might be valuable to them, sure, but in this sort of dynamic not to you. As such your focus instead turns to what you need to observe. There becomes inherently no value to their observation of you and, as such, no real impetus to actually listen and pay attention to what they say.

In one sense, this might seem in line with the values of this work that are deeply concerned with your partner rather than your intentions, desires, or objectives. At the same time, however, this training does not place your own experience of the moment on the back burner. You are the actor that is going to be inhabiting the moment. Just because observation is key doesn't mean it is the only thing that matters. Rather, the Meisner technique works on two mechanisms. Observation is the first that you have been training diligently in the past few chapters. Richly connected to observation, however, is the second half, and that is response. These two phenomena operate dependently. Your observations generate responses, and your responses will organically generate new observations in your partner. An actor who can only respond but not observe clearly has no real connection to the moment in any meaningful way. An actor who can only observe but hasn't learned how to develop a healthy relationship to their organic impulses is equally at a disadvantage. They are both important. One cannot exist without the other and still serve your technique.

When your partner makes an observation of you, it is going to have an impact. Sometimes the impact might be minor, but at other times it could be major. The repetition is that moment when you own your partner's observation of you. Consider the example of baring teeth. This is more likely than not going to be an essential behavior, and having that observed can bring up impulses within you. These impulses are organic, spontaneous, and entirely rooted in the moment – the perfect fuel. As we've said, what you will do in the moment is up to the moment itself, but the repetition in moment 2 offers you the possibility of a response. It brings a level of depth to the experience wherein there is a harmony of both observe and respond. Take away the repetition and you'll find the exercise loses its depth. Add it back in and suddenly the observations feel much more important within the experience. That depth is why we are going to put the three moment exercise on hold for now and expand on it with perhaps the most well-known staple training exercise of the Meisner technique.

Exercise: Repetition, Version I

Set-up: Two actors sit in chairs facing each other. The distance between them ideally should be knees close but not touching. What this gives is the dynamic of no contact but very much "in each other's space."

As usual, let's set up the exercise using the examples from two individuals. Kate and Susan have done a great job so far helping us clarify the three moment exercise, so we'll ask them to spearhead this new one.

Who begins doesn't really matter so we'll start with Kate. Kate is going to look at Susan and notice something about her. What she notices has to be a fact; it can't be a speculation, a question, opinion, or simile. She is, in effect, going to make an observation of her partner. That begins the exercise.

The exercise then falls to Susan. Susan is going to repeat word for word what she hears Kate say. While this looks identical to the start of a three moment exercise, the repeat will be word for word rather than from that person's point of view. Still, the layout is similar: an observation followed by a repetition. This is where the twist happens. Kate is now going to repeat word for word what she hears Susan say. Then Susan is going to repeat word for word what she hears Kate say, and the two will go on like this until the exercise finishes (when either the facilitator or coach calls for it to end).

If any or all of that sounds complicated or overly worded, let's see an example.

> **Kate:** You're moving your hands.
> **Susan:** You're moving your hands.
> **Kate:** You're moving your hands.
> **Susan:** You're moving your hands.
> **Kate:** You're moving your hands.

Et cetera.

Most repetitions like this can run for 2–5 minutes, and later they can go for up to 20 minutes. That's pretty wild. Of course those will look much different than this does, but it's day one for this exercise. Still, what's the value of repeating the same phrase over and over to one another? I know we talked about the idea of depth and all, but this doesn't seem like a very surefire way to get it.

Let's start with the first clarification around this exercise: this is not a drill in repeating the same phrase over and over. Hang on, that's exactly what they did, and it's what they were prompted to do. It's close, but this wasn't the prompt. The instructions were for each to repeat word for word what they *heard* the other person say. That means the phrase will likely stay the same but the moment could throw a few curveballs in. Let's see some examples. We'll start first with the exercise Kate began. In this version, let's say at one point Susan is going to move in her chair and her keys accidentally fall from her pocket, making a jarring sound as they hit the floor.

> **Kate:** You're moving your hands.
> **Susan:** You're moving your hands.
> **Kate:** You're moving your hands. (while saying this Susan readjusts in her seat, her keys accidentally falling)
> **Susan:** (under her breath) Shit. (normal tone) You're moving your hands.

Now this is a very interesting moment. Notice that Susan wasn't planning for this to happen. This isn't a bit she had concocted. Happenstance occurred and her keys fell to the ground. What, however, happened to the text? Clearly since it was under her breath her utterance of "Shit." was meant to be just that, for herself, and if politeness were of value in this exercise Kate could just ignore it and return to the old observation. But the instruction is to repeat word for word what you hear, and the unintentional nature of the moment has introduced a new piece of text. Should Kate ignore the moment in favor of repeating the same phrase over and over?

> **Kate:** You're moving your hands.
> **Susan:** You're moving your hands.
> **Kate:** You're moving your hands. (while saying this Susan readjusts in her seat, her keys accidentally falling)
> **Susan:** (under her breath) Shit. (normal tone) You're moving your hands.
> **Kate:** Shit. You're moving your hands.
> **Susan:** Shit. You're moving your hands.

Et cetera.

Again, it happens rarely at this stage, but that it could happen reveals something about the repetition exercise. If it's not about repeating the same phrase over and over, then what is important is a degree of *listening*, as well as catching changes in the moment. One time I was working with a lovely actor from France. Stunningly gifted, she was a joy to do this work with. At the same time, however, we hit a snag early in this work. She has a particularly thick accent and I observed she was raising her eyebrows. I'm sure she repeated what I said but for the life of me all I heard her say was, "eye rose." Again, I could have just ignored my experience of the moment and gone back to what I believed she said, but this would have been a poor choice. After all, I know what I said. Maybe she really did say "eye rose" instead of eyebrows when repeating. My insisting she said one thing when she might have said another would have been a subtle way to impose on the moment how I wanted the exercise to go, insisting we stick to "my call." Recalling how my desire to control the moment had created so many problems for me as an actor I decided to trust the exercise and so I repeated word for word what I heard her say: "You raised your eye rose."

Catching subtle changes like this in the text isn't about making fun of your partner or trying to trip them up. "Fuck polite" is a very different experience than bringing in an agenda to be rude. Outside the exercises would I have ever let my colleague's accent make me feel entitled to point out it made some words sound a different way? Of course not. Within the exercise, however, that is simply what I heard, and it came from my partner. Having said that, just as these subtle, spontaneous changes in the text tell us one thing the exercise is about, they also point to something it is not. From the very first session with a partner, inventiveness, especially when it comes to how you interact, has been continuously discouraged. Clever, intricate calls pale in comparison with the power of a simply accurate observation, and an organic response generated by the moment is the most preferable. Intentionally feeding your partner behaviors or responding in a way to juice the exercise for more intensity, play, provocation, or any other coating on the moment is a sub-optimal strategy and not in line with the values of this work. It may scratch the inventive itch you feel, but it ends up giving you weaker technique at the end of the day.

In repetition, especially at this early stage, if I go the whole class without mentioning the minute changes that can occur in the text, almost none will appear. If on the other hand I mention these examples early, funnily enough what begins to appear are little "slips" in the text, happy "accidents" of the moment. See where I'm going with this? Being inventive with the text might feel impulsive, or as though you're in the moment because you're creating something with your partner, but in reality it's all coming from you. Your intentions may be good, and to be fair at this point many actors still don't know the difference between an idea that comes from them and an impulse generated by their partner. Discovering that in practice involves recognizing when something comes from you versus when it is being demanded by the moment. We mention the possibilities of the text changing to highlight the value of listening and not taking the moment for granted. If they keep appearing, however, it almost certainly has little to do with the moment in the way we're interested in it. A spontaneous slip you didn't know was coming is to be welcomed, and this is why listening to each call is important. Changing the text of the repetition because you just felt it was the right thing to do only happens because the attention is on yourself rather than where it needs to be.

Floating Words

Given that we've started to get a sense of some of the parameters of repetition, it's helpful to ask: what are the deeper values it offers in training at this stage? Let's see another example to try to begin fielding the immense value this exercise has for your acting technique.

> **Susan:** You're still.
> **Kate:** You're still. (laughs)
> **Susan:** You're still. (playfully pushes Kate)
> **Kate:** You're still. (goes quiet)

Susan: You're still.
Kate: You're still. (goes red)
Susan: You're still.

Et cetera.

Even though these examples are abbreviated for time, they do accurately reflect how quickly rich and authentic experiences can arise. What began as a playful exchange quickly turned into something heavier and possibly darker. We don't know what Susan's playful shove did for Kate but it created quite a large shift. It may have brought up pain, surprise, even joy, but the response appeared spontaneously. On the job, it's best to hold off on surprise physical contact until you know it's safe territory. In training, however, spontaneous behaviors like this are great for your acting. They open the door for an entire journey of possibilities, in terms of both observation and response. It's rather incredible to consider that, in an exercise with only a very small likelihood for changes in the text, this type of experience is on offer. And yet, here it is, and this tells us something valuable about repetition. Repetition at this stage has almost nothing to do with the words being said but rather the interactions underneath them. This isn't to say you shouldn't listen to your partner; on the contrary observations like "You're still" can have a massive impact on you, but notice what's been removed here. In the three moment exercise the repetition took point of view into account. In that exercise the call pattern would have been:

Susan: You're still.
Kate: I'm still.

Here, however, we have deliberately removed point of view for now. Why? For one, it shows us how much on the back burner we are placing text at this point. For many actors this is a pretty shocking concept. So many approaches to training and entire processes are built around the value of "honoring" the text, filled with tools and techniques about how to intentionally play with words, inflect, or do colorful things with text. In this work, however, we are pushing against the idea that you need to be creative with the text, and for some that is hard. In repetitions I often see actors trying to do something with the text. They attempt to add new spice to each line, infusing it with novelty, only to eventually hit the burn-out wall. It's only when they stop trying to do anything with the words, opting instead just to put their attention fully on their partner, that the quality of their acting improves dramatically. Their entire being suddenly takes on qualities unique to the moment, a level of spontaneity that, if we layered actual scripted lines on top, would be incredibly compelling to watch.

It's only when we de-centralize the power of the text that we can explore the possibility that the more you leave it alone the more honesty, aliveness, and uniqueness it will have. This isn't to say there isn't any analysis work at all, or we just throw away the text from now on. If that was the punchline of Meisner you wouldn't need to spend so much time and thought on your process. There is analysis in this technique, but it comes at the end. The circumstances of a script, however, will have a much more specific relationship to your acting than other approaches in which the text is king and dominates nearly every facet of a performer's process. It's a scary thought to consider the possibility that the more you leave text and how the lines will sound up to the moment, opting instead for connecting your attention to the people around you, that you may be doing more to honor it than the dozens of exercises devoted to making a meal out of lines but not adding any additional life into the experience itself.

If through any of this you've inferred that I'm being judgmental of an actor for wanting to take care of the lines, this couldn't be farther from the truth. There is a real, perhaps the ultimate, career-oriented pressure around ensuring the lines are handled and delivered with the care we expect from great actors. Repetition exposes this pressure in unique ways. For example, sometimes I'll see actors feeling the need to make an observation true and keep it true throughout the exercise. Here's what that would look like:

> **Susan:** You're still.
> **Kate:** You're still. (goes intentionally still)
> **Susan:** You're still. (goes intentionally still)
> **Kate:** You're still. (remains still)
> **Susan:** You're still. (remains still)

Et cetera.

This can be considered the pressure of literalism – that if somebody tells you you are being still, the best, and politest, thing to do is to actually remain still. Except there's no instruction built into the exercise that you have to replicate an observation as if it were a command. The text can be one thing while the behaviors underneath it are another. You know this full well in just about any scene from a play or film in which one character says to the other, "You're mad at me," and the reply is, "No." Shouldn't the actor saying "no" be throwing their arms up in fits of rage and thrashing around the place?

Instead what you often see is a denial we in the audience can read but the other character might not be able to. Drama and comedy alike thrive on contradiction. Literalism that denies subtext is a problem for your acting, and in repetition it will also deprive you of nuanced and spontaneous exchanges. All of the organic behaviors in previous examples would be lost if this were an exercise in imitation and conforming to the observation.

What repetition immerses you in is what is often called the river of experience. Working with your partner, especially now with heightened observation skills and organic responses slowly emerging, is going to reveal a whole world of interpersonal experiences on offer that run beneath the text. Some have nothing to do with the words, and rather than ignoring them, you are asked to embrace them. That connection between you and your partner was likened by Sanford Meisner to a river, with the text being a canoe on top. The river determines the direction of the canoe, not the other way around. The connections between you and your partner in the moment determine how the text will come out. It's not what you want to do with the text that matters but what the moment is doing to you and how adeptly you can flow with its demands.

Tongue-Tied by Reality

This type of discussion often brings up a reasonable concern and fear. We can talk about being free and spontaneous all we want, but you know that oftentimes in projects you are going to receive a script and the lines are going to have to be delivered in a certain way. You can't just let any spontaneous inflection of the text take over the experience. After all, what if it's a "sad scene" but you continuously get joyful impulses from your partner? How do we reconcile this idea of artistic freedom with the very real and important constraints imposed by the work environment?

The good news for you is that this work isn't at odds with those types of needs. Yes, it will always ask you to put your attention on the other person, and to let your responses be determined by them. Whether on day one or one thousand that core value won't change. At the same time, however, there are also ways to prime or filter your impulses, which we will accomplish in exercises you haven't seen or encountered yet at this stage. To help bring some context around this, let's first start with where we are. In both the three moment exercise and especially in repetition you have begun to find differences between moments when you are being authentic versus inauthentic.

The moments in this work demand you be connected richly to your partner, and so this involves clear and accurate observations of their behavior. Those observations will bring up impulses within you, sometimes ones you are comfortable with, other times impolite ones. The ever-growing challenge for you that we will take on is how you can express these impulses rather than sitting on them. Those impulses, after all, are entirely authentic to the moment. In other words, they are truthful.

Truthful observations and responses drive the Meisner technique, and they also form the first half of Meisner's definition of acting which we'll introduce here: living truthfully. The act of living truthfully has in my view always been summarized the most cleanly by my Meisner teacher Scott: "an impulse generated by a clearly observed moment of behavior." That already is a very powerful tool for an actor to bring into their work. As we've begun to see, however, living truthfully isn't the only important element of this equation. Your script is going to have scenarios, character arcs, big moments to hit, and so on. Any acting technique, no matter how seemingly free and authentic, that cannot handle the simple demands of a script is not worth your time. It must deal with what is in the story you are being asked to live out – in other words, the given set of circumstances.

Meisner understood the importance of both elements, and so the complete definition of acting according to Sanford Meisner is *living truthfully under a given set of circumstances*. Sometimes he referred to it as "living truthfully under an imaginary set of circumstances," while at other times "an imaginary-given set of circumstances." That last one tells us something very important that is going to become more obvious in this work: any imaginary components of the given circumstances refer to the author, not to you. This shouldn't come as much of a shock given the past few exercises, all of which have asked you to forego inventiveness and creativity in favor of letting both your partner and the moment take you on the ride. While there is some small use of imagination down the road, it's not going to be anywhere near the level that other approaches to acting prioritize. Reality, as we are going to test, is more than enough to give you the fuel needed to propel your acting from moment to moment dynamically. This of course may be different than your process is used to and, as we've said, our job is to test and seek evidence for these ideas.

If that's what Meisner's definition is, then it's easy to identify the "living truthfully" components so far. You've been working on clear observations and are now beginning to deal with the impulses arising from them. How about the given circumstances, however? Have we done any of that? The easy answer is no. We haven't done anything involving scripts or scenes, or tackled any of the numerous questions actors bring about objectives, tactics, actioning, and more. Hopefully that clarifies some of the questions about scripts you may have. It's easy to want to bring those up early. In most Western acting classes I've been in, we were onto scene work on the second or third day. In this training, however, scene work will come at the end. So, for now, if questions arise about how what we are doing at this stage can be applied to a full performance, just remind yourself you are only working on the "living truthfully" elements for now. The "given circumstances" work is coming and will have those answers for you.

Repetition is in itself a vehicle for training "living truthfully." It asks you to make clear observations based on the skills acquired in the three moment exercise, but also now to begin confronting the impulses arising from your work in the moment. Though this exercise will evolve just as the three moment exercise did, the chance to experience a deep interpersonal exchange between you and your partner cannot be understated. When I trained as an actor in this work, four weeks of training were devoted to nothing but this version of repetition. The waters on offer within it run deep. In the next chapter, we'll make a change to the exercise and gain a better understanding of its usefulness in developing an acting process based on authentic truthfulness in the moment.

Summary

Great acting is rooted in an understanding of your experience of the world. Discovering your own experience lays the foundation for building a technique. Rather than trying to achieve this through some kind of psychoanalysis, exercises on headlessness from Zen can bring the truth of your experiencing of the world home in a simple way, further igniting your own curiosity, fueling your mindfulness practice, and aiding you in observing and managing your thoughts. The Meisner technique thrives on the concepts of observe-and-respond. These are the engine room that powers the results in this technique. It is in the exercise known simply as repetition that both observe and respond begin to arise. The first incarnation of repetition still values observations, but now responses and the challenges of expressing authentic impulses manifest. Repetition's exploration of this through firsthand experience introduces Sanford Meisner's definition of acting: living truthfully under a given set of circumstances. Repetition is perhaps the finest vehicle in the actor's toolbox for training truthfulness, even though at this stage the given circumstances have not been introduced yet.

8
Arising Before Thought

Sinawali

Sitting across from her, the teacher looked puzzled.

"Did I not answer correctly?" she asked.

"Am I to understand this is your reason for meditating?"

"Of course. I want to become awakened."

"Awakened?"

"Yes! Like a Buddha."

Having heard her correctly, the teacher stood up. In the corner of the practice room were a few bits and items for tending to the garden. One of these was a single brick. Returning to her, he brought out a cloth and began to wipe it. He did this for some time in silence until his student could not stand it any longer.

"What are you doing?" she asked.

"I'm making a mirror," he replied, continuing to polish.

"But how? How can you make a mirror by polishing a brick?"

"The same way you expect to become a Buddha by meditating."

—

In an early chapter we looked at the dance between practice and theory. Far too often, actors are not given enough reasons or explanation for why they are being asked to do something. Even more surprising, this is usually by design. Meditation can equally suffer from similar issues, particularly when it comes to exercises like the headless ones you have been experimenting with, experiences that almost seem as if they must be cerebral and highly philosophical and yet are the complete opposite. Rather than a practical meditation in this chapter, let's take a few steps back, looking over not only the journey thus far but also expanding on some of these valuable ideas.

Looking at the story from earlier, even to those of us who aren't as familiar with meditation and Buddhism in particular, this may sound counter-intuitive. To many students, the way to spiritually awaken is by following the form of the practice. Sitting meditation, sometimes walking meditation, are the steps to enlightenment. Our experiences can even confirm this. We sit in meditation and feel more awake, aware, surely closer to some form of awakening. Yet, here in this example the teacher is trying to tell her that her chances of finding what she is seeking following this path are about as likely as him making a perfect mirror from a brick.

As you know by now, none of the meditations you are being asked to do have a belief component built into them. They are derived from formal practice systems but don't ask you to believe in any tenets or values of those approaches. At the same time, however, this story about the dangers of expectation in meditation can also tell you about yourself as an actor. The first great error this student commits is in believing there is a correct form of meditation, a way it looks if you're doing it properly. There is something admirable about this belief: at its core it is a very studious way to think about the process. But much later in the parable her teacher says this: "Meditation can be done sitting or lying down, in temple or the street. It's your attachment to the form that prevents you from really doing it." This is incredibly paradoxical. If it can be done anywhere, with no seeming boundaries, then where's the value of formal practice?

Great acting runs into a similar set of issues when you try to boil it down. You may have an image in your mind of what you will look like when you've achieved the level of quality in your acting you hunger for. At the very least we think we know what great acting looks like, and as an audience member that's a fair point to make. One of the ways we learn what good acting is by seeing enough bad acting. Theatre, I find, is often a far better exercise in this than film. In film, editing and effects can help the actor's performance a great deal. In a play a good performance will jump out, especially when compared against other mediocre or just plain bad ones.

At the same time, however, while we can recognize the type of acting we don't enjoy, it actually becomes very challenging to identify the components of great acting we do like. Make a list of the top five or ten actors you adore. How similar are they really? Perhaps one of them is always recognizable but is totally true and authentic in their work, while another might be a total chameleon that always disappears into the role to the point of being unidentifiable. Maybe one did a run of so-so movies until something happened and they just seemed to ignite with a new fire. Perhaps another did high-quality dramatic work for their time, and so has become beloved by history, but was limited in the types of roles available as well as what could be put on screen in another era. Maybe a different choice doesn't have a knack for drama but is a dead shot in comedies. Consider also the casting dilemma – take any one of the roles an actor on your list is famous for. Now cast someone else from your list in the same part. Would they have done as well? I'm sure Robin Williams would have made a great Stanley in *A Streetcar Named Desire*, but would he have brought the legendary status Brando did to the role?

What comparisons like this reveal is that, aside from very broad, general qualities, the nuances of great actors are hard to identify across larger groups. We can identify what makes Viola Davis a wonderful actor, but Kathy Bates is considered by many an equal powerhouse, though what makes her great is arguably quite different than Davis. Identifying individual qualities of greatness is far easier than trying to pin it down across a group. It seems that great acting has the potential to be almost anywhere, expressed in a multitude of ways with many different processes at work. Likewise, great actors can also do poor work when cast in the wrong roles, just as bad actors can sometimes magically turn things around when working with the right people. Even more odd, sometimes the stars simply don't line up. You can have a stellar cast full of great actors and for some reason things just fold. With so many unknown variables, it calls into question the value of any type of standardized training practice as well as the expectations, both explicit and unstated, actors are working towards when they begin training.

Believing that there is a universal form, or appearance, to great acting can lead to another issue that also arises in meditation. In our example, even deeper than just the attachment to a form or image in the student's mind is wanting a result from her practice. Meditation offers insights and realizations, but it's often said that looking for these can lead to years of wasted time. Likewise, sometimes it's only when people stop looking for the result that it arrives at their feet. Wanting results is fine and reasonable. Otherwise why would you invest the time? It's the expectation of results that look a certain way, however, that can often land you in hot water, more confused and less confident than when you started.

Looking back, we first clarified some of the expectations around mindfulness by dropping the idea of using it to induce a relaxed or calm state. It may be a temporary balm for an episode of anxiety or depression, and there's nothing wrong with that, but the more valuable things it offers go into deeper waters that at times may be uncomfortable, making you more anxious or feeling less good. By learning to pay attention without judgment, you stop trying to break up your experience of the moment into things you like or don't want. Instead, you simply notice them, allowing yourself to feel however you feel. This may sound simple but, at its core, it is using your intention to cultivate awareness. This leads you to notice things as they spontaneously arise without looking for them, whether they are sounds or sensations. The ability to see and feel the moment without needing to impose onto it is what is known in Jeet Kune Do as responding with non-intention. You are aware and present, richly enmeshed in the moment.

The key ingredient to this process is attention. In mindfulness you don't constantly direct your attention but instead follow where it leads. If it becomes too scattered you might direct it back to a single point, like the breath, but especially with more practice eventually you begin to use your attention to become curious about attention itself. This isn't a cerebral or deeply analytical process. It's simply becoming aware of what's right in front of you, the happenings in each moment in real time. You can think of this as becoming interlocked with the moment rather than letting yourself be pulled out of it, swept away due to constant distractions or inessential things to do.

Being interlocked with the present moment has another name you might be familiar with: interconnectedness. Of course the concept of interconnectedness stems from far deeper than just your relationship with the present moment. The more you practice the more you begin to realize you are constantly interconnected with the outside world. This can be a scary realization for some of us. We wish to believe we have the agency to detach and protect ourselves, but the more you investigate your conscious experience of the present moment the more you may begin to encounter the possibility that you are inseparable from the world around you. Fewer exercises bring this home more clearly than Douglas Harding's Zen exercises on headlessness, which both reaffirm your own uniqueness alongside your inseparable connection with the world around you. This type of realization is not only healthy for your acting but downright wonderful. Embracing the interconnectedness constantly on offer takes away a lot of pressure you put on yourself to be unique or constantly delivering something novel or "interesting." Softening both the burden of identity as well as the rigid definitions around it is a superb gateway to allowing your responses to be determined by the other person. These are the core values of living truthfully you began working on in repetition.

Starting to think about identity in this way can bring up some larger questions. In acting identity is a very important issue, something many artists are passionate about. We don't want to attack that in any way, but rather to ask if your attachment to the form, the image, you have of yourself as an actor limits you or create problems in your work. For many it does. Many actors place the responsibility for their performances all on themselves, expecting to be masters of analysis, character work, relationships, and movement, and somehow be spontaneous on top of all that. What if, however, the interconnectedness you have been uncovering in your meditations is slowly revealing that your insistence on yourself as the solution disconnects you from both the moment and also the values of great acting? On one hand many of us like the idea of being as interconnected as possible. In my experience actors are deeply empathic, relational beings. At the same time we still see our work, craft, and technique as separate from all other actors in the room. Could it be that the insistence on your identity is limiting the actual freedom and depth of performance you seek? This is, to mildly understate, a controversial position to suggest. Actors are often told they have to develop an artistic identity. It's uncomfortable to consider the possibility that while knowing yourself and your experiences is vital, rigidly defining yourself could be perilous for the freedom you seek in your work.

Recapping up until this point provides several clues to answer these concerns. In Meisner training you have very little time to think and plan. In each exercise you temporarily dissolve the part of your self that considers planning your responses as the key to its success. What is put in the place of that, however, is an experience in which you flow entirely into the behavior of another human being. Using heightened skills of observation, authentic, uncensored responses rise up and flow freely, with no need for self-regulation or modification. This is developing values about acting you find exciting. Being spontaneous and unpredictable with text is a golden aspiration for so many actors. If you're familiar with To Be or Not to Be, just imagine the moment when you finally see a Hamlet who embodies the values of living truthfully. You know what words are coming next, but you have absolutely no idea what they are going to *do* next. That is an immensely exciting virtue to adopt into your technique.

That these experiences parallel and are complimented by the meditations you have been engaging with should continue to clarify the value of meditation and Meisner alongside one another. The ability to interlink yourself with the moment reveals that mindfulness is not dictated by speed, as many often believe, but can be present throughout numerous tempos and rhythms in the actor's experience. It can be an active rather than passive tool, sharpening the experiential nature of the actor's life, regardless of whether in chaotic or still circumstances. It doesn't depend on quiet spaces to exist, and can be practiced equally near an active construction zone during morning rush hour or a church yard late at night. Its applications extend much farther than most people expect.

On rare occasions I have talked about meditation with experts in the field of acting, specifically whether they practice or not. Though I've met some vocal proponents, from a surprising number I've gotten the same response: "I can't do that. I just don't have the focus or patience for it." This is similar to people saying they don't go to yoga because they aren't flexible. Just as the physical purpose of yoga is to increase flexibility, so the value of meditation is in sharpening your ability to pay attention and focus. The more we convince ourselves that mindfulness must look a certain way the more attached to the form we get, as well as the expectations we place on it. The same is true also of the pressures you place on your acting and process to be a certain way. The question the Meisner technique asks is this: what if some of the tools and approaches that sound great in theory end up creating far more work for you than necessary, feeding your attachment to an outcome rather than nurturing your process to embrace the reality in front of you now?

Bringing together not only this recap but also the growing areas we are expanding on in each chapter, we are starting to get a better working understanding of this concept of the self, and the roles it can play in your acting as well and even your expectations on your career. In our hybridization of the Meisner technique, wherein its principles of reliance on the other person are infused with the selflessness techniques of mindfulness, the training provides actors with the tools needed to thrive in environments filled with contemporary challenges where the interpersonal element has been heavily moderated, such as face masks, social distancing, being separated by screens, or working from home. Even with interpersonal closeness removed, the impact of being witnessed, including self-witnessing, does not diminish and can provide a constant source of mindful sensations and materials. By broadening the limits of practice you will never be without something to observe, respond to, or be mindful of. This interplay between selflessness and truthfulness is where the real long-term value for your process lies when these two seemingly differing approaches are combined.

Let Them Row Your Boat

Of all the experiences an actor can have in their work, I would argue the holy grail above all else is flow. By flow I don't mean any type of imposed pacing, rhythm, or any other element crafted for a performance or take. It comes entirely from you. It's a complete experience in which time seems to become suspended and you are completely in your element. In sports it has been called being "in the zone," but it is also an area of interest in the behavioral sciences. Researcher Mihaly Csikszentmihalyi has dedicated the entire span of his career to understanding it, having produced several compelling books that cover the topic. When it happens while acting, finding yourself in a state of flow might feel as though everything is occurring in perfect harmony. Though you remain completely aware, there is a seeming undercurrent of effortlessness to everything. When it does happen it is magical, and audiences absorb it just as readily as the performers.

Unfortunately for most of us, flow also seems to be the unicorn experience of most actors' careers. I remember several times speaking with seasoned professionals with decades of experience, asking them to recall their best moments in performances, and almost always I would hear a flow story. Just as often, that actor would only experience it a few times in their career, unable to consciously find or replicate it again. Though that might sound disheartening, the good news is that it likely is possible to replicate states of flow in acting, or to at least lay the groundwork for them to arise. The bad news, however, is that we haven't cracked it yet. There are intelligent researchers interested in it, but in acting we haven't yet made significant progress on the topic. If there were a training system that could teach flow in a replicable, technical way every trainer I know in the field, myself included, would be flocking to learn that approach. As a field we remain in the dark on how to incorporate that element into training, but we are getting closer. Luckily I think there's a clue to be found within the Meisner technique.

One of the defining aspects to a state of flow is, despite how effortless it feels when in it, it's surprisingly not achieved by doing something easy. Consider just about any task for which there is zero challenge involved. Ever had to do a repetitive assignment at work? Did the ease of it put you into that trance-like flow state where everything just worked in perfect harmony? Probably not. More likely the monotony began to drive you up the wall. This is why psychologists interested in creating flow recommend that people in monotonous, repetitive jobs find some way to make the tasks more challenging, such as creating a pattern or making a game out of it, anything to drive up the difficulty and thereby get your mind engaged. You can see a minute example of this in repetition. In a repetition exercise the instruction is not to repeat the same phrase over and over. Instead it is about repeating what you hear the other person say. It's a slight difference, and most likely the words won't change, but being able to catch and accommodate organic changes in the text, however slight, keeps the exercise engaged at a high level of attention. If the instruction were simply to repeat the same phrase over and over there would be no Meisner technique as we know it.

A key ingredient to flow is difficulty, but here the researchers also give caution. You can probably think of several times in your life when you were caught off guard and totally in over your head. Perhaps you thought you were prepared for a certain job, project, commitment, or class, and then on day one were completely blindsided. Almost all of us can recall an audition we were drastically unprepared or underqualified for. The sting and residual anxiety from those experiences don't go away any time soon. Inside this training a subtle example can be found in the earliest stages of the three moment exercise. It's quite common to hear participants talk about a tunnel vision effect, in which the exercise becomes so intense their field of vision literally begins to narrow. The experience of having to deal with really seeing a person, without veneers of character or lines to hide behind, can be so powerful that the first few exercises are spent just trying to get through it. The first time I tried a three moment exercise it took me about fifteen minutes to even make one third moment observation. Luckily I was blessed to have a patient partner and the support of my teacher Scott Williams guiding me through it, but even with such a simple, calm format the exercise hit me like a wave. In an environment of constant anxiety where we just focus on surviving and getting through, flow isn't really a possibility.

Flow states are likeliest to happen when the challenge we encounter is equal to our ability to handle it. We interlock with it in a unique way, balancing difficulty with skill. See why this is an incredibly tricky thing to standardize when it comes to training? My capacity for the challenges I can handle as an actor might differ from others, so what creates flow for me might not work for you. Still, there are some metrics the Meisner technique offers us for how an actor can possibly measure their own moving towards flow as part of their technique. It's not perfect, we have to be honest about that, but in my view it's far cleaner than just treating flow like a happy accident rather than a replicable experience an actor should strive for.

In this work, there are several elements that I believe can contribute to creating optimal conditions for the flow state. Some might want to look at the tempos of the second version of the three moment exercise, or they may reference repetition. Both feel like a flow state. While I agree there is something flow-like to them, neither exercise in my view inherently can train flow in a transferable way. Different scenes, for example, will ask for varying speeds, rhythms, and tempos. Flow in performance is far more complex and nuanced than a single tempo so instead we might want to consider two points that hinder flow. Firstly, weaker observational skills can lead to distractions, or the ability to give less attention to what matters. Sharpening your ability to observe other people, to specifically hunt for behaviors unique to the moment, re-orients you from being constantly distracted to continuously present. Being unnecessarily preoccupied either on set or stage with thoughts or other less-relevant factors can compound the difficulties of acting. Reducing them doesn't make acting easy, but brings the challenges down to a manageable level.

Paired right alongside the need for developed observational abilities, however, is the insistence that the actor bring a level of spontaneous freedom to their work. Since you most likely won't be surprised by static elements of the production (the lines themselves are only going to have shock value for so long, if they ever did at all for you), what will surprise you are the people around you. Fellow actors may have to commit to the same lines and blocking take after take, but new behaviors will abound in each one. Being attuned to them means impulses will arise within you, and they will come up on the spot. They may be unexpected, and they may feel inappropriate, but with very rare exception expressing a truthful impulse is one of the healthiest things you can do for your acting. The audience loves it and it ratchets up the aliveness of the scene considerably. Our own impulses, however, are not the easiest things to express. We spend a fair amount of our lives being conditioned that authentic expression is not something to be desired in society. Politeness acts as a balm for our authentic, primal responses, a necessary lubricant to keep the gears of civil society turning. As you begin to recognize your own authentic impulses arising in response to another person, you'll find them uniquely tied in with the moment, giving them the very essence of spontaneity. Dynamic spontaneity like this, however, doesn't hang around long. "Will you express the impulse or not?" the moment asks, giving you no quarter to hesitate. If observational skills make the process of acting easier, then giving yourself permission to express your responses, however impolite, can crank up the challenge factor of it considerably in a good way.

Being able to truthfully observe and respond to those around you can act as a kind of homeostasis, balancing your capacity to see new variables arising in the moment with your organic responses to them. It's when this dance between your skills and challenges are in equal balance that I believe flow becomes a likely experience. The goal of any training system interested in flow should be to prioritize developing the actor's ability to see clearly and respond fully to what they observe. These are transferable skills that can confer a major advantage in seeking that effortless quality that seems to define the great performances we see and love.

Exercise: You-I Repetition

Set-up: Two actors sit in chairs facing each other. The ideal distance between them is knees close but not touching. What this gives is the dynamic of no starting contact but very much "in each other's space."

In the previous repetition exercise, one partner began with a simple observation based on the hierarchy of observations (if you need a refresher on this reference Chapters 5 and 6). Their partner would repeat back word for word what they heard. Then the person who began the exercise would repeat back word for word the phrase they heard, and the exercise would go on like this. Let's ask Michael and Richard to give us an example.

> **Michael:** You're smiling.
> **Richard:** You're smiling.
> **Michael:** You're smiling. (*nods*)
> **Richard:** You're smiling.

Et cetera.

One curious thing about this exercise is that it doesn't seem to prioritize truthfulness in the text. Richard was smiling when Michael observed it, but Michael wasn't, and so Richard's observation is a lie. If Richard stops smiling and keeps repeating, now the text is untrue 100% of the time. The lack of instruction for the actors to make it true, to keep smiling regardless, implies this exercise is not about prioritizing the text. This version of repetition thrives entirely on the current of ever-exchanging behaviors between two people. The words might on occasion dip in and out of meaning, but this is the value of completely de-empowering the text. It allows the actors to explore a world of observe-and-respond without the pressures of worrying about literal meaning.

Now we're going to make a small but important modification to the exercise. It will feel familiar in some ways, but will also give us an expanded perspective on an important element of the actor's process. The change is simple: since Michael began the previous exercise, Richard will start this one. He will begin by making an observation of Michael, same as before. The change comes when Michael repeats. He will now repeat word for word what he hears, but from his own point of view. The exercise will continue on in the same way until they are stopped. Let's see an example.

(*Michael opens his bag to get a tissue*)
Richard: You're Mary Poppins.
Michael: I'm Mary Poppins. (*goes red, wipes his eyes, puts the tissue away*)
Richard: You're Mary Poppins. (*laughs deeply*)
Michael: I'm Mary Poppins. (*shakes head, then laughs*)

Et cetera.

In some ways this is a return to familiar territory. The repeat looks very similar to the one in the three moment exercise. Why then begin repetition a step back if only to return to old ground? The answer has to do with the value of the repetitions themselves. We've already explored how the repetition in the three moment exercise facilitates a small amount of interpersonal depth, as well as clarifying the structure of the experience. In the three moment exercise, the depth is more of a hint as to what is on offer, a means to get you further engaged and sharpen the specificity of your observations. In repetition, however, the values are flipped, wherein a specific observation unveils a vast world of possible dynamics between you and your partner. Since you are releasing impulses brought out by them, the experience becomes more personal, the depth compounding significantly and quickly.

This new version of repetition slightly shifts your relationship to the text. In the previous incarnation we made it fairly clear that throwing away the text has immense value, granting you access to many interpersonal dynamics beneath the words. That's largely still a great value to train for your acting since so much of what matters in a performance happens between people being with one another rather than fixating on the words. If you want a great example of this in acting, treat yourself to Yasujiro Ozu's heart-warming comedy, *Good Morning*. Towards the end of the film two characters clearly infatuated with one another, but having refused to admit it the entire length of the movie, meet at a train station by chance. Waiting for the train to arrive, they strike up a conversation about the weather. It's charged with tenderness, an expression of the affection they both feel for one another, and the text is entirely meaningless. The exchange is all about the subtext, and subtext makes for incredibly powerful acting. This makes the you-you repetition exercise, with its entire focus on exploring the life beneath the words, a superb training tool for your acting.

At the same time, however, it doesn't paint the entire picture. Meaning is a crucial component to a set of given circumstances. Often in both comedy and drama there is extreme meaning driving the characters – what they are doing is important because it matters so much to them. In the circumstances of a script, the words can have a high degree of meaning. What you'll continue to discover, especially later when we introduce scene work, is that the moment will still be the determiner of what has meaning when. Since text is part of that, we want to keep the door open for the possibility of text having meaning in the moment. Bringing point of view back into the experience implies the possibility for ownership of the call on both sides. When the text has meaning is still largely a mystery that you won't know until it arrives, but now the possibility for the words to have equal or more impact than the behaviors underneath them has been reinstated. That opens the door an exciting set of possibilities.

The Loudest Moment in a Room

At this stage, the biggest hindrance to your training in repetition is the desire to play word games with the text, to turn the exercise into a type of improvisation in which one actor makes an offer in the form of an intentionally, and therefore artificially, created tone, behavior, gesture, or so on. The other actor usually takes the bait, and an entire bit emerges wherein both are busily trying to drive the exercise, discarding nearly all of the benefits of repetition. Here are a couple examples of what that might look like:

> (*Michael opens his bag to get a tissue*)
> **Richard:** You're Mary Poppins.
> **Michael:** I'm Mary Poppins. (*puts on an English accent, makes a gesture of wearing an imaginary hat, and waves tissue*)
> **Richard:** You're Mary Poppins. (*bows low*)
> **Michael:** I'm Mary Poppins. (*slaps him lightly with unused tissue*)

A partner making the observation that you are Mary Poppins might be amusing – or not – but no matter how novel the observation, or its precision to the moment, every observation at this stage in this work loses steam. This is not only due to the text possibly being a lie now most or all of the time, but also relates to the immediacy of the moment. In that moment Michael's behavior was a perfect capture of Mary Poppins, at least from Richard's point of view. It's a great metaphorical call provided it plays by the guidelines of any observation in this work, but those behaviors will pass. The call will lose its steam, the text seeming to float on top of the interactions between you and your partner, and for the duration of the exercise it may never have meaning again. This is not only acceptable at this stage but is the point by design. Making a meal out of the text foregoes the potential for the words to be a free and easy conduit for whatever behavior is occurring underneath them. Suddenly repeating will feel like hard work, creating immense pressure on both actors to continue performing when there is zero requirement to be performative in the first place.

This is perhaps one of the biggest shifts in your process that the Meisner technique asks, which is to cease trying to be interesting. This runs counter to so many things an actor is taught. As an actor you must grab the attention of the audience, make bold choices or extreme offers. It's a tough, competitive world out there, and any way you can be noticed is a chance worth taking. Even if you've never been told this outright but have worked enough jobs, you may have discovered the more "intense," "big," or "extreme" your choices are, the more attention you get. Don't worry, if this is you, we've all worked with an actor like that or been there ourselves, no one is being judged. Let's instead ask if this strategy really brings in the rewards some actors believe it does.

Beneath any tool or strategy is a belief. This is true of every tool in the Meisner technique, as well as any approach you've learned either in a class or on the job. You base your actions on beliefs about how the world works, and your views about yourself within that world. One belief that drives many actors to adopt strategies oriented towards being interesting to an audience is the idea that an actor starts out as fundamentally deficient. You are not convincing or interesting enough by yourself. You need to learn ways of moving, different accents, varying emotional tools, and so on, because these allow you to "become" the character. I'm not talking about accents or movement tics that are directly called for by the script; I'm referring to all the extra hard work you do for the sake of it, that compulsive desire to learn one more tool, approach, or accent, as well as the judgmental belief of not being worthy enough if you aren't "working hard" for your craft. It's a belief that is going to inform a lot of the decisions you make, from how you spend your time preparing for a role, to what training courses to take, and what jobs to seek out.

Rather than exploring questions of self-esteem or the psychological components of this mindset, it's instead more worthwhile to examine it from a technical perspective. Seeing yourself as constantly lacking, in need of just one more class or skill, is one of the least advantageous positions to put yourself in. The viewpoint that you've entered the industry as fundamentally "not enough" is one of the best ways to sabotage yourself. After all, how will you know when you're enough, when you've changed the dynamic and can shift that label? You may hear the phrase "we never stop learning," but this is true of everything in life. It's such a vast blanket statement that it really doesn't have any meaning. If you don't even have a clear concept of what it will look like when you've finally surpassed being deficient, I would suggest considering that this mindset is a superb way to blind you from knowing when you are actually qualified to take on a job versus when you really do need to learn an additional skill for a role.

Taking Control of Nothing

The pressure to be interesting as an actor is so intense that you often easily forget how unique your experience of the world is. In both the meditations and the Meisner technique, reconnecting with your authentic experience of the moment and another human being within it is such a powerful eye-opener for actors. It counters the notion that you have to work harder to be more interesting. If you've ever seen an actor, or been there yourself, who was trying to upstage a visibly better actor, you probably witnessed them showing their effort first and foremost as they tried to dominate the scene. Displaying effort is a superb way to make the work of everyone around you look more effortless, and if you're acting with another actor whose skills lie in observation and response, your straining to capture the audience's attention will only backfire. If you've ever had the chance to see a great actor live, you'll know what this is like. Two of the best actors I've seen on stage are David Suchet and Christopher Walken (alas, not together in the same show), and they each bring the most unique ability: even when doing seemingly nothing, either listening or waiting for their cue, nobody can keep up with their presence. There's no scene stealing at work, no effort to be interesting to us, and yet these two forces captivate our attention without even trying to. What's going on when that happens?

Attempting to explain this phenomenon brings us to a divide: either great actors have some magical X-factor that somehow gives them monstrous presence, or they have figured out the more the desire to be interesting drives you, the more it will dominate you and rob you of your uniqueness. Repetition is excellent for exposing these ingrained habits, offering actors a way to see their own expectations of the moment draining them of their individuality. It also encourages you by design to keep putting your attention back on your partner, to let them take the responsibility for the success of the exercise. If both of you are doing that to one another, now nobody is really "in control" and exercises go to rich, deep places with very little time expended and no preparation required.

Control is very much at the heart of the Meisner technique, asking how do we recognize it and what do we do with our relationship to it? It's the need to control that can lead actors to game playing in the repetition exercises. Game playing is slightly different than playing word games with the text, but it can reveal more questions about your process that are worth looking directly in the eye and resolving. Let's watch Michael and Richard encounter this problem directly.

> **Michael:** Your hands are shaking.
> **Richard:** My hands are shaking.
> **Michael:** Your hands are shaking. (*places his hand on Richard's arm*)
> **Richard:** My hands are shaking.
> **Michael:** Your hands are shaking. (*moves in, touches Richard's face*)
> **Richard:** My hands are shaking. (*goes red*)
> **Michael:** Your hands are shaking.
> **Richard:** My hands are shaking. (*suddenly raises eyebrows and speaks in a silly tone of voice*)
> **Michael:** Your hands are shaking. (*laughs*)
> **Richard:** My hands are shaking. (*says this in a lavish accent*)
> **Michael:** Your hands are shaking. (*imitates the accent*)
> **Richard:** My hands are shaking. (*playfully slaps Michael on the hand*)
> **Michael:** Your hands are shaking. (*playfully slaps Richard's hand back*)
> **Richard:** My hands are shaking. (*playfully slaps Michael on the hand again*)

Et cetera.

We can see that the exercise changes considerably about halfway through. Michael notices that Richard's hands are shaking, an already provocative essential call. Michael's comforting of Richard soon turns to intimacy, and it almost seems possible that the two will embrace or kiss. After Richard goes red, however, something shifts. He becomes playful and silly . . . too playful and silly. To be clear playfulness is fine in an exercise, as is silliness, but there is a key difference between the *impulse* to play versus the *idea* to play. We can start to get a sense of this by asking about the accent Richard puts on. What in Michael's behavior called for it? Nothing. Instead Richard decided that the moments between them were getting too intense and that creating a playful game was a safer option. In self-defense, he forgoes the reality of the moment for safer ground. Michael quickly follows suit. The jovial one-up slapping at the end is further evidence that whatever truthfulness the exercise might have started with has been drained. Agendas and games have replaced impulses, and the authenticity of the exercise has dried up.

Playing games, whether it is directly with the text or one another, is a natural thing to be seeing at this stage. As this work progresses, the impulses on offer in the experiences become deeper. Real intimacy, for example, can show up, and for some people this is a major borderline. To be entirely clear, you can be uncomfortable with your boundaries being tested. The impulse to retreat, or to retaliate, is perfectly natural. Just because Michael introduced moments of intimate connection doesn't mean Richard needs to be polite and either reciprocate or even appreciate them. Our goal is to keep the door open for a wide spectrum of the human experience, and sometimes this can become intense. There's no question that there is safer ground in trying to make the exercise more creative, interesting, and lively, but the moment asks of you what it does, and the more you obscure your sensitivity to its needs the harder it becomes for you as an actor discover organic aliveness.

At the heart of this example is the inability to release control. Letting go of the need to control things is a challenge. Some actors have made control such an essential part of their life and survival that loosening their grip over a situation or interaction can be extremely painful. Learning how to be open and surrender to the moment, however, is a quality prized in acting. As my Meisner teacher Scott would always tell us about repetition, "You win by losing." That's hard for some people, and changing that habit takes time.

So, the question on your mind might be, what should have happened instead? Why don't we see an example of that? The short answer is because it doesn't exist. There are any number of outcomes that could have occurred. Perhaps Richard would have embraced the intimacy of the moment. Maybe it would have thrilled him, or made him cry. He could have become angry about it, too, feeling either offended at Michael or overly vulnerable. Then again another set of impulses entirely could have arisen. Perhaps Richard would have shoved Michael playfully and they would have ended up in a proper screaming match. Maybe all or none of that would have happened. There is no example because we can't say what the moment should have been. What we can say, however, is looking at all these possibilities and many others not listed, it's a shame that all of those potential, truthful experiences were denied because of fear. The answer to what should have happened doesn't matter. In order to not miss opportunities like these, what ideally will happen in the future is that both Michael and Richard go to those truthful places, even if they demand courage. That's a wonderful habit to train in an actor – to live in chaos rather than artificiality, to work with fear rather than try to immunize yourself to it.

Now that we've continued to develop repetition, striving for a harmony between your observational skills and the impulses arising from them, it becomes time to take your acting technique to new depths, reintroducing a familiar face in the process.

Summary

Beneath every human exchange is an undercurrent of experiences. Sometimes words matter in life, other times what is happening beneath them matters far more. In acting it is the same. Actors can become so concerned about honoring the text they forget that the words, even of the greatest writers, are still only a part of a vast potential series of organic exchanges between the actor and those around them. To embrace the chaos of the unknown rather than seeking shelter in game playing or agendas that obscure the moment is to move towards a set of values that compound truthfulness in one's acting. Truthfulness generates a sensitivity to the moment, and ultimately the moment is the only thing that will determine what has meaning and where that meaning is coming from.

9
Floating Moments

Behind the Mask

On a beautiful autumn afternoon a few Noh actors-in-training went to see a performance at the Noh Theatre in Tokyo. Our sensei insisted we get a sense of what we were moving towards and, while the performance itself was unique and striking in many ways, I have to confess I remember much more about our lunch afterwards. I was in some ways the squeaky third wheel, having only been with the group for a month or two. Sitting next to students who had been practicing for years, even small talk and banter about Noh training offered a valuable learning opportunity. I asked one of my colleagues, for whom I had a particular affinity given her sharp sense of humor and tell-it-like-it-is attitude, what is acting in a mask like? I was months, possibly years away, from being able to even consider training with a mask, but my curiosity overrode the need to be patient.

"It's an absolute pain in the ass," she said, and I couldn't help but laugh as my sensei shook his head when hearing this. "It's two small slits, and if you think moving in a costume is hard enough, here comes the mask which practically deprives you of all sight. Not as much light gets in as you hope! I've almost broken bones nearly slipping while wearing it." She then became quiet. "The thing is . . ." she said, trailing off for a few moments.

"Thing is?" I asked gently, bringing her back to the present.

"When I performed with it, in front of an audience, it was different. I put it on, couldn't see for anything, but it was like something almost inhabited me. I felt this force, and the mask took on that energy. It didn't matter that I couldn't see: something else was guiding me."

I never got to the stage of putting on the mask for myself, let alone in front of an audience. I switched schools halfway through my year there, finding that

DOI: 10.4324/9781003255321-9

a different style suited my individual needs and questions far better. From this second school in Kyoto, as a gift I was given the opportunity to purchase some masks and fans before I left. When I look at those masks I remember the things my colleague said about the energy she felt behind them. It's an experience that she put years into, one of those moments in a performer's career that can make their work feel almost transcendent. An experience of pure flow.

A few years later, I heard something similar, this time in a meditation session. I had just begun to encounter Douglas Harding's teachings, and the question of where the self is located came up. From the first-person experience, we tend to see ourselves as being just behind our face, as if we are looking out from a vantage point. It makes sense, too, given how important vision is for almost everyone. Our intertwining of identity and sight is one of the most common reasons people give for believing that they have a face and head. So let's continue to explore this in your mindfulness practice.

Exercise: Meditation 9

Set-up: Set up your practice.

Part one instructions: Set a timer for 5 minutes. In this meditation you'll focus on sensations related to the body. Notice any feelings of temperature, pressure, discomfort, etc. With each sensation, give your full attention to it. To orient yourself you can take a few deep breaths, and if you find your attention getting scattered you can always return to the breath. Start your timer and, when ready, close your eyes and begin.

Part one notes/questions: When we think of ourselves, we tend to position our identity in our head. Objective science tells us this is the seat of thoughts and consciousness, but also our visual field informs a great deal about where we orient ourselves in the world. At the same time, however, in meditation practice, especially with your eyes closed, sensations arise in only one space, which is your conscious awareness. At the start they might appear to be located in geographically different areas. A tingling in the foot, an itch on the elbow, a bit of pressure on the temple. The more intensely you focus on each sensation, however, the more you'll find they lose their geographic relevance.

If you focus on your hand and its outline, for example, you can give it so much attention it feels like it begins to lose its perceived shape. The same is true for any sensation in the body. It is entirely possible for the feelings in our body to begin to shed a sense of space, especially if we give them our full attention. This can highlight a valuable insight in your practice: though we think our body is essentially a series of separate feelings in different places, all of those feelings arise in the space of conscious awareness. You cannot experience any sensation independent of your consciousness, and without your consciousness these feelings simply would not exist. Our sense of self, positioned we believe behind our face in our head, is really just a series of sensations that arise in consciousness. Our consciousness, however, is the constant factor.

Part two instructions: Set up your practice again if necessary. Set a timer for 5 minutes. In this next half, you'll continue to focus on sensations, only now it will be sensations of where you believe your face and head are. Again, if you find yourself becoming distracted, return to the breath and then expand your attention to other sensations again. If distracting thoughts arise, actively look for who is thinking them for a moment or two, and then return to the practice. Start your timer, close your eyes, and begin when ready.

Part two notes/questions: Pressure, temperature, tingling, itchiness, pain. Do these sensations confirm you have a head, or do they confirm you experience reality as a conscious awareness where feelings and senses are arising? Maybe you feel more inside your head when your eyes are open, but especially when your visual field is limited you discover a far more fluid relationship to where you position yourself in the world. Even more so, you may find you can start to carry over this feeling of unification when you open your eyes. Your consciousness is a uniform space where all of your thoughts, sensations, and feelings arise. In practice you are beginning to become curious about the space itself rather than the contents of it.

Exploring consciousness in this way can produce a major shift in how you experience the world, but it often begins as a more subtle event. Things may simply start to feel more "together," or "whole," an experience you don't necessarily need to think about but can simply bask in. Beginning to recognize the world as manifesting in your consciousness isn't necessarily a wonderful feeling either. It can induce joy, anxiety, numbness, or a different type of reaction altogether. The important thing to realize is that, whatever the hue of your experiences in these sessions, they all share one unique trait: each arises within consciousness, the essence which you are continuing to explore and become more mindful of. This is making contact with the reality you continuously exist within, the same reality you will act in. Fewer things are more truthful than being able to recognize what is really in front of you, even if it differs from how you may have thought about yourself for decades.

Cage Go in the Water

Repetition can seem baffling at first. Even an actor who doesn't go through an extended Meisner training program may encounter it in short courses or tasters, getting exposed without having a clear understanding of the framework of its values and how it bridges into things like text work and scene analysis. It's a great exercise, loaded with potential for training your abilities of observing clearly and responding authentically to the needs of the moment. At the same time, this isn't the whole picture of acting in this work. Repetition, as do all other exercises in this technique, sits within a very specific context. That context is living truthfully under a given set of circumstances, Sanford Meisner's definition of acting.

As a training tool repetition covers the first half of that equation. It is concerned solely with your ability to develop truthfulness in your acting. Though we haven't yet broached the given circumstances element of this training, you've might have begun to get glimpses of your progress in this work. You've come a long way from day one, when concerns about audience observation and pressures might have been creating problems for you. By now those concerns are long in the past. As you've progressed, the questions about your process have become more specific, refined, and nuanced.

Venturing deeper, what you will continue to find is that the Meisner technique doesn't offer many tools in the traditional sense. There are a few, but not many in a prescriptive way. By this I mean a specific tool for a specific situation. "Finding yourself stuck with X, Y, Z? Use this technique, exercise, etc." In Meisner, the concept of a tool is slightly different. Rather than training to give yourself more to do or learn, you work at shifting your priorities and perspectives. In acting we become so preoccupied with solving problems that we forget even better is preventing them in the first place. An actor who knows how to handle the audience, has a healthy relationship with their nerves, and can work with the nuances and sometimes chaos of the moment won't have nearly as many problems as the actor who can't handle their anxiety, sticks to a plan even when it excludes the unique variables of the moment, and is convinced that they've started the performance off as fake and unconvincing, and the only hope of being believable rests entirely on your shoulders. That's a painful, unsustainable set of expectations to put on yourself. Learning how to discard unhelpful habits in the first place will prevent problems from arising and instils a healthier relationship with your process.

Repetition answers some questions related to your acting process, and it also poses deeper, more profound ones. To get those answers we have to do something very special, which in my view is leading towards an immense step forward in owning your technique and liberating you from some of the constraints we've had to impose on these exercises. Let's see something new and start to get a sense of how it not only fields into the hard work you've been doing but builds upon it.

Exercise: Switch

Set-up: Two actors sit facing one another in chairs. Their knees are close but not touching. This gives the dynamic of no starting contact but being "in each other's space."

Instructions: The pair of actors begins a "normal" repetition exercise. This just means that the structure is similar to the previous session, nothing has been altered since then. At a certain point the coach, facilitator, or teacher, will yell out, "Switch!" On hearing this the actors immediately go into a three moment exercise, the interlinked version we explored in Chapter 6. After a period of time the coach will call, "Switch!" again and the actors will immediately return to repetition. The exercise continues this way, with the call to switch prompting oscillations between repetition and the three moment exercise, until the instructor calls for it to finish.

Before we can explore the values of this exercise for your acting, let's see an extended case study between Lena and Nigel. I won't be marking the moments of the three moment exercise, so if you look at it and could use a refresher, feel free to quickly revisit some of the examples in Chapter 6. For context, however, I will list the behaviors that prompt the next observations and the responses that arise as a result. They'll begin with a repetition exercise.

> **Lena:** You're smiling.
> **Nigel:** I'm smiling.
> **Lena:** You're smiling. (*pushes Nigel's leg*)
> **Nigel:** I'm smiling. (*goes red*)
> **Lena:** You're smiling.
> **Nigel:** I'm smiling. (*goes quiet*)
> **Lena:** You're smiling. (*puts her hand on his arm*)
> **Nigel:** I'm smiling. (*begins to tear up*)

Lena: You're smiling. (*strokes his arm*)
Coach: Switch!
(*there is a noticeable pause; after a moment they laugh*)
Lena: Uh . . .
Nigel: You said, "Uh."
Lena: I said, "Uh." (*moves back*)
Nigel: You leaned back. (*wipes face*)
Lena: You wiped your face.
Nigel: I wiped my face. (*is still*)
Lena: You're a volcano. (*furrows brow*)
Nigel: You scrunched your forehead.
Lena: I scrunched my forehead. (*speaks with some irritation*)
Nigel: You're baring your teeth. (*opens hands*)
Lena: You're a fucking politician.
Nigel: I'm a fucking politician. (*moves back*)
Lena: You're running away.
Coach: Switch!
Nigel: Your hands are shaking.
Lena: My hands are shaking. (*goes still*)
Nigel: Your hands are shaking.
Lena: My hands are shaking. (*deep sigh*)
Nigel: Your hands are shaking. (*laughs*)
Lena: My hands are shaking. (*laughs with him, buries her face in her hands*)
Nigel: Your hands are shaking. (*kisses her on the head, takes her hands in his*)
Lena: My hands are shaking. (*looks into his eyes*)
Nigel: Your hands are shaking. (*they kiss*)
Lena: My hands are shaking.
Coach: Switch!
Lena: You have coffee breath. (*laughs*)
Nigel: I have coffee breath. (*covers mouth, horrified, and laughs with embarrassment*)
Lena: You're a little schoolboy. (*pushes him*)
Nigel: You pushed me!
Lena: I pushed you. (*raises eyebrows*)
Nigel: You raised your eyebrows.
Lena: Your leg is twitching.
Coach: Switch!
Nigel: My leg is twitching. (*looks bewildered*)
Lena: Your leg is twitching.
Nigel: My leg is twitching. (*moves back*)

Lena: Your leg is twitching.
Coach: Switch!
Lena: You're moving your head.
Nigel: I'm moving my head. (*laughs and goes red*)
Lena: You're blushing.
Coach: Switch!
Nigel: You're gripping the chair.
Lena: I'm gripping the chair.
Coach: Switch!

Et cetera.

To See or Not to See

Let's divide this experience into two segments. In the first we'll look at the structure of the exercise and examine some of its unique facets. Though this might seem like just a Frankenstein version of two exercises stuck together, in the joining some unique opportunities are created that don't exist in either exercise on its own. We'll first look at one of the more obvious components, which is the length of time between switches. To start, there's no set time limit for how long the actors are meant to stay in each exercise. Having said that, you'll notice the time spent within each got progressively shorter. This isn't just for the sake of reading on the page – varying time lengths is an important aspect of switch, and tells us something about what it is doing under the hood of your process.

The two essential components of living truthfully are observation and response. While in life we often observe and respond to ourselves, especially our own thoughts and actions, living truthfully for an actor is far more concerned with your capacity to observe and respond to another actor. Acting is a highly relational event. Not only is listening an important skill for an actor, but also knowing how to read and respond truthfully to the behavior of those around you. Observe and respond are uniquely tied to other people and, since we don't often spend most of our lives so richly intertwining with others, some training is needed to develop these skills in the unique ways they apply to your acting.

The three moment exercise is intimately concerned with developing and honing your observational skills, including the ability to capture the micro behaviors which yield rich information about complex internal states. It's also an incredibly prudent exercise in that it doesn't ask you to try to read the emotions of other people or to infer what is happening within them. Before we go further with how this ties into the switch exercise, it's important to note this is a break from classical Meisner training, in which observation of emotions is quite common. In these exercises, observations usually take the form of calls like, "That pissed you off," "You're sad," "You didn't like that," and so on. In the many sessions I've both witnessed and participated in, behavior often gets put on the back burner. Maybe one or two out of every ten calls will be related to behavior, the remainder inferences about the emotions the other actors are going through. This to me implies an assumption both Meisner himself made as well as the many teachers of his technique: in acting, emotion has a higher value than behavior.

On the surface this may seem paradoxical or just an incorrect statement. Meisner was highly interested in behavior. The quintessential phrase ascribed to him was, after all, "An ounce of behavior is worth more than a pound of words." Here, however, is where the waters become murkier. If behavior is of higher value, one has to ask: where are all the behavioral calls in transcripts or recordings of his classes, or in the majority of Meisner classes happening across the world? Most of the observations relate to inferring the other actor's emotions, and this is where the split in the road is created. Emotions are rich experiences for us, usually made of networks of behaviors rather than just one. Joy, after all, can involve many physiological processes that include changes in breathing, face color (that infamous blush), tone, posture, and so on. It's understandable that we could conflate observing emotion with observing behaviors, but this is where several errors in thinking about emotion occur.

The first problem point for Meisner teachers and the actors who train using this approach is the belief that we can become better at reading a person's emotions. To an extent, that is true. If you take someone with very little understanding of reading people and train them they probably can get better at accurately describing the emotional state of other people. Actors by and large have more emotional intelligence than non-actors, so the cards weigh in your favor here. Up to a point. The problem becomes a directional one. We base our understanding of emotions on our previous experiences. The brain is very quick at categorizing them in real time, but the best it can ever make is a guess about what the other person is feeling. If you've ever had a miscommunication with somebody wherein you felt they were irritated when they were not, or worse when you didn't notice their irritation, you know first-hand that this guessing mechanism doesn't always work perfectly.

You might also have experienced that in situations in which the emotional temperature was higher and your own ability to clearly read another person's emotions decreased. In an argument a comment intending to make peace or de-escalate can be taken as condescending or inflammatory when its intention was the opposite. As we become more engaged in an interaction, our observational powers do go up in one sense, but they can also easily misread the dynamics of a situation.

At this point some Meisner experts might say that this actually isn't much of a problem, that when an actor misreads another actor they are misreading their behavior from their point of view. You might have thought your partner's redness in the face and heavy breathing meant irritation when in reality they were experiencing attraction towards you. From your point of view the reality is one thing but from theirs it is another, and aren't conflicts like these the essence of great dramatic moments? This isn't a bad argument, but it fails to take one thing into account: the given circumstances. Currently you have no given circumstances, and this is true of any actor working with the training at this stage. In living truthfully without any circumstances, your point of view can actually become a problem rather than a solution. It's not a good habit to train in your acting to keep misreading both the moment and the behavior of your partner and then chalk it up to a virtue of some sort.

Reading emotions is a tricky business. We can get better to an extent, but the intensity of certain situations can hinder our capacity to try to guess the feelings of others. As such there is always going to be a potential level of error present when trying to decipher an emotion. What complicates the problem of emotion even further is what I've heard referred to as the primary colors problem. If we take anger as an example, there are many ways it can be expressed, not just between people but in different situations. The anger you might feel at a loved one's betrayal could be expressed as markedly different than the flare-up when you stub your toe, or when you receive news about a job you desperately wanted, maybe needed, but didn't get. Your behaviors could be wildly different – in one scenario you might scream, in another you may cry, or perhaps you'll laugh, or go entirely still. "Anger" becomes a blanket term that doesn't capture the nuances of how an emotion is being expressed in these individual circumstances. In effect, it becomes a general label, a primary color, even if the behaviors in that moment are wildly different from other times you've experienced it. To observe in your partner then, "You're angry," doesn't capture much of what makes their anger unique in that moment.

Similar to the primary color dilemma, the final hurdle in making emotion part of your observational arsenal is that emotions are usually package deals rather than singular experiences. In the scenario of losing a job offer you might feel anger mixed with despair. In an argument with a loved one that anger can be woven with pain and regret. Another event might see you laughing while boiling with rage. Emotions are complex, interrelated experiences. How does a call account for sadness, joy, and irritation all in one? Behaviors are specific to our emotional experience in a given moment, whereas simply naming the emotion itself is adding a generic label onto a moment. This violates another core tenet of the Meisner technique: be specific. Generic labels are not specific, and the high levels of value we give them shows a critical error in many approaches to the Meisner technique. These errors teach you habits that impact your work in problematic ways on the job. Your observational skills, and ability to read the moment, won't be nearly as accurate as you believe.

That Old Double Sword

Examining how this version of the three moment exercise breaks with classical tradition reveals that the Meisner technique has a level of flexibility built into it. The switch exercise itself is not from classical Meisner but was developed by Scott Williams at the Impulse Company. Certain elements of this training can be modified, developed, or updated, strengthening its values. The three moment exercise shows that you don't need to observe emotions to have a deep growth experience. Behavior is profound enough, often bringing up powerful responses within you.

This is where the exercise of repetition steps in. It begins with a singular observation which tends to become largely irrelevant. After a few repeats the call loses its immediate relevance and instead becomes a piece of structure that facilitates you and your partner exploring surprising moments of spontaneous interpersonal connection. Repetition is concerned with depth. If your attention is fully on the other person, powerful and sometimes large impulses will be constantly rising. Repetition quickly puts you in touch with your authentic responses, uncensored by politeness or social conventions, and the question you continuously confront is, "Do you express the impulse or not?"

This question doesn't have an easy answer, and so it will keep returning in future exercises. For now the helpful way to treat it is to recognize that, by the time you realize you are stuck in your head about whether to act on an impulse or not, the moment has already passed. Unexpressed impulses tend to feel unpleasant. They linger, your inner critic berating you for not expressing them. When this happens, and it happens to all of us, the habit to train is to put your attention back onto your partner and *not* express the impulse of a moment passed. That moment is gone. Rather than judge yourself, continue to give yourself the opportunity to express the next impulse that arises, and this can only be accomplished by taking the attention off of yourself and putting it back onto where it matters most. Over time, you'll get better at just letting an impulse out without thinking about it, even the ones that for now feel taboo or not acceptable. Just as your observational powers improve, so do your responsive ones, though these usually take longer to develop. It's far harder to give yourself permission to organically express an impulse than observing the behavior of another, however profound what you are witnessing may be. If you find the issue of expressing truthful responses a growing problem area for you, don't worry, you're in good company.

Now that we can boil down the three moment exercise as being about specificity, and repetition about depth, you can start to see the contributions each can make to one another. The three moment exercise infuses your repetition with far more specificity, the observations becoming sharper. Repetition bleeds depth into the three moment exercise. Switch joins them like links on a chain, creating a more efficient way to unify these values than if they were trained separately. When it comes to the time spent in each, shorter durations tend to break the actor out of any comfort zones they might find, whether it is a particular flow, rhythm, or pattern of expectation. Though in the example you see only decreasing time intervals, in training sessions we play with them, oscillating between longer spans in each exercise with short bursts of change. It's a great way to keep an actor on their toes, hyper-attuned to changes in the moment.

At the same time, however, switch is also a transition exercise, a bridge into the work you are going to encounter in the next chapter. Let's give the brave actors in our example some helpful feedback that will illuminate more about both switch and the needs of their own individual processes.

Feedback in Real Time

Though the exercises are simple, there's a lot to unpack about them at times. Feedback is very much the same way. We've only touched on it briefly up to this point, since getting the ideas first has been of more value. Passing the halfway point of this training, however, we need to start shifting our attention to the experiences of those inside the exercises, moving from the conceptual to the personal. This allows you to begin exploring how this training becomes attuned to your unique traits and needs as an actor. How you are spoken to as an actor matters, so let's then take some time and explore the type of feedback that I think is most optimal for your acting, as well as types that can set your technique back.

I've got something to say about most acting teachers. As soon as I do, however, you'll probably suggest I go look in the mirror first. But it has to be done, and so I'll say the thing that I myself and most of my colleagues know but is a sore point for some of us: acting teachers often talk way too much. I know, right? It's true, however. Often in training sessions we'll dole out five, ten, sometimes even more pieces of feedback. Though some of it will be said with the tone of "feedback," other times it will be more conversational, but nonetheless comments about your physicality, movement, emotions, tone, expressions, connectedness, and imagination work will all add up. Being an actor myself and so having also been in this position many times, I think in hushed tones we can all admit something: after the first or second piece of feedback, any more becomes an exercise in futility. Actors are by and large deep, intuitive thinkers, and so even a single suggestion can be mulled over for hours or days on end. There's an introspective nature to many great actors that ponders over the minutiae of a comment, sometimes to the point of overthinking it. As teachers it is easy for us to give impressions in a stream of thought, but we often forget that feedback carries a certain weight to it. Actors go to training to improve their artistic process and as a result their career prospects; our first words of feedback often have a far greater impact than we realize.

In training sessions that focus on your process, whether the material is from Meisner, Grotowski, Suzuki, or elsewhere doesn't matter: there is a level of openness required to hear what is being advised. Information burnout is a very real issue in this work, and so, to bring it back to our training, when a Meisner teacher begins making a laundry list of moments they didn't like it becomes very easy to overload an actor. With overload often comes an emotional response. What could be intended as helpful feedback can begin to seem like a list of insults or attacks if the teacher doesn't recognize they are giving too much input. I've seen this happen far more times than it should have. It's amazing to me that as Meisner teachers we work so hard to teach actors to read behavior and yet can be so poor at it ourselves when it comes to seeing the impact of our words on a student.

If it sounds like I'm framing actors as these emotionally sensitive people unable to take a piece of criticism, this not only isn't true but plays directly into a pernicious narrative that swims around in some training scenes that, as an actor, it might help to become aware of. Feedback should be meaningful; it should target what you need in the moment to help you overcome a challenge to your process. Meaningful feedback requires you to have a level of openness to what is being said, even if you disagree with it. At the same time, however, being open often comes with a feeling of being vulnerable, and for good reason. It's only when you're receptive and available that the empathetic exchanges so crucial to great acting can occur. Sometimes when you go to those places you can't necessarily immediately put your guard back up and so there will be a period of time when you are more vulnerable and easily hurt. This can last for seconds or even days if the experience is meaningful enough.

In Meisner training there is a long tradition of brutal feedback, and it's often coated as "tough honesty" or "cutting through the fakeness." It certainly happens in other approaches to acting, but Meisner teachers are no exception when they attempt to present themselves as having some sort of magical third eye, able to see when you are being inauthentic and insincere and to cut through it with razor-sharp ferocity. They'll spot your bullshit, and they'll tell you without any sugar coating when they do. To many actors, it sounds like just the honesty you've been looking for, right? Except when we prod a little bit deeper, we can see there are problems with this approach to feedback.

There's no question that after having done this work for years it becomes much easier to spot behavior that is not in line with the values of this technique, but just as easily a teacher can get it wrong. This is why, especially as actors advance in this training, it's vital for a teacher to continue asking actors if their assessment matches up with their experience. Questions like "Am I on the right track?" and "Does this line up with what you experienced?" alongside encouragements to let us know when we get something incorrect helps keep the feedback on track and, most importantly, accurate. When a teacher doesn't ask these types of questions in good faith, or forgets to remind themselves that an actor who agrees with feedback given in hostile or confrontational circumstances may be agreeing more out of self-defense, there's a major risk that they are going to misread the room and end up causing more damage than good to your process.

Decades of research from psychology on authority tells us when situations are too hostile or confrontational an individual will agree with what an authority figure says even if it goes against their instincts. Actors who come out of an exercise feeling open and vulnerable and then feel attacked in feedback may become overwhelmed. The tendency from the teacher may be to tell you to get a thicker skin, that it's a tough industry and you won't survive if you can't even take feedback in training. This is a trick of smoke and mirrors. Rarely will you find environments as confrontational as some approaches to training, and sometimes teachers even rationalize this by saying, "Yes, but if you can handle this you'll be able to take on anything!"

Feedback that leads you to close up can create a vicious cycle. When you are told you need to develop a thicker skin, you'll have a harder time opening up in the next exercise. An old field of psychology known as behaviorism has shown that our bodies have a remarkable tendency to remember what caused pain or fear in certain environments, and that we become unconsciously avoidant when in similar situations. That research is over *one hundred years old*. Do we ever chalk this up to a correctable fault of the training and feedback environments? No, more often than not the actor ends up blaming themselves.

Most of us, I suspect, particularly after some time in an industry hub, have experienced some degree of the type of environment and teaching I'm writing about. Maybe it was in Meisner, or method, clowning, Grotowski, or any other approach that confused aggressive overloading with compassionate honesty. From my experience I've worked with actors who actually mistrusted me because I wasn't being harsh enough. They had wrongly conflated someone being an asshole with healthy communication. Rarely could I get the actor to budge or acknowledge the problematic situation they had put themselves in; if the value of feedback is determined by how beaten you feel, then you're going to miss a lot of worthwhile feedback. You'll also mistake a lot of poor ideas for good ones. This conditioned broken communication loop becomes one of the most long-term damaging habits for your process.

Healthy feedback recognizes the openness asked of an actor as an element of their process to be nurtured and honored. It also doesn't give too much information at once. Sometimes in an exercise I'll easily see four or five areas where a suggestion could be made, but what I first try to do is see if all of these issues are circling around a common theme. An actor afraid of feeling open, for example, may adopt certain habitual responses such as behaving like a bully whenever their partner has an impulse to be kind, attempting to steer the exercise into confrontational waters since this feels safer. If that manifests several times in an exercise, there's really only one piece of feedback that is of value, which is to address the innate fear of being open to one's partner. Sometimes there will be multiple areas to be improved on, and in this case I start with just one for the actor to work on. Gradually we'll wear that number down. Through many mistakes I've learnt that patience must be incorporated into feedback, and one relevant point at a time is more than enough for an actor. One or two pieces of meaningful feedback are far more valuable than a laundry list that starts sounding like archaic Latin after a while.

Sensitivity to the Moment Itself

Having clarified some components of how feedback should be ideally handled in training, I'm now going to do the *wrong* thing and give multiple pieces of feedback on the same exercise. This is only due to this being a chapter in a book, with the exercises serving as an in-depth case study where we can go into many points of the experience more thoroughly. In a training session feedback would be one bite-sized idea at a time.

Rather than having you continuously referencing the example of Nigel and Lena, what I'd suggest is go back and read through it once to refresh yourself. I'll paste the relevant sections of it here for us to analyze together. Go ahead and give it a quick read-through, and then come back to this point.

Let's start by looking at this moment between Lena and Nigel:

> **Nigel:** *I'm smiling. (begins to tear up)*
> **Lena:** *You're smiling. (strokes his arm)*
> **Coach:** *Switch!*
> *(there is a noticeable pause, after a moment they laugh)*
> **Lena:** *Uh . . .*
> **Nigel:** *You said, "Uh."*

So, these two are having a beautiful moment of connection, and then I call for them to switch. That's just the pain I am. What did happen, however, is something very interesting. Lena and Nigel were richly connected, deep in the moment between one another, and then when the call to switch came they adopted a deer-in-the-headlights attitude of, "What do we do now?" The long pause, and Lena's "Uh," tells me two things. Firstly, they were connected in the moment with one another, engaged in a rich display of public solitude. Secondly, they interpreted the call to switch as an impetus to exit that moment.

There are a couple of reasons this happens in this exercise. Firstly, for now repetition and the three moment exercise still largely feel like separate experiences. There's a different flow and rhythm to each. When the call to switch happens, you can almost see the gears grinding as the actors transition between them. This is normal, and it goes away fairly quickly. They've never incorporated both into one experience, and so the pause and "uh" on one level is just technical acclimation and not much more.

On another level, however, the pause and general confusion marks a divide in the actor's psychology that can come up in this exercise. Actors come to train in the way they will experience acting on the job – interconnected, alive, and open. At the same time there can be another part of the actor which is the dedicated student side, the side that needs to show the teacher they are hearing the instructions and doing a "good job" on the exercise. Nigel and Lena encountered this first-hand. They were in the land of the former, working on the acting muscles they will take into the job, and then the call to switch pulled them into the realm of being the good student actor, the realm of knowing they had to switch and needing to make sure they did it right. In that moment, however, they realized there were a lot of instruction *not given*.

Consider this question on their behalf: when the call to switch came, who should have begun the three moment exercise? Was it Nigel, since he was the last to speak? Or perhaps Lena, since it was her turn to talk next in the repetition? Maybe the repetition has nothing to do with it. Maybe it should have been Nigel since they were repeating the observation Lena made, or should Lena have just cut in and made another observation to start the new exercise? These are questions you'll realize you didn't have until they arise in the moment, and you have fractions of a second to answer them before the exercise descends into the awkward silence and tension that inevitably crept in. So why doesn't switch have these instructions built in? Why doesn't it tell us who begins an exercise or not?

The short answer is the exercise doesn't tell us this because it's not up to the exercise, and it's not up to either of the people in the exercise. The way we can better understand this is to examine the subtext at the heart of the question, "What should they have done?" The reason an actor asks that is not just for novelty, but because another question is buried within it: "What should I do when this happens to me in the future?" Questions about how to handle the future are tricky, and they point to a growing challenge we are going to keep navigating in future chapters. Actors constantly deal with the unknown. Chaos rears its head, popping up in unexpected ways that must be juggled. Basing your responses on your partner compounds this. We have a degree of control over our own actions but little to none over those of other people. Even greater than the unexpected actions of other people, however, are the unknown demands of the moment, an experience that we cannot know until it arrives. The transition in switch feels like a moment of freefall chaos because it is. It's the first moment we've introduced so far in which there's no structure within the exercise to keep you safe. Who begins the next exercise? That depends entirely on what is profound and meaningful to that moment. We won't know what that is until the moment reveals itself. Or, to put it another way: I have no idea, and neither do you. That is not an accidental lack of planning, but the point by design.

Up until now the coach, in this example myself, has handled the majority of the experience for you. Sure, you have dealt with many unknown variables, but I've guided other elements of the experience, such as who begins the exercise, how long they run for, and so on. This has been very helpful, since it's allowed the actors to get comfortable with the structure of exercises as well as the rich experiences within them. But what hasn't begun to be encouraged enough yet is your sensitivity to the moment itself. The call to switch is one of those moments of absolute chaos when the entire thing could fall apart. It will feel different than just about any other moment you've encountered in this work so far. This is what we need to keep moving towards. It's only when you can not only live truthfully but also be sensitive to the needs of the moment itself that you can start to take more ownership over your process in this work, to begin leaving the good student side of yourself behind and go to work as the keen actor you are.

That transition moment in switch is the first of many in this training in which you will begin to develop that intuitive sensitivity to what the moment asks. Do you begin the new exercise or does your partner? Will both of you speak at the same time or nobody speak at all? Only the moment knows. There's no "right" way to transition between exercises in switch. Becoming comfortable with chaos, even if unpleasant at times, is a superb habit to bring into your acting.

One technical comment could be directed at Nigel. When Lena's eyes effectively glazed over and the exercise began to lose its momentum he valiantly jumped in with the call: "You said, 'Uh.'" We understand that Nigel did this to stop the leak in the experience, a call made more out of agitated helpfulness than anything else. That was the reality of the moment and, all things considered, it's a fine and true call. One piece of input could be for any actor to be careful of being too literal with the calls. That someone said something is acceptable material for an observation, but it has ironically less to do with them in a broader sense. The relationship you have to text at this stage is fairly minimal, so commenting on what someone is literally doing rather than the behaviors underneath can feel less rewarding. Was Lena still when she said that? Did her mouth fall open in total dismay? Was she shaking? There are numerous behaviors on offer which tend to be more exciting than an observation of the literal content of someone's speech. It may be minor, but it's a bit of tool sharpening that yields great benefits over time.

The Courage in Openness

A piece of input attuned to the actor's process can be found in this exchange:

> **Lena:** *You wiped your face.*
> **Nigel:** *I wiped my face. (is still)*
> **Lena:** *You're a volcano. (furrows brow)*
> **Nigel:** *You scrunched your forehead.*
> **Lena:** *I scrunched my forehead. (speaks with some irritation)*

This exchange immediately follows the tension of the first call to switch, when neither actor was sure of what to do. Nigel wipes his tears and goes still. Lena, seeing there is a lot going on under the hood, makes the great metaphorical observation that he is a volcano in that moment. And what do volcanoes do? Not this one, it seems, since Nigel doesn't erupt but goes still. Lena detects this, and becomes irritated.

The first element we have to praise is Lena's willingness to say "fuck polite" to Nigel's discomfort. Impulses not being expressed rarely feel good, and she could sense this, finding Nigel's stillness infuriating. Expressing that, especially in the face of a complicated experience that involved playfulness, tears, and confusion all in the span of several seconds takes a lot of courage, and we love that. What we also want to ensure, however, is that Lena knows there is a difference between wanting to get something out of someone's behavior versus just having a response to it. If she had sensed Nigel wasn't expressing his impulses, whatever they were, and began to become irritated because he wasn't letting them out, then we've identified an expectation on her end. In expecting Nigel to behave a certain way, to give her what she wants, Lena has shifted the dynamics of the exercise and put the responsibility for the experience back onto her shoulders. Not only will this create more unnecessary work for her, but it goes against the core value that what happens to her is not dependent on her thoughts, intentions, or desires but rather what Nigel is doing to her and making her do. The solution in this case would be to remind herself that she doesn't need the other actor behave in any particular way to do her best work. She can still observe him sitting on his impulses and respond fully without the added pressure of making herself responsible for taking care of him and his impulses.

On the other hand, if Nigel's stillness had simply triggered the irritation then Lena's response would have been in line with all the values we are working with so far. She would neither need to justify nor explain her response, since the exercise obeys the logic of impulses rather than asking our impulses to obey the rules of logic. Impulses are unpredictable and hard to pin down, and so long as it comes from the other person one impulsive response is as good as the next.

Inverting the feedback, we do need to address the elephant in Nigel's room: the impulses not being expressed. We can tell his observational work is strong. He is present with Lena and catching a range of her behaviors. The experience has brought up a wide array of responses within him, responses he is not giving himself permission to express. This can lead to compounding issues in the exercise. Let's take a look at what happens immediately following Lena's observation of him being a volcano:

>**Lena:** *You're a volcano. (furrows brow)*
>**Nigel:** *You scrunched your forehead.*
>**Lena:** *I scrunched my forehead. (speaks with some irritation)*
>**Nigel:** *You bared your teeth. (opens hands)*
>**Lena:** *You're a fucking politician.*
>**Nigel:** *I'm a fucking politician. (moves back)*
>**Lena:** *You're running away.*

These are some extremely detailed, powerful observations of behavior. The baring of teeth in particular is a stunning essential call of behavior, one that conveys so much about the primal experience on offer in this work. At the same time, however, observations and responses exist within a context. Lena observes Nigel is a volcano, sensing a brewing within him. This irritates her, and when she becomes irked, he opens his hands, attempting to calm the situation. Rather than succeeding, his actions stoke Lena's fire further and she calls him a "fucking politician," accusing him of running away. Nigel's attempts to diffuse the situation don't go exactly as intended. That's the beautiful nature of spontaneity in this work, and it parallels both comedically and tragically with our human experience. Sometimes we try to make peace and it backfires. Nigel's impulse to calm the situation is a perfectly valid response to a situation of growing discomfort. Impulses to soothe, be kind, and defend oneself can all be perfectly valid.

The learning experience for Nigel is that impulses not expressed can rattle around, leading to knock-on effects in the exercise. This doesn't "ruin" the experience in any way. Our work is about dealing with what arises in the moment, whatever that is. For his process, however, Nigel's refusal to give himself permission to express his responses can create a large amount of tension related only to him. Tension in an exercise is great so long as it emerges from the exchange between the two of them. Tension unrelated to an exchange makes acting harder. So let's explore a few possible impulses that Nigel may have sat on.

Provided he's comfortable with sharing, let's say the first example relates to a moment that came just before switching. He's begun to express some pain, and Lena is comforting him by stroking his arm. At that moment, the impulse to hug her arose, and this became the problem impulse. To some this may sound surprising. In my experience many actors are tactile people who enjoy gestures of friendship such as hugs. For you the impulse to hug somebody might be no big deal at all. This begins to show how individual this work becomes in the latter stages. We will all have our moments in training when we hesitate to express an impulse for fear of the consequences. Nigel isn't comfortable with hugging too often. We don't need to prod his background, but for context here let's say in his past hugs weren't something that were given often, and so hugging someone on impulse is a big deal for him. Rather than express the impulse, his thoughts begin to tell him, "Don't do it. You'll get rejected, pushed away, laughed at, etc." He sits on the impulse, and begins to judge himself for it. A series of moments go by wherein he struggles to bring his attention fully back to Lena.

In the case like this, what Nigel has to learn for his acting is that giving yourself permission comes with a variety of agreements and conditions, from credos such as "fuck polite" to the importance of a response being dependent on a clear observation. Since he has met these conditions, he doesn't need to deny himself. It takes courage to express that which is taboo for us, and on one level his fears are justified. There's nothing in the exercise that says if he hugs Lena she has to embrace him warmly and praise him for his courage. Any number of responses could occur. He might be laughed at. He could get slapped. She may embrace him back, or something different entirely. Everyone in training has agreed that we all have a right to our impulsive responses, provided we meet the basic conditions for their arising. There is also the agreement that anyone can stop an exercise at any point if it crosses their comfort threshold and there will be no fear of repercussion from me.

Nigel doesn't need to "take care" of Lena by not burdening her with impulses he feels ashamed about. Lena is strong and can handle herself. If she doesn't like what he does, he's going to find out quickly, but nobody will judge him for expressing a fairly won response. I often say in this training we are far more afraid of our own impulses than other people are, and this makes sense. For us our responses don't exist within a vacuum. We drag behind us a past body of experiences that tells us some things are okay and others just not permissible. That learning curve has not been easy. For your acting, however, other factors must be taken into account, such as the unique conditions and agreements related to living truthfully.

The Excitement of Safe Danger

An intimate response is one thing, but let's consider an entirely different type of impulse that could have arisen. Suppose instead of it being a hug, Nigel had the impulse to shove Lena hard when she was stroking his arm. Something about her comforting felt insincere, and a fairly large violent impulse arose. Out of concern for safety, Nigel chose not to express that impulse. In this case, on one level I fully agree with his choice. There's no learning benefit to harming your colleagues at all, and it's a terrible habit to take that type of spontaneity into your acting. At the same time, impulses to be violent are valid if they arise from what your partner is doing to you. Sitting on them tends to have the same impact denying any other impulse does, and so we need to ask how we handle those types of responses. The first thing to remember is that Nigel doesn't need to take it out on Lena to express that impulse. He could kick her chair. He could move back. He could stamp his feet or wave his fists in the air. He could also stand up, slam the chair on the ground a few times while screaming at the top of his lungs, and then sit back down. There are many ways to express an impulse like that without putting your colleague in any jeopardy, and so in Nigel's case he now knows if any impulse like that arises again he can channel it into a different expression and keep his partner safe.

When talking about violent impulses, some discretion has to be used since we don't want to suppress touch unless you don't wish to be touched at all in the exercises. Though rare, I have worked with a few actors who, for whatever reason, did not wished to be touched. One admitted she had particularly painful arthritis, and so even a light amount of contact could induce pain. This is all perfectly fine, and simply requires that, before beginning an exercise, you say, "I'd like to not be touched." I won't ask for a reason, and a wide range of possibilities are still on offer with touch limited. That said, unless there is a reason, we want to welcome touch, including contact that can become appropriately aggressive. You've seen examples where light, even moderate, shoving and other examples of physical contact have emerged. This keeps reinforcing the value of not denying the tactile elements of this work. It's only when you feel the impulse will be particularly problematic for anyone's wellbeing that you need to channel it elsewhere to express it safely. As the exercises progress we'll continue to cover more about how to handle dangerous impulses in this work and also why there is almost never a risk of anybody actually being hurt in this training.

When the Moment Has Passed

Some suggestions can also be applied to Lena's work in this exchange. Her observation of "You're a fucking politician" implies to me large responses were held back on both sides. The swearing in particular could be a good indicator. It's very true that swearing can be an expression of anger, but in these exercises it tends to appear as more of a controlled release. It's a great way of threatening to be impulsive without actually expressing the impulse itself. It's possible Lena felt an impulse to rage at Nigel over his stillness, or to express pain or even laugh at him. For whatever reason, she also sat on some of these responses, and while they weren't fully repressed they did come out in small measurements. The swearing is one example, but how about the call that Nigel was running away? Running away from what, exactly? If a conflict were brewing, that's as far as it went, and impulses stewing without expression can become a problem in these exercises. As we've seen, they tend to hang around, but even more problematic is that they can eventually give rise to agendas that have nothing to do with the moment itself. If Lena doesn't express an impulse to laugh at Nigel, for example, she runs the risk of self-commentary coming in: "Oh, I should just do it. Why can't I? What's wrong with me? You know what, to hell with it, I'm just going to laugh in his face and mess with him."

This running parallel commentary has nothing to do with the values of good acting. It's entirely separate from the moment and is pulling attention away from the relevant variables. Even more pertinent to you, there's nothing unique to our training when it comes to this type of experience. This scenario happens regularly to actors on the job. In a take, a truthful impulse might not be expressed for whatever reason, and then the next three or four will be spent partially present with your scene partner and the rest of the time mulling over what you should or shouldn't have done. Eventually when you do express it, does it still feel organic and spontaneous? The answer is almost always no. An impulse not expressed runs the risk of turning into a piece of prescriptive blocking that may no longer apply to the moment anymore. Having this experience doesn't make you a bad actor, it puts you in good company with just about all of us, but we need to find a solution.

If Lena and I discuss these possibilities, and we agree that I'm on the right track with appraising the challenge she ran into, then the first step we can prescribe sounds simple but can have profound implications: if the problem is a train of distracting thoughts when something doesn't go "according to plan," then becoming aware of them is a first key step. In repetition exercises there are a lot of things happening at once, and an acting performance is very much the same. Attempting to juggle several things, sometimes we simply aren't aware of being distracted – our thoughts might be loudly nagging at us in the background of our awareness but in the foreground they could just be manifesting as a persistent anxiety, image, sound, or something else. Being able to recognize you are distracted in the moment as it is happening is a critical first step. The ground you've been covering in meditation sessions will be of aid here. The ability to clearly differentiate between feelings arising from interactions versus your thoughts offers a clear path towards being able to fully redirect your attention outside yourself and not deny the impulses that wish to be expressed.

If Lena can clearly catch herself when distracted, then she can start to get a visceral sense for when she is being pulled away from her partner. To accomplish this, she has to "break the rules" of the Meisner technique for a few sessions. This means taking a moment or two to fully put her attention back on herself, recognizing the distracting thought, and then consciously redirecting the attention to her partner. It's only a few moments that will be lost in the exercise, and over time the need to do this will diminish. Impulses not expressed can distract for more than just a couple moments, so the trade-off is worthwhile, and again it is temporary.

Rather than telling Nigel he is running away, this strategy opens the door for Lena to clearly observe once again the behaviors telling her he is running away. It's how you ensure you stay in the moment in a relevant way, able to make observations like, "You have coffee breath," one of my all-time favorite examples of "fuck polite."

Summary

Understanding who we are may seem like a large, daunting task. It's a big-picture question that seems to offer no real path towards arriving at a satisfactory conclusion. Breaking this question down, however, reveals that a major component of our identity is rooted in our experiences. Misunderstanding our experience can give rise to habits and expectations on ourselves, and so investigating our conscious experience becomes a valuable way to not only reconnect with our actual experience of life as it is happening in real time but to recognize habits and thought patterns that can distract us in the moment. This question of the moment is of equal value in the Meisner technique, and by hybridizing two of its early exercises, repetition and the three moment exercise, an entirely new experience is created. The switch exercise allows actors to oscillate between the interpersonal depth on offer in repetition and the specificity of the three moment exercise. This marks the first step in entering the deeper stages of this training, where questions of the moment will become even more paramount.

10
Losing I Within You

The Challenge of You

At the end of the day, what matters most to you is consciousness. That's a pretty bold assumption given we've never met. After all, there are probably many more experiences that take up bandwidth in your life than thinking about the role consciousness plays in it. Your acting career, for example, the jobs you are working on already, waiting to hear about, or bitterly have missed out on. There are emails to be written to agents and casting directors, networking to be done, and technique to be learned. There are other factors of life that also take up space: relationships, bills, side jobs, health issues. Take a moment to think about four or five deeply important things in your life right now. I'm guessing exploring and understanding consciousness didn't make the cut?

At the same time, you may want to ask yourself why you don't consider consciousness to be of more value. Everything you do is going to be dependent on being conscious in the world. Consider all the examples I listed of meaningful things in your life: every single one of them has to pass through your consciousness to be experienced. Consciousness is the domain in which every joy and regret lives; without it you wouldn't be able to experience them. Without consciousness you couldn't make plans, think strategically about your career, form and break relationships, and exist in the ways we consider being alive. It's even more important than the body: is it possible to not have a functioning body and still be conscious? Of course. A marvelous pair of films, *The Diving Bell and the Butterfly* and *The Sea Inside*, both explore true accounts of able-bodied individuals who lost the capacity to use their bodies and re-discovered the vibrancy of life. Stories such as this are a celebration of the value of consciousness and its many triumphs.

DOI: 10.4324/9781003255321-10

In the same vein, the thought of a body without consciousness can inspire immense pain and argument. I can still remember the many heated debates raging across the United States regarding a 26-year-old woman named Terry Shiavo. Shiavo was found in the hallway of her apartment, collapsed and unresponsive. The story that emerged was that, in an effort to keep her weight down, she had been drinking a high volume of liquids (including caffeinated beverages) and the over-hydrating had depleted her potassium levels to the point that she went into cardiac arrest. By the time emergency workers revived her, she had suffered immense brain damage due to oxygen deprivation. Years of efforts to bring her back ensued, but the Terry that people knew and loved never returned. She remained in a state of brain death for fifteen years before the authorization was given to remove her feeding tube. On many fronts, from political to religious, and even personal, it was one of the most emotionally painful cases the country has been through, bringing directly into the spotlight some of our most intimate and taboo views regarding life and the limits we should or should not be able to impose on it.

Even in the case of Terry Shiavo, at its core was the question of consciousness. There are many lenses this case can be seen through, but one defining aspect is how much we value even the possibility of consciousness returning after an absence. A major percentage of those invested in the case held some element of the belief that, if there were even the shred of a chance some level of consciousness could return, it was worth the wait. We may rarely think about it, but consciousness is very much a personal and at times violently contentious issue.

Existing from Within

The perspective you wake up in every day, how you come into contact the world and handle both its blessings and trials, only exists because of consciousness. If you had no consciousness, your experience of this world would be replaced by a nothingness we cannot comprehend. Consciousness is the forum in which you will experience the entirety of your life. In the same vein, it's also the space in which your acting will take place. Being able to discover and train your consciousness doesn't mean that all of your problems will suddenly go away. You won't explode into this radiant light that nails every audition. There often isn't a mystical experience to investigating it and, if there is, it never lasts. What getting to know your experience of the world better can do, however, is help you identify what in your own mind contributes to your challenges. We can talk about getting distracted as if it's a minor thing, and in some situations it is, but the habit of being perpetually lost in thought, unaware of what is happening in the present, can magnify our own suffering and contribute to its prolonging. This includes the griefs, fears, and challenges you run into as an actor. Even if you consider yourself a diehard method master who can change just about every facet of your personality, your conscious experience is still the only one you get.

Paradoxically, the more you train yourself to clearly connect with your experience of reality, the more you find some aspects of your self-identity dissolving. You'd think that mindfulness is about learning to explore yourself, and in one sense it is, but rather than strengthening your identity, aspects of it can begin to seem less relevant or important. The narrative of our life is far more negotiable than we might have previously considered. Let's take a more obvious example in some of these meditations: understanding and connecting with your headless experience. It's objectively true you have a head. No head means no consciousness and that means no experience of life. Subjectively, however, we spend nearly all of our lives looking at the heads of other people and almost none seeing ours. If we didn't have mirrors or reflective surfaces, we would never be able to see what others describe as our head, accepting its existence purely on faith. There's a power to no longer taking your experience of the world for granted, exploring and becoming curious about the space you inhabit. In the past session you developed this further when you experimented with dissolving where senses in your body are located. The more you focus on a feeling in your body, the more it loses its orientation and becomes an experience within consciousness.

Simple explorations show us that some of the aspects we assume about ourselves are more constructs than fact. Some of our judgments are helpful, others create problems for us, and coupled with our distracted mind, can lead to a fair amount of anguish. To be clear we certainly aren't always responsible for our suffering, but sometimes we are, and sometimes we can compound the unfair hand we were dealt. Exploring consciousness in meditation won't instantly tell you what to hold onto and what to let go of. What it can provide however, is the forum for you to begin recognizing and making decisions about what elements of your identity to keep in your life. That's what we mean when we talk about concepts like dissolution of the self. It's not a process of violently taking away meaning from your life, but providing a means to gain more clarity into what really matters and what is simply distraction.

One of the great paradoxes of meditation practice for actors is that it can seem to run counter to the goals of infusing your acting with more truthfulness and authenticity. How unique are you really going to be if you keep letting go of things you once believed true about yourself? Take the issue of identity. How much time do we spend talking about the importance of knowing yourself and forming a clear identity as an artist? In conventional actor training, quite a lot. Identity seems inseparable from the creative process. At the same time, it might be helpful, and slightly alarming, to recognize that we have much less control over our identities than we may believe.

Consider your thoughts. Where do they come from? Most of us would answer, "They come from me." But is it really as clear as that? Say you're having a deeply important conversation with someone, and then suddenly you think, "I have to remember to get yogurt at the grocery store tonight. I hope those bastards have the dairy-free version this time." Where did that come from? Did you intentionally conjure that thought up at the worst moment imaginable . . . or did it just seemingly pop into existence? The great philosopher Alan Watts would often say, "You don't know where your thoughts come from: they pop up like hiccups!" From the moment we wake up, thoughts, images, and ideas are taking up bandwidth, but how much say do we have in choosing them? In your mindfulness practice you've likely come into contact with this many times already. It seems a great number of our thoughts are unintentional, and the greater challenge is changing the ones you don't want to be there rather than selecting what is going to occupy your mind. With so much of waking life led unintentionally, it really does challenge our notions about how crystal we can make our artistic identity. Maybe we're chasing the wrong set of values when it comes to understanding our artistic process? Perhaps instead of creating concrete pillars to make ourselves more unique, the better process is removing habits and aspects of yourself that bring more grief than help.

Several approaches to actor training also directly base their techniques on this set of possibilities. Meisner certainly is one, but more so in my view is the work, particularly the earliest chapter in his career, of Jerzy Grotowski. By whittling down the elements of our personality that get in the way, Grotowski suspected that what was at our core was not a boring blank page but pure artistic expression itself. Removing habits and hindrances to the point of expressing pure impulses was not the lowest thing an artist could do but the highest. In my time training with Eugenio Barba and his company Odin Teatret in Denmark, I found that Barba's dedication to preserving this chapter in Grotowski's research led to the creation of some profound training techniques. In my view, the work I encountered there is the physically embodied equivalent of the profound experiences on offer in repetition and the forthcoming exercises in the Meisner technique. The work is deep and rich, and you leave with the sense of not having gained more but having lost habits and ideas that didn't serve you in the first place.

Exercise: Meditation 10

Set-up: Set up your practice.

Step one instructions: Set a timer for 5 minutes. In this meditation you're going to experiment with a few different techniques for sharpening mindfulness, specifically your attention to both the body and breath. In this first half, you'll start with what has been described as "noting" the breath. This version comes from Thich Nhat Hanh's work on Zen, and was the first breathing exercise I encountered with his members of his sangha, or meditation community, in Colorado. To note the breath, you're going to silently repeat a phrase on both the inhale and exhale. In Hanh's work, there is often a full sentence and a shortened version for practice. Here is the one you'll be working with:

Breathing in, I know I am breathing in.

Breathing out, I know I am breathing out.

You may recall that on the topic of the breath we've been careful not to force it, but to rather let it come naturally, even if it is shallow or uneven. Repeating a longer phrase runs the risk of artificially lengthening the breath to make sure you get everything in. To allow the breath to come and go naturally, the short version of the phrase I recommend you use is:

In.

Out.

On the inhale, you'll silently say to yourself, "In," while on the exhale, you'll silently say, "Out."

Try this for the full 5 minutes and then return here. Start your timer, close your eyes, and begin when ready.

Step one notes/questions: Noting can be extremely helpful for meditators, sometimes for surprising reasons. It's common to lose track of when we become distracted. The current of our thoughts is so strong that we find ourselves pulled along for minutes at a time before awakening to what has happened. Noting can be an excellent metric for catching yourself when you become lost in thought. When the added layer of a mental note disappears, there can be a sort of lightbulb moment that makes you go, "Oh, I was completely lost, I stopped repeating to myself." This can be an excellent way to sharpen your practice. When you find yourself lost in thought, notice the thought, and search for any feelings of annoyance or judgment at yourself. These are just more thoughts, so observe them as well and then return to the practice of noting your breath.

Step two instructions: Set up your practice again if necessary. Set a timer for 5 minutes. In this next half, you'll continue to focus on noting, though of a different kind. Once you begin, start by counting backwards for 21 breaths. This means when you inhale you silently say to yourself, "20," and then same for when you exhale. Then on your next inhale you say, "19," and so on, all the way until you reach zero (include the zero in your counting). Here's one additional component: every three breaths, consciously relax the corners of your eyes. When you hit zero, start over again, until your timer beeps. When you are ready, start your timer, close your eyes, and begin.

Step two notes/questions: This approach to noting doesn't come from any strand of mindfulness I've encountered. I learned it from working with a particularly gifted yoga teacher in Arizona, and it always stuck with me as an excellent way to compliment the practice of noting. The practice of counting has largely the same effect as repeating a phrase such as "In/Out," and some people will relate more to the idea of a countdown versus a continuous stream of phrases. Even more useful I found was the practice of consciously releasing tension around the eyes every three breaths. There are a few elements to this worth pointing out. The eyes, particularly the corners of them, are an area we don't pay much attention to throughout our day, and yet they hold reserves of tension. From squinting to habitual facial expressions, our eyes can be a major tell about our unconscious habits. If you're like me, you might have found that in between each round of three breaths some or all of the tension you had released crept right back in. If that wasn't your experience it's completely fine, but a large number of people I've spoken to about this exercise have a similar experience in discovering habits of their body that operate independently of conscious intervention. In mindfulness practice you begin a process of discovering your body in a unique way, particularly the sensations that accompany it. Focusing on a minute sensation you don't give much thought to offers another means to sharpen your attention and train yourself to be aware of elements you might not have noticed before.

Noting works wonders for some people. It can open up entire avenues of awareness, and some strands of mindfulness base their entire approach on it.

For others it won't be as effective, and knowing where it lands for you is just as valuable. Even though meditation practice is gradual, there are some tools that can expedite the quality of your technique, and noting the breath can have this effect on some meditators. It's also a useful tool in the event you find yourself especially distracted. In its functionality there is depth, so feel free to continue using it in the future meditations within this book even if I no longer mention it.

When You Really Feel It

This chapter marks the first major turning point in this work. After what has been a thorough, in-depth, and at times trying journey for your process, you will begin to see more concrete rewards for your labors. These will compound even further in the next chapter. At this stage in the work actors often feel that things accelerate, that suddenly the exercises become more "advanced." While it may seem that way, in truth the exercises you'll encounter from here on aren't necessarily that much more complicated. They are simply the result of all the legwork you've done up to now, a tipping point for your acting process. Having said that, the newness of these experiences is palpable, and can be wonderfully intense and feel like a true rollercoaster of experience.

In the past chapter, you encountered a Frankenstein exercise known as switch. Switch is essentially repetition and the three moment exercise stitched together, with the changes in the exercises being guided by the coach. Though switch does indeed have some valuable lessons for your process, we also discovered that it seems to act as more of a bridge, rather than being a concrete exercise in itself. But a bridge to what? That's what we're going to discover now, as we take switch to its newest incarnation.

Exercise: Auto-Switch

Set-up: Two actors sit facing one another in chairs. Knees are close but not touching. This gives the dynamic of no starting contact but being "in each other's space."

Instructions: The actors do the switch exercise, beginning first with the three moment exercise and then transitioning into repetition. If any clarification is needed on the individual components or steps, refer to the previous chapter. There is no difference in the exercise itself; it is the exact same version of switch you encountered before. The key difference, however, is that now the coach won't call for the switch to occur, and neither will anyone else in the room.

At this point a sense of panic almost always floods the actors who hear this. What do you mean you won't call it out? they ask. How will we know when to switch? What if it never happens, what if we don't do it right, what if, what if, and more what if. The answer to all of this is the same: I have no idea. Rather than try to pre-empt the future, let's just do one and see what happens. Courtney and Gina graciously, and bravely, agree to try it out.

>   **Courtney:** You sat down.
>   **Gina:** I sat down. (*smiles*)
>   **Courtney:** You smiled. (*moves chair in*)
>   **Gina:** You're coming in.
>   **Courtney:** I'm coming in. (*nervously laughs*)
>   **Gina:** You laughed. (*touches Courtney's arm*)
>   **Courtney:** You're touching my arm.
>   **Gina:** I'm touching your arm.
>   **Courtney:** You're touching my arm. (*goes quieter*)
>   **Gina:** I'm touching your arm.
>   **Courtney:** You're touching my arm. (*laughs and tears up a little*)
>   **Gina:** You're crying.
>   **Courtney:** I'm crying. (*nods*)
>   **Gina:** You nodded. (*gives Courtney a hug*)
>   **Courtney:** You're holding me.
>   **Gina:** I'm holding you. (*speaks comfortingly*)
>   **Courtney:** You're still.
>   **Gina:** I'm still.
>   **Courtney:** You're still. (*Gina pulls back*)
>   **Gina:** I'm still.

Though it hasn't run for too long, let's say I stop the exercise here. There's much to talk about both in terms of the exercise and what each actor went through. Before we get to that I want to point out something that is often a concern among actors, and it relates to the presence of the tears. We've also seen some crying beforehand. Is this a goal, for the exercises to get this emotional? When actors come to this training they bring a variety of concerns and needs, and one of the most consistent ones I've noticed relates to emotions, specifically how to generate them on command. It's normal to hear discussions about creating real emotion in just about any conventional actor training, whether it is Stanislavski, the method, Uta Hagen, Stella Adler, or numerous other name approaches, so let's address it here.

On a surface level, trying to generate emotions using many classic tools, whether from your imagination or memory, seems a forlorn quest given that it violates the core principle of the Meisner technique. With the other person being of such primary value, and all exercises attuned to observing and responding to them, taking the time to focus on your own experience to try to consciously alter it doesn't sit cleanly with our values. That, however, really is just scratching the surface of the issue. If it's just a matter of rules, then who really cares? What's more interesting is the possibility that you can have a richer, more honest emotional experience by *not* putting much attention on yourself.

That seems counter-intuitive. With emotions being such an important part of acting, how can you have access to deep emotional experiences without needing any input from yourself? One answer lies in the way this training reflects our human experience. Consider life outside your acting. For many of us, feeling emotion really isn't much of an issue. Ever had someone bump you on the street and before you knew it a surge of rage flashed up? How much premeditating did you need to do? None. The stimulus came from outside you and before you knew it an authentic response had arisen. Have you ever been shamed at work, either by a colleague or superior? You might have felt tears welling up and fought to push them back down. Or what about the experience of a stranger you found attractive suddenly noticing and smiling at you? Your whole heart feels like it's welling up. Do you express your rage and throw your scone at the person who cut you off, burst into tears and wail uncontrollably in front of your boss, or jump up in excitement at the smile you've received? Of course not. You work hard to stop these feelings, to contain and moderate them. A fair amount of life is spent grappling with emotions we have little control over, not trying to generate them.

At the same time, though entangled with the world around us, we also generate feelings. Thoughts can just as easily guide your behaviors, especially when you are ruminating over something. Take that horrible incident at work: do you let that go as soon as it hits 5 o' clock and your shift is over? Chances are, not. You mull over it, stewing for days over what happened as well as what you should have said or done in the moment. Our thoughts about an event can color thousands of moments after it has occurred. This isn't necessarily a bad thing. People can think deeply on a troubling experience before coming to the conclusion that a proactive action needs to be taken to ensure it doesn't happen again. What is worth recognizing is that we do spend time generating our emotions without much issue, so then why does it feel so hard for many actors to create an emotional experience in a class, in rehearsal, or on set? Something isn't adding up. The argument that you just need practice equally doesn't make much sense when you consider how much of our lives we spend engaged in prolonging certain emotional states.

One possible issue with the classical emotion-creating approaches has to do with the nature of acting itself. Acting is largely a relational experience. The overwhelming majority of drama involves people speaking and interacting with one another. The majority of Shakespeare's great monologues are written with the intent of addressing the audience, directly or indirectly. Even one-person shows involve working with the audience. Acting trades in the interconnectedness between you and at least one other actor or the audience. Why then are we so fixated on you needing to use your own personal history or imagination as fuel when such a large amount of both your personal life and acting work involves outside stimuli? Where's the value in getting better at using yourself as material when nearly the bulk of every line you'll have to speak relates to what is *out there*?

I would argue that many traditional ideas about acting make it harder to learn how to act because they go against our natural instincts and a large majority of our human experience in general. They might be brilliant, but they're brilliantly wrong. The unfortunate thing is that actors convince themselves that if their acting training doesn't feel hard before it feels natural then something must be wrong. Hard work, however, doesn't necessarily mean *better* work. Why all the self-chastising and brutal criticism for not being able to do things humans simply don't do well? Emotions that are directly generated by us don't have nearly as strong a connection to outside stimuli as ones that are unexpectedly triggered. As far acting is concerned, it seems far more likely that training to engage with what is outside our thoughts and body is of more importance than trying to first mine some authenticity from within and then somehow connect it to our colleagues.

Before we return to the example exercise, I just want to clarify that I'm not saying there is zero value in focusing on yourself. The ability to engage with our thoughts and imagination to alter our experience is also a part of the human experience. Any acting technique that denies an element of our personal experience is incomplete. In just a few chapters we're going to begin introducing new concepts, some of which ask you to engage with yourself in ways you have not yet experienced in this work. We also need to deal with how you handle specific moments within given circumstances that call for an emotional result, such as crying on a certain line. Personal engagement is still a component of this training. What you will notice, however, is that it is minor. The majority of this training is invested in connecting you to what is outside you and letting that take care of most of your work as an actor. That's a far healthier balance in my view than exaggerating the importance of our own introspection. The greater value in acting will always be what happens outside you and, as Courtney experienced, that can lead to surprising and complex rich emotional experiences without reaching for them, such as laughter through tears.

Moments, Not Mistakes

If you need a quick refresher on the example exercise feel free to do that now. Courtney and Gina had, by and large, a superb exercise. Part of what makes it superb is that there was evidence of strong technique at work, and the other part is that it raises a lot of questions that will target their process and learning needs. So, here's the first big question: without the coach to call it, how did they know when to switch? With no seemingly clear guidelines, how will you know when to switch? The short answer is it isn't up to you, nor is it up to your partner. That leaves us at a bit of a strange divide: if the coach doesn't know, and neither person in the exercise knows, how did the transitions happen anyway?

In the previous incarnation of switch we encountered some questions about the nature of the transition. Who, for example, begins the new three moment exercise or repetition? We concluded that there was no easy answer that didn't involve either or both partners breaking the values of the technique and introducing an artificial agenda or decision. It seemed that while you wouldn't know beforehand, when the call to switch comes the moment itself reveals that answer. It might be chaotic and messy, but it will be apparent. This newest experience of switch behaves in a similar way. It seems that when you change between exercises doesn't depend on you but rather the needs of the moment itself. For many actors, especially when they feel what that is like in practice, that can be terrifying.

Auto-switch is an escalation of your sensitivity to the moment. It asks you to release your dependence on a change coming. Wait, but doesn't a change have to occur? The answer is if it doesn't arise in the moment, then a change won't occur in the exercise. Most of the time it will, but now you have to trust that the moment will take care of the call to change if it comes at all. Furthermore, you also must release your dependence that, if a change comes, you will do the right thing. That targets perhaps one of the biggest challenges in this training, revealing a value that very few actors are comfortable with: in this work, there is no such thing as a mistake.

Most actors depend on mistakes existing, especially in training. You'll attempt an exercise and make several mistakes in it, which then are corrected by the instructor, coach, or facilitator. The hope is that by fixing a mistake in an exercise you strengthen your process. It doesn't feel good to make mistakes, especially when you're on the job, but they are seen as an essential component to your growth as an actor. And though I've said there are no mistakes in this work, in one sense you could identify a few. In the three moment exercise, for example, if no one ever repeats the second moment that could be considered a "mistake." What if, however, a moment comes that is so profound it breaks the rules of the exercise? Let's say something happens with your partner that is so profound you have to call it, even if it isn't your turn? Do we deny the truth of the moment just to ensure we did the exercise correctly? How is that going to be better for your acting?

Obviously in this example there is a balance. Too much noise in the signal and the exercise falls apart, losing its steam and ability to facilitate a rich interpersonal experience. But the occasional moment that demands a response? If we ignore the possibility of this happening, we set your technique back rather than forward. This also mirrors experiences that happen on the job. Spontaneous moments not supported by the text or direction can become some of the hallmark moments of a film, or create an interaction so good that your director asks you to do it for every performance thereafter. We have to recognize that there is a difference between a lack of structure versus emerging chaos. One has to be addressed, while the other embraced. This possibility, however, challenges the idea that you can ever have a process that is mistake-free, or that by correcting every mistake you're becoming a better actor for it.

Mistakes, by nature, are binary events. They either happen, or they don't. That's great for a classroom setting. If the acting training is going to serve you, however, that can't be the whole picture. In your work, whether on stage or screen, there are going to be fewer black-and-white examples of mistakes; rather, you'll more likely encounter instances of serendipity that present themselves as moments. Do you break track and respond to them, or stick to the previously laid out plan? You may not know before the moment arrives, but adopting the habit that mistakes are a problem and that eliminating them is your goal is going to set you up for unnecessarily challenging experiences in the work environment.

At this stage, we need to replace the concept of a mistakes with a continuum. At one end of the continuum is "stronger technique" while at the other is "weaker technique." If a moment comes that breaks the rules of the exercise and you were all the smarter for embracing it, then you would place that on the end of having stronger technique, of possessing the sensitivity to register the value of such a moment and organically respond to it. If you find the exercises falling apart because you forget where you are, are distracted, or trying to drive them with your own agendas, then you can pin that towards "weaker technique."

A sliding-scale technique is much more attuned to the nuances and moments of great acting. Sometimes the best acting keeps to the rules, while at others it breaks them. In this training, then, there are no mistakes, only moments. Will the moments go according to plan or not? We won't know until we get there, but the most valuable thing is you developing the sensitivity to those moments and being able to work with them, whatever they throw at you.

Seeking Depth in One's Acting

Thus far we've focused on the transition points in auto-switch, but we haven't considered an equally important element of the exercise that also has no clear guidance: when you do transition into a new repetition or three moment exercise, how long do you stay in it? Is it possible to stay in one for too long? What happens if you never leave one of the exercises, for example transitioning into a repetition exercise and then just staying there until the coach calls for the exercise to finish?

This is not a simple question to answer, and it needs an example to help clarify it. Let's look at a scripted hypothetical conversation. Two good friends, Law and Kathleen, haven't seen each other for a month. They're meeting at Kathleen's apartment for a catch-up. Kathleen owns a dance studio.

> **Kathleen:** I can't believe you haven't been by the studio yet. We've totally updated the lighting system.
> **Law:** No more cutting out in the middle of practice?
> **Kathleen** *(laughs)*: I'm still waiting for the flicker to turn our choreography into an '80s flash mob.

Law: You better record it when it happens.
Kathleen: Or you could just come by more often.
Law: I know, I've just been busy.
Kathleen: With?
Law: (*casually*) Just some health stuff happening.
Kathleen: (*pauses*) Everything all right?
Law: I think so. I needed to get some tests done.
Kathleen: What's going on?
Law: High white blood cell count on my last labs. They think it's my allergies, but they just want to rule out anything else.
Kathleen: And?
Law: Everything's come back normal so far, I'm just waiting on the last two.
Kathleen: Thank God.
Law: Fingers crossed. Besides, I knew I had to get them done. Otherwise I'd have you chasing me down.
Kathleen: Please, you love my persistence.
Law: I seem to remember walking home after a sprained ankle . . .
Kathleen: (*elbows him and laughs*) Hey, that was your fault for ordering us those five-gallon margaritas!

Pausing this interaction, let's examine two sets of moments that occurred between them. In the beginning when Kathleen and Law are bantering, their dialogue has more of a humorous and light tone. Kathleen asks Law about what's been keeping him from visiting her and he very casually mentions he has had some health issues. Rather than continue the conversation as it had been progressing, Kathleen senses something else might be going on. She stops the flow of the conversation and shifts gears. They go deeper into the topic of Law's health. Once they've covered the matter, the conversation organically shifts back into the light tone, with Law starting to recall the story of Kathleen spraining her ankle when they were drunk.

Notice that there are transitions in this conversation. The talk was at one level, proceeding organically, and then Kathleen sensed a moment when they needed to go deeper into a topic. Once that ground had been covered, for as many moments as needed, the conversation shifted again. That idea of a moment that demands to go deeper is deeply woven into auto-switch. See if you notice it in the exercise between Courtney and Gina:

Gina: *You're crying.*
Courtney: *I'm crying.* (*nods and laughs*)

Gina: *You nodded. (gives Courtney a hug)*
Courtney: *You're holding me.*
Gina: *I'm holding you. (speaks comfortingly)*
Courtney: *You're still.*
Gina: *I'm still.*
Courtney: *You're still. (Gina pulls back)*
Gina: *I'm still.*

What's happening here mirrors the conversation between Kathleen and Law. Courtney's tears move Gina to hug and attempt to comfort her. Something in that moment, however, shifts, and Courtney senses it. That moment was demanding more depth. Repetition is the go-to tool for mining interpersonal depth. In auto-switch the three moment exercise offers a heightened means to both catch moments that demand observation as well as intuit the ones demanding more depth. If we'd asked Courtney and Gina who made the decision to go into repetition, the most likely answer from both would have been, "I don't know, it just happened."

Some moments will require depth, and others won't. The question of how long you stay in each exercise depends on the moment itself. If the moment called for it, you could stay in either exercise the whole time. More likely, however, a balance will still be found. That's what we mean when discussing the sensitivity to the moment developing within your process. It requires intuitive, not analytical skills, and that is a highly transferable tool for any job you walk into.

While auto-switch has its benefits, it still is largely the same switch exercise, and as we uncovered in the previous chapter switch is simply a bridge exercise pointing the way towards something new. Auto-switch has gotten us closer to what this is all leading towards, but now is the time for us to complete this leg of the journey that began with switch.

Rinse and Repeat, Rinse and—

What grows out of switch and auto-switch? To answer this, let's consider moments when a change is demanded in repetition. Repetition is the forum where deep, meaningful discoveries can be made. Transitioning out of that means something equally profound or attention-getting in the moment has demanded to be observed. Up to now the three moment exercise has been our means of getting out of repetition. But we have to ask ourselves, if something so profound happens it demands a change out of repetition, shouldn't that observation be repeated as well? There's depth on offer, and repetition is our tool for exploring depth. Rather than fluctuating between two different exercises the natural outgrowth is to repeat until the moment itself demands a new observation. That new observation will be repeated until a new one is called for. How long each repetition goes on for is unknown. It could be just a moment, or the remainder of the exercise. Let's see an example of what that might look like.

> **Gina (*noticing Courtney has a big smile*):** You're the Cheshire cat.
> **Courtney:** I'm the Cheshire cat. (*laughs*)
> **Gina:** You're the Cheshire cat.
> **Courtney:** I'm the Cheshire cat. (*playfully swipes at Gina*)
> **Gina:** You're the Cheshire cat. (*buries face in her hands*)
> **Courtney:** You're hiding.
> **Gina:** I'm hiding. (*nods*)
> **Courtney:** You're hiding. (*touches Gina's hair*)
> **Gina:** I'm hiding. (*raises her head*)
> **Courtney:** You're hiding. (*moves chair in*)
> **Gina:** You're coming in.
> **Courtney:** I'm coming in. (*leans in*)
> **Gina:** You're coming in. (*kisses Courtney*)
> **Courtney:** I'm coming in. (*shocked*)
> **Gina:** You're still.
> **Courtney:** I'm still.
> **Gina:** You're still. (*smiles and laughs*)
> **Courtney:** I'm still. (*with noticeable irritation*)
> **Gina:** You're still. (*face turns red*)
> **Courtney:** You blushed.
> **Gina:** I blushed.
> Etc.

For the purposes of the book I've condensed the number of repeats. Generally, though not always, observations tend to be repeated a bit more, but for the sake of your time I've done my best to strike the balance between getting the example right and giving a feel for the amount of time one might spend in a repeat. There is no prescriptive number of repeats in Meisner. Sometimes an observation might only be repeated once before a new one commands to be called; other times it might be repeated thirty times. The moment decides, so if these seem shorter here it's just for the sake of space and not having a living example in front of you.

So, is this just repetition but now with changes? Yes, but what makes it different from just about any other approach to Meisner is how you earned those changes. Generally, in many Meisner classes, repetition changes are often allowed within the first couple of sessions. You'll be working with your partner in a repetition exercise and the instructor will interrupt to ask, "But did you notice when they did *this?*" to which, if you caught that behavior, you'll say yes, and the instructor will say, "Then call that!" At that point you'll observe what the teacher wants you to and go on repeating until you think you've seen a new piece of behavior in line with what you're supposed to be calling. All of this can eventually lead to a repetition exercise that looks similar to what we're working on now, and the time-saving element is tempting at the outset. Why go through all the challenges of the three moment exercise and integrating it with repetition in switch as well as dealing with the stress of when to change and all that heaped onto it? Isn't it much easier for the teacher to tell you what to do and when to do it? I agree, it certainly is easier. And toxic to your technique.

In a technique interested specifically in the other person, it's easy to think that repetition can accommodate changes by just observing when they do something unique or interesting. The exercise, however, isn't about what you find compelling. As we've seen in this and the past few chapters, it thrives most when conjoined with the demands of the moment, and that requires a heightened level of sensitivity and observation. What you think is interesting, or juicy, doesn't really matter. Your primary tools are observation and response, and while there is quality among observations, the moment itself is what tells you when a piece of behavior is essential, or if a metaphor is needed to capture the entirety of the moment.

With my experience I probably could coach you to observe what I think is the most relevant in a given moment but then where would that leave you? I won't be with you on set, or in rehearsals. If all an actor does is learn their teacher's preferences then they still won't have trained and developed their habit of reading the moment and working with it. It's far easier to learn skills help you thrive in a class, even if they don't translate to working environments. By doing better in a training session you might feel as if you are growing as an actor, but you might just be getting better at being a student under that particular teacher. Far harder is learning tools that translate across different environments, worked on in a class but tested on the job.

To expand on this more, let's have Courtney and Gina show us a common example of how Meisner training is taught. Let's say Gina has a problem with expressing her anger. She laughs when nervous, and instead of expressing the impulse that terrifies her when conflict arises, she seeks safety in laughter and other disarming tactics. This is a common challenge actors encounter. We all have our impulses that we consider taboo, and expressing aggression, especially in an exercise wherein you could be met right back with it, rightfully ranks up there for a lot of us. While nervous laughter is a perfectly valid impulsive response, in our example it's become Gina's habit that denies other valid impulsive responses.

Here, generally, is how a fair number of Meisner teachers would help Gina in this scenario. Let's say in a repetition exercise tension has started to arise.

>**Courtney:** You're staring at me.
>**Gina:** I'm staring at you.
>**Courtney:** You're staring at me. (*shows teeth*)
>**Gina (*laughs*):** I'm staring at you.
>**Courtney:** You're laughing!
>**Gina (*laughs again*):** I'm laughing. (*holds hands up in gesture of peace*)
>**Teacher (*calling out*):** Don't run away, Gina! Stand your ground!
>**Courtney:** You're laughing at me.
>**Gina:** I'm laughing at you. (*lowers hands*)
>**Courtney:** You're laughing at me.
>**Teacher:** Come on, Gina, let your rage out! Don't let her walk over you!
>**Gina (*suddenly screams*):** I'm laughing at you!
>**Courtney:** You shouted.
>**Gina (*screams*):** I shouted!
>**Courtney (*going quieter*):** You shouted.
>**Gina (*calming*):** I shouted.
>Etc.

In one sense, we could say that progress has been made. Gina has finally let out that rage she's habitually bottled up for a long time, possibly years. That's a great step forward for her technique. From now on, when that impulse does arise she'll have an easier time expressing it. The benefit of this in the long term is that she will re-attune her relationship to anger in her acting work, so that when the time comes to express it in a scene it will be much easier for her to let those responses flow freely without censoring them. All of this is theoretically possible, except in this scenario a problem has been created, not solved, for Gina.

Owning the Top of the Climb

Ownership is a major component of this work. Even after years of teaching not just Meisner but other training approaches I am familiar with and believe in, the importance of an actor being able to own their tools still keeps me up some nights, going over what I teach, and how I teach it, all in the hopes that I've made it as transferable as possible. Ownership to me is synonymous with portability, the ability for a learned skillset to translate outside the environment it was learned in. In actor training we don't consider this nearly enough. If you learn a set of tools and it fails we normally chalk it up to individual learning. "It wasn't for you," we may rationalize, "you'll find something else that works." Sometimes this is true. Sometimes, however, what is believed to be rock solid technique is actually filled with holes, able to produce beautiful results in a training session but wilting as soon as the actor exits the room. In the future I believe better research will be done to understand this, but not anytime soon. Since we don't know cleanly where that line exists, taking great pains to ensure that a system still answers to reality beyond the training environment is paramount, even if it means changing elements of that approach once thought rock solid.

When a coach helps you obtain a result through pushing or encouraging, it seems benign. In some contexts, it's very helpful. If a coach is directing an actor in a filmed scene for example, this type of feedback could be useful. In the case of a film take there's a specific outcome the actor is aiming for, while in training the outcome has more to do with strengthening a wider process. In this context pushing you to obtain a result might make a teacher feel better, and it could be done with the best of intentions, but now you have been robbed of owning that discovery. Circling around expressing a certain impulse for months or longer isn't a pleasant one, but when you finally break through that inhibition and express it, the sense of ownership will be enormous. When a coach helps you, all that has happened is that they've achieved a result for a training session, but that only adds up to you getting better at what the teacher wants to see, not what you sense the moment asks and having the courage to go there for yourself.

To be clear, addressing an ingrained habit preventing you from doing your best work is extremely important, but it needs to be done after the fact, once the exercise has ended. The frustration at not being able to express an impulse is a key ingredient to the moment when you are about to do it again and then say, "To hell with it, this time I'm just going to let it out." Self-granted permission is a far more potent tool in one's arsenal. Repetitions are not directed scenes. They aren't exercises meant to be coached into a certain result. They're a venturing into the unknown, and the courage needed is the one to embrace the chaos of whatever happens, not the ability to replicate a teacher's instruction for an emotional result as if they are actors taking direction in a scene.

This type of ownership is the primary difference in having taken all the steps to discover the moment when a change in repetition is needed versus me on day one telling you to change the text when your partner does something new, unique, or interesting. It's why you've gone through the steps of fusing the three moment exercise and early repetitions in switch and auto-switch, only to have it all now merge into one complete technique of repetition, able to train truthfulness in your acting in a fully portable way. These added steps are a progressive approach to the Meisner technique, developed by practitioners interested in cleaning up elements of classical training that don't sit cleanly with its concepts and wider goals. It is a fine-tuning of application, not a reworking of the deeper ideas Sanford Meisner pioneered when creating a truly remarkable approach to contemporary actor training.

So, how does one make a change in the text of repetition? Rather than me telling you when to, the far healthier answer is, to quote my teacher Scott, "You don't. A change happens, and you're in the room when it does." The ability to be present for that type of event makes your acting a whole different type of animal.

Summary

Recognizing and understanding your conscious experience of the world offers a unique way to connect with yourself. Meditation's ability to provide a set of tools for exploring consciousness can bring you into direct contact with the conceptions about your identity you believe to be true. In practice, the technique of noting breaths can be a useful tool for further sharpening your attention. Attention is one of the least discussed and yet most profound attributes for an actor, especially attention to the demands of the moment. The auto-switch exercise in the Meisner technique raises many questions about the growing role of the moment in our work. Eventually, auto-switch evolves into the full technique of repetition, when changes can now be accommodated in the text. Successfully engaging in a repetition exercise at this level implies that an entire series of values have been learned – values that are transferable beyond the confines of a training environment and applicable to where they matter most: in practice, doing the real thing.

11
Circle Without Beginning or End

Shifting Currents

Given the size of this chapter, and the importance of material covered, for the sake of time we won't have a meditation exercise. In the next chapter, however, we will begin conjoining your mindfulness work with a new approach to practice, one that eventually will be directly applied to text analysis.

The journey of the Meisner technique can feel like an entirely different pathway into the actor's process. It doesn't begin with scene study, or abstract physical exercises, nor does it emphasize the importance of developing yourself and your powers of sense, imagination, or memory. It won't ask you to forward plot, devise scenarios, or be inventive. It simply requires that you learn in practice what it means to truly see another person, clearly and without preconceptions, and then discover what it means to respond to them without thought. To let the empathic, more primal side of yourself act before the rational voice.

Though Meisner training foregoes many of the steps found in other training approaches, this doesn't reduce its complexity. Many questions still spring up in this work –questions about the nature of your impulses, why you sit on certain ones when others are expressed so easily, and what to do when the experiences themselves lose the veneer of feeling like an "acting exercise" and instead become something more honest and human. What does it both feel like and mean for your acting to seek truthfulness and authenticity over pretending or imitation? These are huge, big-picture questions for your process. Whatever your answers to them will be, this training reveals that you have a well of insight, thoughts, and intuitions you might not have realized before. You share this attribute with every great actor you've ever admired, the ones who lived before you and those who will come after.

DOI: 10.4324/9781003255321-11

For the next two chapters, the format for introducing a new exercise will shift. Until recently every exercise in the Meisner technique could be considered top-down. You were handed down a series of instructions and steps for how to develop your technique in each exercise. Less attention was paid to the individual experience and more to ensuring you developed a level of technical strength. That has served you very well. It allowed you to learn the ropes and values of repetition so that you could have the necessary boundaries in place to facilitate a deeply individual experience between you and your partner. The past two chapters, however, have shown a shift in our work. There's no secret formula for how to perfect a repetition technique, and we gave up the idea of mistakes as a relevant part of your technique. The top-down model was great in the beginning. Recent developments, however, demand a new outlook.

That Which We Carry

The examples and feedback in this and the next chapter will be largely bottom-up. Bottom-up experiences have more to do with you and your unique encounters in each exercise. Now that you have a working technique of repetition, far less focus needs be paid to developing the bones of that technique than to the unique flesh you put onto it. Rather than introduce the basics of an exercise and then give some examples, it might help to see it written out as an extended case study, a condensed hypothetical of what usually happens in training sessions.

One note I believe is worth making before we progress is that today's exercise will go deeper than before. When you do it you will most likely encounter some of your oldest habits, even ones that stem from childhood when you were learning how to be a civilized person fit for society. I can't pre-empt what yours are, and so the examples here won't lay out your journey but will instead give you a sense of what could arise either for you or your colleagues in training. The purpose of this exercise isn't to draw out those habits, but it does happen as a natural byproduct.

We'll journey with two actors, Raoul and Jennifer, through their first encounter with this exercise, and I'll cast myself as the coach in this session. In the room we are in the group seated at one end, and close to the opposite are two empty chairs. There is also a door the leads into and out of the room.

When I ask for two volunteers, Raoul and Jennifer raise their hands.

"In you go, brave souls!" I say, and they chuckle. They sit in the empty chairs in front of us, keen and ready.

"So, in the last session we finally worked out the technique of repetition. Any questions about that before we take it to the next step?"

"I've got one," Raoul says. "How often do we make a new call?"

"There's no rule for it but as a general value I'd say be careful of too many changes in the text of repetition. Obviously the moment will let you know how long to repeat for, and that could change very quickly, but usually in the beginning if you have to err opt for the side of fewer changes."

"Got it."

"Anything else?" Both actors shake their heads. "Perfect. This next exercise, then, is called 'the knock at the door.' It's a repetition exercise that begins with a knock at the door."

They wait for me to say more, but what they don't know is actually I don't have much more to tell them.

"So . . ." Raoul says, and Jennifer laughs.

"One of us knocks . . ." she asks.

"Yes," I agree.

"And then the other answers?"

"I actually don't know that."

"When do we do the repetition, then?" Raoul asks.

"I don't know that either."

"Soooo . . ." Raoul says even more emphatically, and everyone in the room laughs. Up to this point I've rarely said, "I don't know." I've almost always had an answer, but today marks a new step in pushing for more independence. I'm not being intentionally vague, either, I honestly don't know the answers to those questions. If I did try to answer them I would be pretending to know the future, and when it comes to the nature of impulses, no human has that power. I'll need to do something to prove to the actors that not only do we all collectively not know the future, but also that I'm not deliberately withholding information from them.

"Let's try one and see if things become more clear. How does that sound?"

The actors nod, and I ask Raoul to step outside with me. We go into the hallway and close the door.

"So, you mind if we chat for just a couple of minutes?" I ask.

"Sure . . ." he says, unsure of what I mean.

"Well, right now they're probably thinking I'm giving you some secret instructions."

"And you're not?"

"I don't have any, unfortunately."

"Oh shit."

"You were hoping for some?"

"Yeah," and he chuckles.

"Sorry to disappoint. But hey, have you tried the noodle place across the street?"

"Oh it's good."

"Really?"

"Yeah, last time I went I got the . . . was it chicken? No, well, maybe, it was basil and lemongrass. So nice."

"I'm a sucker for lemongrass."

"I know! It's totally worth it."

"Thanks for the recommendation. So, while I don't have a secret instruction, here's what I'm going to ask. Silently count 30 to yourself, nothing strange, just normal counting. Then knock."

"Okay. And then I repeat?"

"I have no idea," I say sincerely, and then head back inside.

When I enter the room I can sense the tension. They think I've just 180'ed on them, that after sessions of training with no secrets now I've suddenly asked one of them to withhold a piece of information about the exercise. This tells me something not only about this group of actors but, sadly, every group I've ever worked with. I sit down with the group and give Jennifer a genuine smile. Now up there alone, she nervously smiles back.

"That new series you were telling me about earlier," I ask her.

"Which one?"

"The Mike Flanagan one."

"It's amazing."

"Can I find it on any streaming service . . ."

"I think it's just on Netflix for now."

"Netflix, got it. Without spoiling it what stuck out most to you?"

At this moment the knock comes. Jennifer freezes. She looks at the door, looks at me. Total deer in headlights.

"Uh . . ." she trails off.

"Great," I say, and I sincerely mean it. I call for Raoul to come in, and we stop the exercise. Both actors sit in confusion.

"So, let's start with you, Raoul," I say.

"Okay . . ."

"So we went outside together, and we had a chat."

"Yes."

"Do you remember what we spoke about?"

"Well, you asked me to count to thirty and then knock."

"Yes, and before then?"

"Oh! Right. You said everyone in here was probably thinking you were telling me some secret about the exercise."

There are some chuckles and amused head shakes from the actors in the room.

"And did we?"

"No. We just talked about the noodle bar up the road."

"That was it?"

"That was it."

"Great. So, was my guess right? Did you all think I was giving him some piece of information nobody else had?" Collectively, everyone nods. "Why is that the case? We haven't had any secrets up until this point. If anyone had a question I would either answer or say, 'We'll get there soon.' So, why? What makes us as actors think this withholding is part of the learning process?"

"Maybe it's how a lot of us are taught?" one actor asks.

"How so?"

"Well, when I first started my acting classes we had to do these poses, these physical gestures. I'd do mine and the teacher would always say to me, 'You didn't do it right because you didn't think about this or that.'"

Other similar stories support this actor's example. Though I'm writing a hypothetical here, this is largely, with some exceptions, how I was taught acting as well. That's not to say we were all being taught by manipulative psychopaths (though there are more in the actor training scene that anyone should be comfortable with). Acting is often taught by the teacher asking the actor to do an action, a bit, or a piece of scene work, and then when the actor finishes they are critiqued with *the one thing* they didn't take into consideration beforehand. To help clarify what I mean by this, I once took a Shakespeare workshop with a name teacher in London. This person had a lengthy track record in the industry, particularly when it came to the classics. I was working on a great piece from *Measure for Measure*. We were asked to read it in front of the class and just see where things went. For an early read I thought it went pretty well. My partner and I connected a few times, it wasn't perfect, but when we finished I could see the instructor was not happy.

"Royce," she asked, "why weren't you listening to the changes in the rhythm?"

I paused, looked at the paper, and back to her. I thought I had been listening to the other actor. Genuinely confused I asked, "I'm sorry?"

"There are two succinct rhythm changes in the scene. The text almost descends into blank verse at one point, and the iambic pentameter even changes to trochaic at another."

"I didn't notice that."

"Well, that's your problem, isn't it? That you don't pay attention to these things."

"I can look for it next time. I just didn't know that you wanted me to pay attention to it this time."

Though I meant well by saying this, and with zero sarcasm, that reply didn't go over well.

"So I'm supposed to be the one to tell you how to act well? That's my job, to treat you like a defensive child and hold your hand through this process? [*to the entire class*] Let me tell you all something about actors like this. When they ignore what's so obvious in Shakespeare, which is the rhythm he gives us, all it does is sap the life out of the scene . . ." and on, and on. For at least a good five minutes that felt like fifty I became her personal teaching example of what was wrong with all the actors like me.

To clarify, if it sounds as if I'm recounting a traumatic story, I had the good sense to realize she was playing a power game and tuned out most of the raking over the coals I received. Of course my read could have been better, that's why I was in the class. What was also clear, however, is that this teacher was attempting to pull the rug out from under my feet. She had asked for one thing and then surprised me with something else she wanted to be considered but hadn't asked for. That's different than a piece of direction phrased like this: "In that read you missed some of the changes in rhythm. It turns suddenly uneven and sounds almost like blank verse. Next time take that onboard more." This is feedback very different than the pedagogical tool I'm talking about. The art of teaching by withholding information is commonplace in actor training, so ingrained that in the simple experiment Raoul and I performed outside the door it ignited that concern and paranoia in just about everyone. If you find yourself in a training session in which these tactics are being used, my best advice is to avoid volunteering to work until a break comes, and then leave. There's zero benefit in this type of learning by humiliation. It does nothing for your growth as an actor.

"If I wanted Raoul to do something specific," I say to the group, "there's no benefit in my not having told him beforehand. So let's be totally clear: there are still no secrets in this work. You know everything I do about knock at the door beforehand. All we can do is work with what comes up and, as we're starting to see, there are more unknown variables in this exercise than ever before. That's big-picture stuff. So, Jennifer, let's talk about what happened with you."

"Okay."

"We were talking about the Netflix series. Then the knock came. And you froze. Completely."

"Yeah." Jennifer laughs.

"So, what was going on there?"

"Well, I didn't know what to do."

"When the knock came, did you feel the impulse to do anything?"

"I don't really remember. I just got worried about what I should be doing."

"Right. Well, we know this is a repetition exercise that begins with a knock at the door."

"And that's all we know?"

"Yes."

"I'm very confused."

"That's perfectly normal at this stage. Let's do another and we'll keep fielding through the weeds on this one. Deal?"

"Deal."

"Come on out." Jennifer and I go outside, leaving Raoul in the chair. We close the door, and I say, "'So, it's the same instructions. Count to thirty and then knock."

"And he'll answer?"

"Let's see what happens."

"That's code for you have no idea."

"Yep." I give Jennifer a friendly smile so that she knows we're on the same page. We are all now engaged in a process that feels new and different than anything up to this point in training. You, reading this, might also be confused about what is the purpose or even what this exercise looks like. We're all on the same page for now, and clarity is coming.

"You mentioned lemongrass," I say, sitting down and talking to Raoul who now sits alone in the chairs in front of us.

"Yeah, in the chicken."

"Ever had Tom Yum?"

"No, what's that?"

"It's a lemongrass soup. I had it once in Pahoa at this tiny place called Ning's, it felt life-changing for me."

"I'll have to try it."

"You're from Massachusetts, right?"

"Yeah, close to the New Hampshire line."

"How's the food scene there?"

"You like seafood?"

"Oh yes."

"Then you'll be happy."

The knock comes. Raoul looks at the door, and pauses. The knock comes again. "Come in!" he shouts, which is my cue to stop the exercise.

"Great stuff. Jennifer, do come in!" She enters, sits, and looks at Raoul. The puzzlement on their faces is real.

"Lots to talk about. So, Jennifer, you went out, counted to thirty, and then knocked."

"Yes. Then he yelled for me to come in."

"Did you want to?"

"It just confused me."

"There was a confusing element there I wanted to ask you about, Raoul. Why did you say, 'Come in'?"

"Well, she knocked, and . . . that's what you do when somebody knocks at your door."

"True. The instructions say, though, that this is a repetition exercise that begins with a knock at the door. What part of repetition is 'Come in'?"

"It's not . . . ?"

We laugh, and I say, "Bingo. There's no observational component to 'come in'."

"Got it."

"So, I'm more confused now," Jennifer says. "A repetition exercise that begins with a knock at the door. But when do we actually start repeating?"

"I don't know," I reply honestly.

"Right when the knock comes?" Raoul asks.

"It depends. Say the knock is particularly hard, or violent, and you don't feel the impulse to speak. That's fair. The moment is going to be the thing that answers that question for you."

"I think I've figured it out," Jennifer says.

"Great. Raoul, you're out, same instructions."

Raoul leaves, and Jennifer and I chat about various things. The chatting might seem like time-filling, but in actuality it serves a very important learning function. Tackling so many unknowns, it can be easy for an actor to feel singled out. Keeping the tone of the room warm and recognizing the frustrations as they arise is important to everyone remaining both open and willing to keep trying. Jennifer and I are talking about a theatre production we both saw on separate nights. We compare notes, going over the lead's work, an actor we both admire. We've just begun to discuss some of the staging elements.

"The set was a little weird, you have to admit," Jennifer says, laughing.

"I have no idea what they were going for. I don't know why in an affluent castle there's literally trash everywhere. But maybe–"

The knock comes. Jennifer gets up immediately and answers the door.

"You were knocking," she says.

"I was knocking," Raoul repeats, and as they both break into awkward laughter I stop the exercise.

"Great work you two. Come back in." They both shake their heads and return to the chairs, but I can tell their frustration is still within a reasonable level. "There's a lot to talk about in this exercise. Jennifer, let's start with you. What happened there?" I ask jokingly.

"What do you mean?"

"You totally iced me! We were just having a conversation, the knock came, and you just ghosted me to answer the door!"

"I guess I did. Should I have done something differently?"

"No, no, and to be clear I'm only joking about the icing. But something did happen there. We were talking, the knock came, and what did you experience in that moment?"

"Well, I'd decided in my mind when he knocked I would just open the door."

"You decided that beforehand?"

"Yes, before the exercise started."

"How well did it work for you?"

"It felt awkward, to be honest."

"I observed that as well. There was a level of comfort in our conversation, and then when the knock came you seemed to go into a kind of 'actor mode' where it was now time to do the exercise right."

"Yes."

"So, a couple of things to unpack there. First, the choice to answer the door regardless of the quality of the knock, who does that exclude from the equation?"

"Raoul."

"Yes. Why?"

"Because maybe I wouldn't have wanted to answer the door."

"Possibly. Or maybe you would have. It seems you decided what the moment would be before you got there."

"I agree."

"That's not a bad thing in itself. Sometimes predictions about the future do come true. But as far as a habit for your acting goes, it's not as strong as the one where you accept you don't know and work with the moment as it comes up."

"That's more scary, though."

"It certainly is for me. Why is it scary for you?"

"Because then you could fail, you might not have the right tools or make the right call . . . I don't know."

"But you could also be wrong when trying to predict the future anyway."

"I guess . . ."

"It's hard to let go of that desire. But we're not here to judge moments. We can look at technique and ask if it could be made stronger, but that's as far as mistakes go. My guess is when you heard the knock you said to yourself, 'I'm going to get the exercise right.' But you lost a value in our work, which is public solitude. That sliding scale relationship between the audience and whatever else it is you're doing."

"Should I have just kept talking to you?"

"I don't know what you should have done. I don't think any of us will know. Besides, what came up in the moment was great because it gives us material to work with. So let's talk about what did come up and the possibilities within it. The knock is the only information you get in the beginning, right?"

"Yes."

"So the quality of the knock will tell you about what is happening within your partner. Is it a hard knock, a soft one, and so on. You might have the impulse to get up and open the door. You might have the impulse to carry on talking with me. Or something else entirely could happen. That's why we don't need to judge what you did in a negative light. We can just say the next time the knock comes, and that's really *if* the knock comes, there might be more possibilities on offer, and deciding that moment beforehand might not aid you."

"I think I see what you mean."

"I suspect more exercises will make things clearer. Raoul, when you knocked, and Jennifer opened the door, what did you see?"

"Honestly? She looked really surprised, she looked like this owl," Raoul says.

"Thanks," Jennifer quips, and they laugh.

"Your eyes were just so wide. I didn't know what to do."

"'So you were just rendered speechless by what you saw?" I ask.

"Yeah!"

"That's a great moment for your acting, to be so struck by your partner the moment demands no words. We like that, but did it also put you in your head a bit, somewhat like, 'Well, what do we do now?'"

"Definitely."

"The solution for that is put your attention back on her and keep it on her. It seemed the moment when the door opened was quite profound, and then the awkward laughter came as a result of the attention coming back onto yourselves. Keep your attention on Jennifer, and see what she makes you do." This time Jennifer goes out. Raoul sits with a puzzled look on his face. "How are you doing?" I ask.

"I think it's getting there. But you said something confusing."

"What else is new?" I say, smiling. "But seriously, what was it?"

"You said, '*If* the knock comes.'"

"Right."

"Can we not knock?"

"There's two ways to look at it. The instructions are that this is a repetition exercise that begins with a knock at the door. Deliberately choosing not to knock isn't really a great strategy then, you just won't start the exercise. But, having said that, let's say you're in the hallway, preparing to knock, and you get a phone call from your agent saying they've got a big role for you in the next Spielberg movie but you have to come meet the casting director right now. Are you really going to knock?"

"Nope. Sorry everyone, I'm out of here."

"Exactly. So generally the knock will come, but that doesn't mean it's guaranteed. Taking it for granted isn't as wise as staying open to the possibility that the instruction to knock has been given, but whether it will actually arrive we just don't know."

The knock comes.

"Speak of the devil," Raoul says, and gets up to open the door. He opens it.

"You opened the door," Jennifer says in the doorway.

"I opened the door."

"You opened the door."

"I opened the door." Raoul gestures for her to come in, and Jennifer immediately goes for the chair inside. They both sit. "You sat down," he says.

"I sat down," Jennifer says, and laughs.

"You sat down." Raoul smiles.

"You're smiling."

"I'm smiling," Raoul says, bashfully.

"You're smiling."

"I'm smiling." He moves in.

"That's great," I say. "I'll stop you there. Getting closer, right?"

They both nod. I can sense that though it isn't fully clear yet, they are starting to grasp some elements of the experience more. The intimidation factor is decreasing and they sense they are part of a process of discovering this exercise.

"So, Raoul, the knock came while we were chatting, and I thought you had a wonderful example of public solitude. You didn't switch off from being you when the knock came, you finished our conversation, got up, and answered the door. That seemed all true to the moment. Was that your experience?"

"It felt a lot easier."

"Good. Easier is good. You opened the door and the repetition began. Then you did something interesting. You seemed to invite Jennifer in."

"Yeah, I wanted her to come in."

"Right. Well, that was a very polite thing of you to do."

". . . Gotcha. So I shouldn't have invited her in?"

"I think the politeness was in response to something that came up for you. You were holding the door open and you said just now you wanted her to come in. Why? What was going on for you there?"

"I just started to feel awkward. It started to bother me she was just standing there not doing anything."

"Do you think she wasn't doing anything?"

"Well, she was standing pretty still."

"And the stillness bothered you?"

"Yes."

"So it seemed the politeness, the gesturing to come in, might have been in response to an impulse you didn't express?"

"Possibly."

"When you registered the stillness, did you want to move towards her?"

"Away, actually. I didn't want to be so close anymore."

"Would that have been okay? Could you have walked away?"

"Well, I was holding the door open."

"True."

"And it would have been rude to just close the door on her."

"It seems to me your observation skills were sharp. You registered that stillness and earned the impulse that came up from it. Something in her behavior was telling you to move back. If that was the truth of the moment, then you have permission to be 'rude.' Just because you close the door doesn't mean she won't have the impulse to come in. She can open a door, you know."

"I've done it once or twice," Jennifer says, and we all laugh.

"In one moment you felt the impulse to answer the door. The next moment told you to back away. You can have both. Working with the moment you've got is a far better strategy than insisting she behave differently to give you a moment you might be more comfortable with."

"I see." Raoul nods, taking it onboard. Politeness is a deeply ingrained habit that comes up in many areas. It's part of that social conditioning we have been encountering in this training since day one. The knock at the door, however, tends to mark the point at which these habits begin arising more potently. We can talk about the importance of adopting "fuck polite" as a value all we want, but it's really only when an actor experiences the opposite, the hindrance of kneejerk politeness, that they can begin to sense those boundaries and start redrawing the lines.

"Jennifer, nice work there," I say. "The repetition might have been short, but you had some strong attention. The moment when he opened the door and you said, 'You opened the door,' seemed to be easier for you than the previous exercise."

"It felt a lot easier."

"That's great. It was a true behavioral call you made, and as the tunnel vision in the exercise gets better so will your observation skills. But there was one moment I wanted to ask you about. Tell me if I saw this correctly: Raoul opened the door fairly soon after you knocked. You two began the repetition, and he gestured for you to come in. You entered, and then immediately made a bee-line for the chairs. He picked up your cue, and then something very interesting happened. When you two were standing there was a noticeable tension in the air, but as soon as you both sat down it seemed to release and the repetition flowed so much more comfortably. Was that what you encountered?"

"Oooooh yes," she says.

"So what was the difference between standing and sitting?"

"Familiarity."

"Familiar as in?"

"Well, this is the first time we're out of the chairs."

"I know. Now you've got to deal with that whole standing issue. In the beginning actors are confused by the chairs. Eventually they say, 'When do we get to get up?' Well, it's day one of being able to get up and how does it feel?"

"Not worth it," Jennifer says jokingly. "Safety in the chairs all the way."

I laugh and say, "Right, you nailed it. Especially in the beginning of learning this exercise the chairs feel like safe zones. It's familiar territory. Now, the chairs can be a trap. If you have the impulse to sit down you certainly can. But habitually going for the chairs as a safety strategy is not an optimal one. Because you're entirely right: once we introduce the possibility of being on your feet, an entirely new range of observations and especially responses open up. That's big territory, and it can feel overwhelming. So, if it's true in the moment, sitting is fine, but avoid the chairs as safe territory."

"Got it."

"Now that the initial shock of the exercise has worn off, and you're starting to find your feet in the experience, we can talk about what the actual point of the knock at the door is. In the previous session I said there was one final impulse we hadn't dealt with, an impulse so big it needs its own exercise. The knock at the door is the exercise that tackles that impulse. Any idea what I'm talking about?"

"Moving?"

"Exactly. Raoul had the impulse to move away from Jennifer, and that was such a major moment it led them both to seek safe ground. Rather than safe territory, however, these new discoveries are exactly where we want you to explore. The purpose of the knock at the door, then, is to discover the *impulse* to move. That's very different, as we'll see, from the *idea* to move, which is what Raoul adopted when he insisted Jennifer come in."

Animal Impulses

It's worth repeating here: the knock at the door finally gives you the means to work with all of the impulses related to movement, and the many implications that come with them. Movement is a profound experience in the animal kingdom. To move towards something implies so many possibilities:

familiarity, aggression, intimacy, conflict, and so on. To move away implies an equally vast constellation of potential. When coupled with the understanding that impulses generated by observations an entirely permissible, fueled by the value of "fuck polite" that strips social veneers away from the experience, movement in this training can become a powerhouse event, filled with uncertainty and an exciting sense of danger. In the beginning of this training the chairs were valuable. Sitting offered a means to compartmentalize and learn the basic steps of this technique. Eventually, however, the act of living truthfully as an actor demands more than just being seated. You will start to notice all the movement impulses you've been denying. Being on your feet, juggling the many variables that are thrown at you, is far more in line with what you will encounter on the job as an actor. Now that your technique is strong enough you're ready to begin importing these values into the possibility of movement beyond the chairs. It's equally exciting and terrifying.

"Now that we've better defined the parameters of the chairs let's see a few more examples before you brave souls get a break." Raoul gets up to knock, leaving Jennifer in the chair. "Is it getting clearer for you?" I ask, and this is a sincere question. Though I think the actors are finding their feet in the exercise, they are the most important judges of their own experience, and so checking in regularly with them ensures I'm on the right track with my feedback.

"Much clearer. See, why couldn't you have just told us all of this in the beginning!" Jennifer says.

"Oh, right, that would have worked well. Me monologuing for an hour and then expecting you two to do something with it."

"For sure. No, I'm kidding. This type of an exercise has to be done a few times to get into it."

"I think so. A lot of Meisner teachers teach this exercise in five minutes. They tell one actor to knock, and the other to answer the door. But do you see how many possibilities we would lose if I just said you'll answer the door each time when the knock comes? We would dampen so much of your ability to read the moment. Because in reality I don't know if Raoul will knock, and I don't know if you will answer if he does, and neither do you. We could artificially say we do, but that wouldn't be a value that would serve your process beyond this room."

"It's all about the unknown, isn't it?"

The knock comes. It's a very rhythmic knock, almost musical in nature. Jennifer seems confused by it.

"Okay . . ." She looks to me and says, "Two seconds." Then she stands and opens the door.

"That was a weird knock," she says.

"That was a weird knock," Raoul repeats, and his tone is disappointed.

"You're still," Jennifer says, and she touches his arm.

"I'm still."

"You're still."

"I'm still." Raoul comes past her, into the room.

"You came in," Jennifer says.

"I came in."

"Your hands are in your pockets."

"My hands are in my pockets," Raoul repeats, shifting from side to side.

"Your hands are in your pockets."

"My hands are in my pockets," he says, taking them out. Jennifer moves towards him, letting the door close.

"You came closer," he says.

"I came closer," Jennifer repeats, moving even closer. She puts her arms over his shoulders.

"You're my big sister," Raoul says, and blushes.

"I'm your big sister," Jennifer repeats, and hugs him tightly.

"You're my big sister." Raoul embraces her, starting to well up.

"I'm your big sister," she says, tearing up as well.

"You're my big sister."

"Beautiful work," I say. "Let's stop there." The actors sit for feedback, both wiping their eyes. "Well, that was a joy to watch," I say, and they smile. "Talk about a beautiful example of the types of intimacy you can find in this work. Actors are so worried about connection and chemistry, but really it's much more simple than a grand mystery. You might notice chemistry has never been an issue in this work. Every pair we've seen work since the beginning has had great, dynamic chemistry. Is that just a coincidence? Probably not. I think the secret ingredient is engagement. The more two people engage with each other the more their chemistry naturally grows. That's the beauty of this work. You never need to worry about chemistry again. By plugging in, observing clearly, and responding truthfully, you're going to have that spark of connection. That's magical, in my opinion. But let's talk about what happened. Jennifer, I think you discovered something about repetition that we circled around at the beginning of the session. Did the first half of the exercise feel differently than the second half?"

"The second half felt much deeper," she replies, and Raoul nods.

"I agree. One thing that might have contributed to that is how many changes there were in the text of repetition in the first half. You didn't really give yourself time to repeat as often, and you drove the changes pretty much entirely in the first half."

"I guess I just wanted to catch all the things he was doing."

"I like that, and as we said earlier, as the tunnel vision effect in this exercise lessens, you'll see more and more. But what you'll also find is too many changes in the text of repetition drains the exercise of its depth. If you put the responsibility for driving the exercise all on your shoulders you're going to miss many opportunities to connect with him. Put the responsibility for it on his shoulders. He's doing the same thing to you. The moment will let you know when a change is needed, and I think you took that on board in the second half. You seemed to give yourself permission to hang back and keep that balance of observation and response, and suddenly you two found yourselves in some very deep waters very quickly. Does that line up fairly well with what you went through?"

"I guess it's just about trusting him, and trusting the moment."

"Actually, it's the opposite."

"Really?"

"I think so. It's about trusting in your own technique, that when you encounter the moment you'll be able to work with what it throws at you. Or when you work with another actor, that they don't need to be doing anything specific for you to do your best work. That's one of the strongest values this work instills: you don't need another actor to be doing this work to you to be doing it to them."

"What do you mean?"

"Raoul was observing and responding with strong technique. But say he hadn't been. Say he was a colleague you were working with and he rarely paid attention to you and seemed so wrapped up in his own head and process. Before you began this training would that have been a problem for you?"

"Of course."

"But now, is it so much? He's still going to be giving you behavior. You can still observe him and respond to whatever he's doing truthfully. He doesn't need to be doing anything specific for you to have that trust in your own technique and to do your best work."

"It would help, though."

"Of course it does, but as a technique I'd say it's better for you to have one that thrives even when working with difficult or unresponsive actors. Observe-and-respond is a metric you can apply to any partner independent of the quality of their own work."

"That's quite liberating, actually."

"Yes. Building that trust in yourself doesn't mean things will go smoothly all the time. It just means that whether everything goes perfectly or you encounter hurdle after hurdle, your technique is strong enough to handle it." I turn to Raoul, and say, "Raoul."

"Yes?"

"'You're my big sister.' Wow."

"Yeah," he says, and even though he laughs he knows he went somewhere personally profound.

"What a beautiful call," I say. "That hit you both like a truck."

"It did."

"That's the level of depth on offer when you put the attention on your partner and let them take you for the ride."

"It surprised me," Raoul says.

"It seemed to, and that's a wonderful quality for your acting. To surprise yourself, in the moment. When that happens we all share that experience with you. And I think you went somewhere you weren't expecting yourself to go."

"There was just something about the warmth in her face . . . that's how my sister looks at me when she knows I need comfort."

"When she knows she has to be Big Sister."

"Yes."

"Great work, and great courage. Really." And I mean it. The biggest discoveries about your process in this work will oftentimes surprise you. Raoul probably didn't realize he had that level of openness so readily available until it just happened. In the future, he'll continue to grow confident that, if the moment calls for it, he has a much more vast range of experiences available to him than he might have previously given himself credit for.

"On a minor technical note," I say, shifting the conversation to a different area of his work, "your knock seemed quite inventive."

"Yeah. I just thought I would try something different."

"To get a different result?"

"I don't know, actually. Maybe it wasn't the best choice."

"For now, give yourself permission to have a boring, normal knock. In the next session we'll introduce a new tool that can possibly change the nature of your knock but, for now, just count and knock. Simple is better, no need to be inventive."

"Got it."

"Now, let's stop the exercise here because, for the next session, I have some homework for you."

A Well of Meaning

Homework? Now this is a new thing. Thus far we haven't had any assignments for training. When it comes to living truthfully there's not much need for preparation. This should tell you something, however, about where the boat is finally ready to sail. In the next chapter we are taking our first steps into the given set of circumstances, beginning the process of training the entire package of living truthfully under a given set of circumstances. All of the time you've spent developing a strong technique is now ready to be put to use. This will of course raise many new questions, and bring up ones that had been previously unanswered. To keep consistent with the format of this chapter, I'm going to script both the directions and clarifying questions I often receive regarding them.

"In the next session you are going to begin working on an exercise known as the independent activity. True to its name, this is an activity you will be doing by yourself, so in your planning don't make another person essential to its completion. A successful independent activity fulfills four criteria. First, it must be physically engaging, and by this I mean tactile and fiddly. Writing a piece of poetry, for example, could meet some of the other criteria, but there's nothing tactile or intricate about it. Building a LEGO or other building blocks structure, however, is definitely fiddly. Other examples might be when a small metal chain becomes balled and tangled. Untangling that requires a high level of tactile attention. A classic staple is gluing together a broken mug or plate. Just make sure it is ceramic, however, and not glass, since I don't want anybody getting cut."

"So we're actually going to be doing this activity?"

"Yes. Whatever you bring in, you're going to be really doing in the exercise, and this is another important thing to note: whatever activity you choose, keep the activity itself as real as possible, nothing imagined in the activity itself. For example if your activity is making cake batter, you'll actually have to bring in all of the items needed, so you won't be pantomiming or pretending to crack eggs or whisk butter. That also might encourage you to keep it simple: the value of the activity isn't determined by how complex you can make it, though for once I'm saying this is your chance to be creative.

"The second criteria is that it must be difficult to complete in the time you set for yourself. This tells you that you'll need to set a time limit, so I would recommend bringing a timer with you. It could be an egg timer, or the clock on your phone, it doesn't matter so long as it can keep the time for you and ring or beep when the time is up. That way you won't need to be concerned about keeping track of time in your head."

"How long should the time limit be?"

"That depends on your activity. What that tells you is you'll probably want to have a good sense of how long the activity will take to accomplish."

"So we need to have done it before?"

"Not at all. Feel free to bring in an activity you've never had any experience with and are curious to try. Since there's a lot of flexibility here, the time limit is your best honest guess. The criterion is to make it difficult to complete in the time possible, so the way you would reach this is by first estimating how long it would take for you to get it done comfortably. If you're building a puzzle that would comfortably take you nine minutes to accomplish then give yourself eight and a half, or just eight. That's the real sweet spot of this exercise, to find the time limit where it's not impossible to get it done but puts a degree of pressure on you.

"On a side note, I will say that generally activities that take longer than ten minutes run the risk of the actor getting distracted. It's hard to keep that pressure on for longer than ten minutes. This certainly isn't a rule, so if you want to attempt an activity longer than ten minutes go for it, but generally in the range of four to eight minutes is a good time limit for your first activity.'

"Just to be clear, we bring something in that's hard to do . . ."

"Right, physically intricate."

"With a time limit, and then we get it done in that time limit?"

"I don't know. You'll do your best to get it done, but I don't know if you will."

"Got it."

"The next two criteria are the first of their kind you've encountered in this work, because they are going to ask you to be inventive. In these two criteria, you'll come up with some imaginary circumstances. Up until now I've asked you to only wear your actor's hat, so to speak, but for this portion you're going to be taking that off and putting on your writer's hat to create them. Once you're done, you're going to put the actor's hat back on, and you'll be testing the circumstances to see if they are strong enough.

"To help put all this into perspective, let's look at the third criterion. The third criterion for a successful independent activity is that the activity has to be done now, and not later. That means you're going to have to come up with a reason that it must be completed right now. If you're making a paper wreath for a friend's birthday, you need to get it done now or you're going to miss the party."

"So, a deadline?"

"Well said. There's a deadline in this activity. This needs to be done right now, and you won't get another chance to complete it if not now. That deadline can come from a variety of places, of course. It could be one you set for yourself, or in your circumstances it could be given to you by an outside person, such as a loved one, colleague, or the situation itself. There really are immense possibilities. Before we get into the specifics of how you set your circumstances, let's look at the fourth and final criterion for an independent activity. The fourth criterion is that there is an extremely meaningful consequence to not completing it in time. That relates to the deadline aspect, but is its own unique element."

"What do you mean by extremely meaningful?"

'This is where you're going to have to look to yourself for answers. Consider what has a lot of personal meaning for you. It could be something happening in your life right now, something that could happen, or something related to your past. The sources of meaning in your life are what will give you the consequences as well as reasons it must be done now."

"This is an imagined scenario then? We're not recreating something from our past?"

"Yes, this is quite important. This is not a re-enactment of something that has happened to you. It's an exploration of something that *could* happen to you. If your grandmother has passed on, for example, then baking a cake for her birthday that she'll enjoy won't have a lot of power. On some level you'll know that she isn't here to actually eat it, and so that knowledge will sap the consequence of its meaning and the deadline of its urgency. Likewise, it doesn't help to be purely imaginative either. If your activity solely relates to winning a million-dollar lottery, for example, that's an interesting premise but it doesn't mean much unless you connect it to your life. What will you do with that money, for example? Is that money a house for your mom so she can get out of that noisy, unsafe apartment complex? That's much more concrete and specific to you than just celebrating you won a million bucks. Not that any of us would complain, but I think you see the difference.

"Having covered the criteria, let me give you a couple examples of independent activities I've seen. The first one involved a very gifted actor named Manuel. Manuel was sewing a torn shirt, and he had given himself five minutes to do it. For his activity, he had imagined his daughter had fallen and hit her head on the playground. She was stable and going to live, but there was a risk of her going blind if she didn't have immediate surgery. There was also a risk, however, that she would become blind from the surgery, so this really was his last possible chance to spend time with her while she could see. On a father-date playdate a year before this happened, she had torn her favorite shirt, and he had promised to fix it for her. Work, life, and other commitments had kept him putting it off. With news of the accident, and the possibility of her losing sight, he wanted to be there with it before the surgery, to show her the shirt and give her something to look forward to when she woke up. This was an extremely powerful activity for him, and he based the five-minute time not only on finishing the shirt but estimating the time he needed to leave in order to make it to the hospital before the surgery. This gave him a profoundly urgent deadline. He couldn't even waste a single second. It was, all around, an extraordinarily strong activity not so much for the dramatic nature of it but the personal meaning he had."

"And his daughter wasn't actually having surgery?"

"No. He really has a daughter, but the surgery was a circumstance he had created, along with the meaning of the torn shirt. The shirt wasn't actually hers, it was purchased from a store and he tore it just before the activity. If this scenario had actually happened it would be too rooted in reality for our purposes. Some grains of personal truth and meaning are essential, but the scenario itself is fictional.

"In another example, a brilliant actress named Rena had brought in some chocolates, syringes, and powdered laxatives. She first began by mixing the powder with water in a beaker to get the precise concentration. Then she began directly injecting 0.1 ml of the laxative into each chocolate. She had to be profoundly careful to only inject in a side corner of the chocolate so the syringe hole wouldn't be visible, and she had to make sure every drop went in. She hadn't brought in any extra chocolates, so the risk of failure was immense, and she had to be precise to ensure she did everything right in her time limit. Her circumstances were that her best friend was moving, and recently had pranked her hard, and she was out for revenge before her friend departed town. They had this kind of a relationship in real life apparently, constantly joking on one another with elaborate pranks, so in her scenario she was inviting her over for a final chat and catch-up, and would present her with a gift of fine chocolate to enjoy on the plane ride. Filled with laxatives, of course. I have to say, I think half the room almost fell out of their chairs laughing, but this was another wonderfully strong activity filled with meaningful consequences and urgency."

"That's a much more fun example than the first one, which was pretty heavy. We don't need a certain emotional tone or anything then?"

"Don't focus on emotion when creating these circumstances. If you try to create a 'sad' or 'joyous' activity you're going to set yourself up for disappointment. Instead focus on what's important to you and what event, if it happened, would have extreme meaning for you. Generally that means something heavier, since tragic possibilities worry us more than joyful ones, but activities certainly can be joyous as well. But don't worry about the emotional tone, we honestly won't know what that is until we get there."

"I guess my question is more of a general one. With our circumstances, do we need to . . . I don't know, 'act' them?"

"No, there's no pressure on you to make anything happen. If the circumstances are strong they are going to take hold of you during the activity, as if what you've imagined has happened has actually just happened. That's why we say we're going to be *testing* the circumstances rather than *forcing* them to work. You want to choose a scenario that ignites the activity for you. What that means is something you'll discover when you get to that point of doing it in front of us, but you'll know when it happens. So, no, please don't go home and spend time thinking about how you are going to show or demonstrate any aspect of your circumstances. We're looking for circumstances that are so meaningful you can't help but be motivated by them once you start your activity. Spend time investigating that; this is your opportunity to come up with a possible activity and then test it in practice."

I'm sure the actors have plenty more questions, but too many questions up front runs the risk of information overload. They've got the essentials to create an independent activity and, if this were an actual class, would have at least a few hours if not a day or week to both think about the activity and come up with their best attempt at fulfilling these criteria. It's finally time to begin developing the facility for connecting living truthfully to a given set of circumstances, for now ones of your own creation but eventually the circumstances found in any text you will encounter.

Summary

Culminating the journey of learning the technique of repetition ends with confronting one of the deepest and most profound impulses: the impulse to move. The implications of this are explored through Meisner's knock at the door exercise, which calls into question many assumptions both about acting and the reality of conditioned habits in your acting. Through a gradual process of exploration, actors discover not only the depth of the exercise but also new questions about their own process. After learning the knock at the door, actors engaged in this work will have the full technique of repetition, able to train their facility for living truthfully whether seated or standing, still or in motion. It is the complete journey of repetition, and the perfect segue into now learning to work with the given set of circumstances. At the end of the session, actors are given a homework assignment that, when completed successfully, marks a major step into training the complete definition of acting according to Sanford Meisner: living truthfully under a given set of circumstances.

12
What Burns Deeply Within

With No Voice, the Cricket Sings

The strands of meditation we have been interested in serve a double function. They offer a simple, replicable means to explore your experience of reality as it is actually happening. This includes how you see the world looking out from your eyes, as well as the sensations of sound, sight, smell, and touch you continuously encounter. We can consider this building a skillset to sharpen your attention to the details you exist in but may not have been previously aware of.

Within this context, however, you'll also begin to notice certain elements of your life that no longer make sense. Perhaps you always considered yourself someone who only gets stressed when other people trigger you. Through practice you may discover how much you add to your own anxiety without having realized it before. Maybe you felt angry because there were so many wrong, misled, or bad people in the world, only to discover a degree of that rage comes from you feeding it when you become slightly irritated at something, encouraging it to grow like a wildfire. These facets of our identity don't just relate to the causes and effects of emotional states, but also big-picture values about ourselves. It's not uncommon after a process of self-exploration to say to yourself, "I originally thought I wanted this for my career as an actor, but now I realize I want these things more." We craft our paths of life from our thoughts about who we are, and when those perceptions can change, so too can our paths become clearer and more relevant. Discovering these elements of self, and dissolving them when they no longer align with your conclusions, are the second function of this type of practice, a process that empowers you to keep aligning your plans for the future with your experience of reality.

Many of the benefits in meditation are gradual. You'll practice for a time without seeing anything, only to slowly begin noticing subtle differences in your daily experience. While normally you might be swallowed up in anxious thoughts when something unpleasant happens, now for just a moment or two you may become aware of the tightness in your chest, the way your breath has changed, or the recurring thoughts nagging at you. Your tools may not yet be strong enough to do anything about them in the beginning but, eventually, you'll be able to move the dial on your experiences from totally lost in thought to aware and present. That's the slow-building effect of meditation that yields powerful, consistent results over time.

Solely focusing on the gradual nature of meditation, however, ignores an equally valid, albeit much rarer, set of possibilities: breakthrough moments. Even early in practice, breakthrough experiences can occur. These may manifest as a sudden sense of greater connection to the world around you, a heightened clarity of recognizing yourself as inseparable from the rest of reality. You might find that even ordinary activities are now uniquely vibrant. Drinking a cup of tea or coffee, peeling an orange, or putting on a piece of clothing can become so crisp and unique that you feel there is nothing like this experience in the rest of the whole universe. The mundane becomes extraordinary.

Whatever their hue or character, another characteristic of breakthrough moments is that they often don't last – a blip that is gone in the next instant. There are, of course, exceptions. Sometimes a breakthrough can last for minutes, hours, or even longer than a day. Regarding them as lasting the entirety of a lifetime, enabling you to go through every day feeling as if you're in some esoteric trip, that's the stuff of poorly written legend. Rather than extended periods of bliss, meditation breakthroughs tend to return to the mundane, the normal. Integrating meditation practice into your daily life doesn't mean rainbows of enlightenment await, but rather going through life with more clarity, more attention, and less distraction from your own thoughts. As meditation expert Jack Cornfield has written, "First enlightenment. Then the laundry."

Breakthrough experiences in meditation aren't simply examples of noise in the signal, or anomalies that are extraordinary for the sake of it. They can and often do serve a unique function in providing you with insights and learning that can fast track certain types of release. A breakthrough insight, like a light suddenly violently flooding a pitch-black room, can reveal misconceptions you had about yourself, cutting through them with little effort. There is a reason we value epiphanies so much in many fields, that elusive "Eureka!" moment, and breakthroughs serve as a type of meditation equivalent of an epiphany.

Unfortunately, there's no clear way to replicate them. Actors who have trained in the Stanislavski system understand the headache this brings. In his work Stanislavski wrote about inspiration, a type of breakthrough insight an actor could have about their character that would negate the need for much of the research or preparation an actor does. An actor's work on a character, Stanislavski reasoned, could provide the groundwork for inspiration to come or, if it never arrived, at least there would be technique an actor could use to see them through the performance. Like flow experiences, breakthroughs are a rare phenomenon in many fields, acting and meditation included. This brings us to the value of koans in meditation practice.

Does a Dog Have Buddha Nature?

Even if the word "koan" is new to you, you've likely encountered some already. Perhaps you've heard an iconic one: "What is the sound of one hand clapping?" If I asked you that now, as a sincere question, you might think it was a riddle of sorts. It sounds paradoxical, and so there must be some sort of trick to solving it. But is that really the right way to treat this question? Riddles thrive on double-meanings. The fun is the reversal of having the first meaning reveal the actual meaning. Take this common riddle:

> I can fly but I have no wings. I can cry but I have no eyes. Wherever I go, darkness follows me. What am I?

Something that flies through the sky but has no wings must be a unique creature indeed. The second sentence tells us it cries, which is of the experience of a living being, particularly something like a human. Yet it has no eyes, so how can it have tears? The third sentence conjures up the possibility of something ominous, such as a cursed being or object, or pursued by a literal darkness where it goes. What's the best example of a traveling darkness? The night. What moves through the sky, dropping water, followed by night? Clouds. We answer a riddle through analysis and an open mind. It may take a while, but we eventually find the *correct* answer.

When it comes to the sound of one hand clapping, however, we're at a bit of a standstill. Very quickly we realize it doesn't have clues buried within it. If you are playing volleyball with a friend and hit the ball, well that's the sound of one hand. So what? There's no reversal built into the equation like a good riddle. It feels more like a nonsensical question. Use your powers of analysis to answer it and not much comes up. Yet that in itself that tells us about koans and their value for meditation practice.

Let's look at the complete version of the koan: "You know the sound of two hands clapping. What is the sound of one hand?" That tells us something unique about the single hand. When two hands come together with enough force to produce a clap there's a sound. But when you ask what is the sound of one hand, you might feel temporarily stumped, your thoughts suspended for a split-second before you even have time to work it out. The question itself is baffling. On its own, without anything else, a hand makes no sound. What if you simply sat with this seeming paradox in meditation? It might surprise you that the insight it offers us has to do with singular consciousness and our inseparability from the world. We won't go into the specifics of how that conclusion is reached just yet, but for here what is important is that this isn't an insight you will find through analysis but rather by incorporating the koan into your meditation practice.

Koans can be best introduced as phrases extracted from stories about the words and deeds of Zen masters who had experienced awakening, similar to the kinds of breakthrough experiences we were describing earlier. Rather than riddles to be solved, they are moments of clarity taken from the lives of others. Sat with in practice, they can be sources of breakthrough clarity for us as well. When this happens, as well as which koans will aid you in your practice, is a mystery, and like any other form of meditation, the power of koan practice builds over time. Still, they offer a unique way to bypass our desire to understand something intellectually and instead experience it viscerally. Let's try one.

Exercise: Meditation 11

Set-up: Set up your practice.

Part one instructions: Set a timer for 5 minutes. In this meditation you'll be working with the koan, "Who am I?" In Chapter 10, we introduced the idea of "noting" the breath. This, as well, is a kind of noting, though you won't be using it to keep track of your breathing. Instead repeat the phrase to yourself on your exhale. When you inhale, simply inhale, and on your exhale gently say to yourself, "Who am I?" Sit with this phrase for the entirety of the 5 minutes and see what comes up. When you are ready, start your timer, close your eyes, and begin.

Part one notes/questions: This particular phrase is so useful because of how many tempting, and irrelevant, things it can bring up. Just as "the sound of one hand" doesn't have a rational answer, repeating to yourself "Who am I?" is not engaging in a thought experiment of sorts. A question like that in any other context might serve as an invitation for us to sit down and "figure" things out by making a list, engaging in deep conversations, buying a positive psychology planner, and so on. Rather than exploring deeply using your thoughts, let this phrase crest gently on your exhales. It may bring up a visceral response, something emotional, or nothing at all. Koans are uniquely attuned to your individual practice. The phrase itself can produce a moment of insight or awakening, or this time it may not do anything. Both outcomes, and the many possibilities in between, are perfectly valid experiences. Having said that, however, if you find yourself getting lost in thought due to a koan or the nature of your mind that day, employ your tools from mindfulness by recognizing the thought, and then returning to the breath and repeating the koan. Each of these practices deeply connects to one another, even if they descend from entirely unique traditions and eras in history.

Step two instructions: Set up your practice again if necessary. Set a timer for 5 minutes. In this next half, you'll continue to work with the koan, "Who am I?" or if you want to try a variation you could use, "Who is this?" Inhale normally, and as you exhale softly repeat the koan to yourself silently. When you are ready start your timer, close your eyes, and begin.

Step two notes/questions: It can be extremely challenging to be told you don't need to do something with an element of meditation. In mindfulness training, for example, letting the breath come and go naturally, without artificially deepening or manipulating it, can be a struggle for practitioners.

Sometimes practitioners sit within a koan for years before experiencing an insight; other times it's in the first five minutes that it can arrive. The important thing is to be present and not attempt to juice the koan of thought, meaning, or a result. Koan practice, like any form of meditation, is a labor of patient love. In future meditations, you'll continue to discover further how koans aren't riddles or problems to be analyzed or solved. They aren't mysteries in the traditional sense with a clearly defined answer. One doesn't need to do anything with a koan for it to have an impact. The trust component is letting the koan work on you, rather than you attempting to seek meaning from it. This stepping back gives us another insight into koans, which is to treat them as Zen Master Henry Shukman (whose work I highly recommend and has informed much of my own practice) advises: as "beckonings from moments in the lives of awakened people."

On a final note, throughout the day, if you find your day being punctuated by moments of mindfulness, feel free to spend a few breaths quietly repeating the koan on the exhale. In different environments and contexts new things can arise. Koan practice, just like mindfulness and headlessness, are designed to be entirely portable into any area of your life.

Rising Tides

In the previous chapter, you may have noticed that we shifted entirely from listing instructions to exploring a hypothetical case study. This is because there's no way to introduce the knock at the door as a blanket set of instructions without first seeing an example of the journey. This shows us the risks of being too prescriptive. Imagine if my instructions had said, "In the knock at the door, one actor goes out of the room and then knocks. The other actor answers the door and thus begins a repetition exercise." Not only would this be a gross simplification of the nuances of the exercises, but I would have sabotaged your work. Your learning would have mostly been aimed at undoing my mistakes. Who says for example that there really will be a knock? Most likely there will be, but the only guarantee we have is that the instruction to knock has been given, not that the knock itself will come. Who says the actor in the room will always open the door? Maybe their partner will come in if they wait too long or another impulse drives them inside? Who says the repetition begins once they are face to face? It's possible the repetition could start before the door is opened, or that when they are face to face there is only silence.

The knock at the door is in many ways an embracing of the unknown variables that surround us constantly. Now the unknowns not only extend to changes in the text but also movement and the wide range of impulses that brings up. These are the unknowns you will deal with on the job, and if we wish to begin moving towards greater portability, taking more ownership over your work is essential. This is why the only instruction I could have provided to summarize the exercise is, "The knock at the door is a repetition exercise that begins with a knock at the door."

This exercise is very much the same way. In today's assignment, the actors were asked to each bring an independent activity. To refresh yourself on the specific components of the activity, as well as an in-depth exploration of the criteria, feel free to visit the final section of Chapter 11. Though there are many versions of independent activities, some of which won't be covered in this book, I find it helpful to begin with the approach to the independent activity used by the Impulse Company, where I first trained in the Meisner technique. It's not the richest or most complete version of the independent activity, but it's a great introduction for the many possibilities it offers. According to Scott Williams, a successful independent activity has four components built into it:

1. The activity must be intricate, or fiddly. Another way to consider this is physically engaging.
2. It must be difficult to complete in the time limit you have set for yourself.
3. There is a reason it must be done now and not later.
4. There is an extremely meaningful consequence to not completing it.

It's worth noting that your first few activities should be treated largely as experiments in finding your feet with what a good activity is and is not. In most Meisner training the independent activity is the bread and butter of an actor's development. It trains the entire package deal of living truthfully under a given set of circumstances. Finding out what is a strong activity takes time, and this is why actors often do many activities in Meisner training. I probably have done in my own training hundreds at this point, if not more, and have seen thousands, so my best advice is don't worry about getting it perfectly the first time. Give it your best guess, and if it doesn't work, you'll find out why. Finding your feet with this exercise is a gradual process by design, and so the majority of feedback in this chapter is targeted for early, rather than more developed, phases of this exercise.

The final element worth noting is that independent activities can be long, often lasting ten minutes or more (your time limit, as you will see, is only one element of what makes this the case). To shorten the examples and focus on the most relevant details, my example repetitions won't be longer than three or four repeats per observation. This is not representative of repetitions in a living training session, in which calls tend to be repeated longer, depending on the moment of course. If you look at the repetitions and they feel short, or you see a consistently patterned number of repeats, just note this is done for the sake of this medium.

Scripting again, we've got four actors who will be working today. Through the successes and challenges each pair encounters you will start to get a sense of how to plan your own activities.

Preparing for What?

The layout of the room is slightly different. There is a table for the actor doing their activity, and one chair at the table. I ask for someone to volunteer. Beverly bravely raises her hand. I then ask for a partner. Sam offers to be first in the mix.

"Great. So, this helps us get a better sense of the day. Today we're going to see four independent activities, so you'll all do yours, but only one actor does their activity at a time. This brings us to the question of what their partner is doing. Remember the knock at the door exercise from the last session, where one person was in the room and the other was out?"

"Yes . . ." Beverly says.

"Well, it's coming back."

"Oh no." She and Sam both laugh, shaking their heads.

"The independent activity has two components. First, the actor in the room is doing their activity. Second, the other actor goes out of the room, and after a period of time knocks. Just as in the knock at the door, a repetition exercise begins with the knock at the door."

"So do I keep doing my activity while repeating?" Beverly asks.

"I don't know."

"Of course you don't," Sam says, laughing.

"But I really need to get my activity done," Beverly says. "How am I going to have time to repeat?"

"Let's see what happens when we get there," I say. I want the actors to know that soon they'll have all the information I can give, and then we'll all be back in the same boat of assessing what the moment brings. "First, however, there's one additional component to introduce."

What Fills the Void of Waiting?

"In the previous session," I say, "during one of the times outside the room, Raoul gave a very inventive, musical knock. He was onto something there: being outside the room, just counting and then knocking, doesn't do much for your acting. Once the repetition starts rolling we're back on track, but that span of time outside the door seems wasted. There's also a practical parallel question, which is how do you get yourself prepared to go on stage or back into a take after some downtime? So, why don't we introduce a new set of tools that you can practice when you're outside the room that also can be applied to your work on set or stage? Let's talk about preparation.

"This version of preparation comes from the Impulse Company, in London. Down the road it will be replaced by a more potent form of preparation from Larry Silverberg's work, but this is a superb way to begin introducing yourself to the concept of it. Preparation has one function only, which is to put you into what at Impulse is called a 'state of aliveness.' How exactly this will manifest in the moment isn't clear, so there's no defined outcome for what a preparation should look like. This also tells you something equally important about it: rather than trying to force anything to happen from it, you are simply going to be testing your preparation to see if it is a strong one."

"Like when we were preparing our activities?"

"Exactly. Just like you won't be 'acting' to show us your circumstances, you don't need to treat your preparation as anything other than a visceral experiment that might have an impact on you. So, when you go out the door, Sam, you'll do a preparation. There are five types of preparation on offer for you to experiment with.

"The first is called the physical preparation. In a physical preparation, you engage in any type of physical activity right up until the point of exhaustion. This could be running up and down the hall or around the building, jumping jacks, push-ups, you name it. The important thing is that you really push yourself to the point of being nearly completely wiped out. Go beyond the point where you just feel a little energized or pumped up, really try to exhaust yourself. The great ballet dancer Nijinsky would work out to the point of exhaustion before each performance. His reasoning? So he would have nothing left to hold onto. When you hit that point, you knock at the door."

"And that begins the exercise?"

"Let's wait and see before answering that, but for the person outside the room, those are your steps: as soon as you are out of the room, you do a preparation, and at the peak of that preparation you release it into the knock."

"No need to count to thirty anymore?"

"No, and don't worry about a time length or anything like that. Generally preparations take longer, in the range of a minute or two. They can of course end up being shorter or a bit longer, it just depends on the preparation and how well it is working. The extra time dovetails really well with the independent activity by giving the person in the room enough time to get into their activity. So, that's it for physical preparation. Physical preparations are excellent. In some senses they have some unique strengths over the following ones. Any guesses as to why a preparation based solely on physical action is a strong one?"

"Well, it's always reliable."

"What do you mean?"

"If all I need to do is exhaust myself, then I can achieve that each time."

"Bingo. There's also no risk of you getting trapped in your head, judging yourself for the preparation not working. If you're not exhausted enough, simply push yourself harder physically. Just as a basic call is our go-to default for observations, so is the physical preparation your reliable base camp for preparation. If you ever find yourself worrying about these next ones, a physical preparation will get the job done just fine. And that brings us to our next four, which we can call the non-physical preparations.

"The first type of non-physical preparation is memory. Generally memory is the weakest form of preparation, and all I mean by this is that it tends to have the lowest success rate of the lot. There's a simple reason for this: memory by nature deals with moments in the past. Meaning has a tendency to change over time. What was once incredibly meaningful to us now may no longer have much relevance. Time and changes in our perspectives change our relationships with memories. The risk of course is that it can end up putting you inside your head by not providing you with the result you're after. You try to access a memory and say, 'Well, I was sad when it happened, but now I'm not feeling anything. What's wrong with me?' The short answer is nothing is wrong with you: it's simply that your relationship with that past event has now changed.

"To avoid this risk, the best advice I can give you for any of these preparations is not to try to use them to generate an emotional state. Don't pick a memory because it was sad once. Focus instead on a meaningful event in your life, something important. Then, once you have the memory, again, don't seek any outcome from it, but do your best to immerse yourself in the details of that memory. Be as specific as possible. If the event you are remembering took place in a restaurant, remember what the seats felt like, the temperature of the table, the texture of your glass or cup against your lips.

Connect with that experience as viscerally as possible. If the preparation is successful, it's going to start filling you with that aliveness. Again, what that aliveness can feel like emotionally is impossible to say. It's entirely likely in revisiting a memory which caused you great pain at the time that joy can now arise, and vice versa. Whatever it is, allow it, and when the preparation has filled you to the point of being almost overwhelmed release it into the knock. Any questions about all that?"

"It seems like these non-physical preparations are mental ones."

"Yes . . ."

"So that means I'm in my head."

"Correct. It's important that once you knock you don't put any pressure on yourself to keep making the preparation happen. Preparation's only function is to get you through the door. Once you're in put your attention on the other actor and see what happens. The preparation might evaporate, it might keep informing the exercise, it might dissipate and return; there are many possibilities but the key is to make sure you don't let it trap your attention onto yourself. All of these cautionary notes aside, however, as great as physical preparation is, it pales in comparison to the depth and power of a strong non-physical preparation. Don't let the warning labels discourage you: as we continue to do these activities, keep experimenting with different types of preparations. If you get too stuck in your head just change to a physical one. That's the beauty of having it as a fallback.

"So, some of us have an incredibly strong relationship with our imagination. We can have rich, imaginary scenarios playing out in our head that we are a part of, and they move us so much it feels like we are actually there. If you're that person, then this next preparation might be for you: imagination. Imagination asks you to imagine yourself in an entirely fictional set of circumstances completely divorced from your current life. You could find yourself as a wizard or queen in a fantasy world, a character in a video game, or living in a completely different era and chapter of history. The sky is the limit but the only criterion to remember is that it doesn't incorporate many elements of your present life; that's material for the next preparation.

"The potential challenges to using a purely imaginative preparation are similar to those of memory. If you revisit a certain place in your mind you are fond of, and the feelings you are used to don't come, it can be easy to start becoming concerned about what has changed or isn't working. The solution, however, is largely the same: specificity in the details. The texture of your clothes, temperature of your environment, the feel of the ground if there is any . . . whatever you come up with, enrichment of the details is your first priority. Let the preparation fill you as you continue to engage with the unique, wonderful elements of that reality."

With no questions, we move into deeper waters with the next preparation, increasing the potency dramatically.

"For most of us memory and imagination play a meaningful role in our current circumstances. We remember important elements of where we have been and infuse them with our desires for where to go. We think deeply about our present and use our imagination to envision how it could change. At the crossroads of memory and imagination is the third form of preparation: fantasy. Fantasy is a bruiser of a preparation. There are few things more potent and powerful to most of us than a rich fantasy. Fantasy also has the added bonus of being far more relatable and, by its nature, often much more meaningful than simply memory or imagination alone. To craft a fantasy, you're going to take an important element of your life and hybrid it with something that could happen which would be extremely meaningful to you.

"Let's say in your real life you have an ex you continue to pine over, that you wish you had a second chance with. Now let's say, also real, your first date was in a park decorated for the winter holidays. You know there's no chance of reconciliation, but now the imagination component of fantasy steps in. What if one day your ex calls and says they want to meet and talk in the park from your first date. What would that mean for you, that possible second chance you would give anything for? Exploring the fantasy could yield a number of emotions, from joy to anger to pain and so on, and so again don't engage with the fantasy looking for an outcome. Explore it to bask in it, to revel in the details of having this one chance again. Engage with the details of the lights on trees, the temperature in the air, the look and, if the fantasy takes you there, the feel of the skin on your ex's face, hands, and so on. Hear their voice so clearly, as if it were a song you loved but thought you'd never hear again. If the fantasy is working, it's going to take hold of you before you're even fully aware. When you are at the peak of it, release the fruits of that preparation into the knock. Fantasy is such a unique, potent part of our lives, so don't underestimate its power as fuel for a preparation."

"Fantasy is then about what could happen?"

"Not just what could happen, but what could happen that would change you and your current circumstances in a profound way. That's the real key difference between it and imagination. Fantasy uses imagination as fuel, but that can only happen because it's so woven into your life and what gives it meaning. And speaking of meaning, this is where we reach our fourth and final preparation. Some would argue this is the most potent form of preparation, more powerful even than fantasy, and I think you'll quickly see why. My old Meisner teacher calls this form of preparation 'spin.' Here is the essence of spin: you'll engage with an unresolved issue in your life." I can hear some actors rustling in concern at this, while others are immediately nodding their heads.

"To be clear, an unresolved issue doesn't mean some great trauma or pain. What makes spin so powerful and effective is that the issue itself doesn't need to be extremely large to have an impact. It could instead be as simple as that *one* phone call you've been putting off making, or that *one* email you need to write. You know which one it is for yourself – the one that makes your teeth grit when thinking of it, or causes your heart to jump an extra three beats in anxiety. Spin asks you to directly focus on something you've been avoiding or that remains unresolved, and to engage with the details of not having done it. If it's that unfinished email to your boss telling them to shove it where the sun doesn't shine that's been sitting in your drafts for months, imagine the writing of that email, and also all the moments that prompted it. Engage with it however it is that injects you with that aliveness we're after.

"So, everyone today will participate in two exercises. One will be your activity, and the other will be you acting as partner. The person who remains in the room does their activity, the person outside tries out a preparation. When the preparation is full, the person outside knocks, and then . . . well, we'll see, won't we?"

The Magnificent Incandescence of Being in a Hurry

Beverly takes her materials up to the table. She has them in two plastic bags.

"Any questions from either of you before we give this a try?" I ask.

"Nope," says Sam.

"I've got one," Beverly asks.

"Go for it," I say.

"My activity needs a little bit of setting up. Do I do that before I begin or do I set up after I start my timer?"

"It depends entirely on the circumstances you've set up. If the circumstances are you've broken your spouse's favorite cup and it needs to repaired before they get home, you'd want to start the activity with the mug broken. You'll break it just before either class or the activity starts. On the other hand, if you're setting up a party, have just brought the supplies home, and you need to start on them immediately, then obviously you'd save all the unwrapping and unbagging for when the activity begins."

"I see," Beverly says. "Then I'm good to go as is."

"Great. Sam, head outside, do a preparation, and then knock. As soon as that door closes, Beverly, off you go."

"Got it," she says. She reaches into her bag and grabs an egg timer. Sam leaves the room. When the door closes, she quickly sets the timer and begins busily emptying the bags. Out of one she pulls a small electrical device, which she turns on, as well as a small set of wire cutters, metal strings in packaging, and some printed instructions. From the other bag she pulls out a worn-looking mandolin. She opens the instructions and begins to read. "Oh shoot," she says, peering over them. She begins trying to remove the tailpiece off the mandolin, but it doesn't budge. She goes back to the instructions to make sure she is doing it correctly. She is clearly becoming more agitated. She begins to force the tailpiece, but it doesn't want to go. "Come on," she whispers under her breath, and finally it gives. She's just begun to open the package of strings when a fairly loud knock comes. She looks at the door for a moment, but then goes back to fiddling with the package. After a lapse of thirty seconds or so, another knock comes.

"I'm very busy," she calls out. "Go away."

There's another pause. She frees the strings from the package. She begins to attach the first one to a hook that had been covered by the exposed tailpiece. As she is attempting to work with it the door opens. Sam enters, still largely out of breath. His breathing is loud and she notices him.

"You're out of breath," Beverly says.

"I'm out of breath."

"You're out of breath."

She realizes she can't get the string over the loop and goes back to the directions. She turns quiet again. Sam stands there, unsure of what to do.

"You don't want me here," he says.

"I don't want you here," she replies.

"You don't want me here."

"No, I don't want you here, so go away." As she says this, Sam spots a glaring essential behavior.

"Your hands are shaking."

Beverly doesn't repeat. She manages to get the first string on. She starts working with the second one, but as soon as she does disaster strikes. The bridge of the mandolin, a piece meant to be held together by the strings, suddenly plonks right off. It falls to the ground.

"Oh dear," she says, trying to look for it.

"You're looking for it," Sam says, trying to contain his laughter.

"I'm looking for it," she says, reaching under the table to find it. It's under her chair but she can't see it.

"You're looking for it." Sam's face goes red as he tries to hold back the laughter.

"I'm looking for it–"

The timer goes off. Both actors suddenly seem unsure of what to do. Beverly stops looking for the item, then looks at me.

"Well?" I say.

"Isn't the exercise over?"

"We can stop it here, yes. So, wonderful work you two. Really. For a first independent activity there were some great things. Some bumps in the road we can address, but overall a fantastic first go."

I make sure both actors have heard this. The independent activity has a lot of components to it, and while this was far from a strong exercise there are many good things to be praised as well as material for growth. This is a learning process, and it's day one.

"For each of these activities, feedback is going to be broken into two parts. First, we'll look at the activity itself, using our four criteria to see how strong or weak each element was. After that, we'll talk about the work each of you did in the exercise. So, let me open these first questions up to the group. The activity itself: did it meet the first criterion? Was it physically engaging and intricate?"

I see nods and hear a few yesses from the group.

"I agree, there were a lot of fiddly components, and that you had brought the tuner in was a great metric to know if you had done it right or not once the instrument was strung. This is quite important with activities. Having a specific outcome, where you'll know exactly what it looks like when finished, is an essential element for the exercise to thrive. Doing makeup for example might be intricate and engaging, but if you don't do it perfectly there's still chance to give yourself an out by saying, 'Well, it's good enough.' We don't want you to have that option for yourself. It's really all or nothing, you did it exactly as it was meant to be or you failed. Either the instrument was properly strung and tuned or it wasn't."

"Oh, we were far from that," Beverly says, chuckling.

"It seemed that way. But that brings me to the second criterion. Was it difficult to complete in the time she gave herself?" Almost everyone agrees unanimously. "I concur," I say, "but I wonder if you cut it too short."

"I've never strung an instrument before, so I thought I could get it done in the time I gave myself."

"Which was?"

"Four minutes and thirty seconds."

"I love that you had never done this activity before, so I fully respect you had to make a best guess on it. Let me ask you about something I noticed: as it went on, did you start to realize there was no possible way for it to get done in time?"

"A little."

"When the piece fell, it seemed to me you were just a bit more relaxed in looking for it. Not that you didn't care, it certainly seemed to matter, but I wonder if the futility of the time had begun to dawn on you and you were starting to see the writing on the wall."

"I think so."

"As you'll see today, there's no way to perfectly predict the time for getting something done. In your next activity you may have a totally different set of parameters. But generally if it's something that is being done for the first time, the referencing of instructions can take up more time than if we already knew how to do it. I wonder if you had given yourself seven minutes, for example, if the possibility of getting it done would have continued to fuel that urgency for you."

"It would have made it seem more plausible, but I still don't think it would have been done by then either."

"You're certainly far braver than I am with trying to string an instrument. By the way, are those wires sharp in any way?"

"Not really."

"Great. A general piece of advice is to take care when planning to work with sharp objects. There is a fair amount of pressure in this exercise so just factor that into your planning. I've never seen anyone get worse than a small nick, and that was incredibly rare, but if any of you were planning on juggling swords maybe opt for something more life-preserving."

"Damn," Sam says.

"That's the advanced class," I joke, laughing with him. "So, onto the third criterion, did it seem to you all as if she had to get it done right now?" I see some agreement, so I ask the group, "Why? And by that I mean what did you see in her behavior that gave you that impression?"

"She kept talking to herself," one member says, "like not for us, she kept saying things to herself. I do that when I'm pretty stressed or in a hurry."

"Plus she kept telling him to go away," another actor chimes in.

"I agree. There was some evidence in her behavior that she needed to get this done in the time frame. That brings us to the fourth criterion. In Beverly's behavior did you sense there was an extremely meaningful consequence to not completing it?"

Here the group is more divided. "Sort of," someone says.

"Okay. Go on."

"Well, she kept telling him to go away and stuff, but when she dropped that piece she didn't look really hard for it."

"Let's go to you on that, Beverly. Did it feel like if you didn't finish stringing and tuning the instrument there would be a big consequence?"

"I think so . . ."

"But you're not sure?"

"I'm not sure how big you wanted it to be."

"Not big necessarily, but meaningful in a way that it's the most important thing to get it done right now. So, let's try something. Before we do, I want you to know if I ever ask any of you a question about your circumstances and you don't want to share, you've got my full support to say you'd rather not. Circumstances usually involve very personal and meaningful things, and thus far we haven't needed to intrude on anyone's past or personal life for their acting to grow. That said, are you comfortable, Beverly, with just giving me a one- or two-line summary of your circumstances?"

"Sure. My son just got a big award at school, and I wanted to surprise him with this gift."

"Does he like playing music?"

"He loves it. He wanted to study it full time but decided on another degree."

"But he still plays?"

"Oh yes."

"And was this instrument once his, or did you buy it like that?"

"I found it a secondhand shop and decided it would make a nice gift for him."

"But it doesn't have strings and so you're going to learn how to string and tune it, even though you don't know how?"

"Yes."

"That's an incredibly kind thing of you to do. Your son is one lucky kid. And why does it have to be done now?"

"Because he'll be home soon."

"I see. And if your son comes home, and you haven't finished yet, what's the consequence?"

"I won't be able to give it to him when he comes into the door."

"And then what happens?"

Beverly pauses, thinking on it. "Well, I suppose we could just do it together, or I could do it later . . ."

"There's definitely some meaning in there, but it seems like the consequence for you isn't as strong. If you get it done in time, that's a great, very thoughtful thing done. But if not done now, a few hours isn't as big a deal. That's the beauty of what the consequence does, it gives you a concrete reason for why a few hours later isn't going to work. So that's one way you can test whether a consequence is potentially strong or not, by asking yourself if there's any opportunity for a takeback, and then to eliminate that possibility. You don't want to give yourself an out so the activity can be done later with minimal consequence. We want something that is so meaningful it needs to get done now, and if it doesn't there's no chance for a repeat."

"So this activity didn't work then?"

"It worked on quite a few levels, so there's no reason to be discouraged. This was a great first attempt. There is a fundamental issue with the activity which we'll cover in a second, but we don't want to deny there were plenty of strengths. The question around the consequence is a major one, but just because that component didn't work well for you doesn't mean it derailed the entire experience. But since we're on the topic of the consequence, can I ask you, does your son live in this city?"

"Oh yes, he's still at home. He was going to move out to be closer to the university, but with everything that's happened in the world we thought it would be better for him to stay at home."

"You don't have to answer this next question if you don't want to, but how do you like your son living with you?"

"To be honest? I love it. When he was first planning on moving out it hit me much harder than I thought it would. I knew I should be happy for him, and I was, but I also wasn't ready to see him go."

"Him staying means a lot to you."

"Of course."

"Well, let me ask you, then, what if instead of an accomplishment at school it was a job offer, or a scholarship to study at the best program in the country? He'd get a full ride but would be leaving home. How would you feel then?"

"I would be happy for him."

"And?"

"And my heart would break."

"So it sounds like this is a pretty meaningful possibility What if then you were stringing the instrument because this was his last day before leaving, the day he was coming by to give you a hug and say goodbye? If you didn't get it done by the time the timer goes off, he'd never get to take it with him on the car ride. Would that have made the consequence more real?"

"Oh I'd have bolted the doors and never let you in!" she says to Sam, and we all laugh. "Come hell or high water I'd have finished that instrument."

"So that's the kind of response we want to our consequence, activity, and circumstances. There's no second chance if you miss it. Sure, you could mail to him, but it wouldn't have the meaning of him recognizing how proud you were of him, and that he could take his next steps into the world with your gift to remind him of how much he means to you. Seeing him off on the start of his journey. You'll never get that chance again."

I can see Beverly is already becoming moved by the possibility. She wipes her eyes and says, "I could try that, sure."

"Don't worry about revisiting it for your next few activities. Allow for some space in between scenarios. It's not like this is a graded activity where if you just try those consequences now you'll get an A. This is a process of testing what areas of meaning in your life can inform your acting. You're more than welcome to try the same activity while tweaking the circumstances, but in these early stages keep branching out with new activities and circumstances.

"So, that's our analysis of the activity itself. Overall, a wonderfully strong first attempt. Let's get into some individual feedback for each of you on what happened between you both. Sam, I have a guess, but what type of preparation did you do?"

"Physical," Sam says, breaking into a smile.

"And how did it go?"

"Awesome. I ran in place until I was nearly passing out."

"You came in like some *Seinfeld* character unleashed. It made you wonderful to watch. When you caught your breath, what happened to the preparation?"

"Well, when she kept telling me to go away it seemed to stop, but I think it wasn't gone completely."

"Why?"

"When she dropped that piece I had to try so hard to stop myself from laughing."

"You got the giggles big time! So, why did you think that you had to stop yourself?"

"Well, it just seemed mean to laugh at her misfortune."

"Did you want to help?"

"I did."

"Could you have done that? Is it okay to help someone in an activity?"

"If it's what the moment calls for."

"I agree. If you'd wanted to help her because it was the 'right thing to do,' that would have been coming more from yourself. But if you see your partner struggling and the impulse to help arises, go for it. It doesn't mean it's going to work out well, but it's worth expressing that impulse. Just like you have a complete right to laugh at your partner's misfortune if it's a truthful impulse. You won both impulses fairly, so you don't need to deny yourself one in favor of the other, even if one of them was incredibly impolite."

"Got it."

"One minor technical note for you, there were two calls you made of Beverly that I wanted to ask you about. The first was, 'You don't want me here.' I agree it seemed very clear she didn't want you there, but there probably were a lot of things she didn't want in that moment. She didn't want a turkey sandwich either. A stronger call might have been to look at any behaviors she was giving you that brought up that feeling of her pushing you away. Stillness, silence, or how she stopped repeating, could have been cleaner observations in the moment rather than a general opinion on her state of mind. The second call has to do with when the piece of the instrument fell on the floor and you said, 'You dropped it.' That's literally true, so it's not a bad call but why did she drop it? Were her hands shaking, was she short of breath, was there tension in her face, and so on? A good strategy is to stay with your partner and keep the calls attuned to their behavior as opposed to what they are literally doing."

"Makes sense."

"So, a great preparation and some fantastic work. Beverly, let's talk about what happened between the two of you. There you were, working hard to get the instrument tuned, and here comes the knock. To which you seemed to ignore it."

"I had to get the activity done."

"That's fine. If the activity is compelling enough that can happen. But then he knocked again and you called for him to go away. When he finally came in, the two of you were repeating, but several times you either stopped repeating altogether or ignored him."

"It was really hard to focus on getting the activity done with him there."

"I agree. But, unfortunately, the big takeaway for you is he isn't going away. He might have the impulse to leave the room, but ignoring him won't make the problem go away. You've got to deal with all of them: the activity, urgency of the circumstances, and your partner in repetition."

"So I can't stop repeating?"

"It depends. If he does something so profound in the moment that no words are needed, silence is a perfectly legitimate response. On the other hand, if you put the attention back onto yourself and think, 'I need to ignore him or I can't get this done,' then that comes from you and your intentions rather than something he is making you do. Had you engaged with him, I don't know what would have happened, but not allowing the exercise to happen because it's challenging isn't the best strategy. You'll have to deal with multiple things in your acting, embracing both challenging, urgent circumstances as well as the people you'll be working with, and both can fuel one another."

"But then I'll never get my activity done."

"We definitely agree that you needed more time to get it done, so in this case completing it wasn't going to happen regardless of whether you engaged with him or not. I can tell you from experience, however, that of the thousands of activities I've seen where the time was well guessed, which is the majority, half were completed, and half weren't. So that tells you something valuable about this exercise: you're going to work your best to make it happen, but there's nothing in the instructions that says you need to finish the activity for it to be of value to your acting. There's just as much growth for your process to be had in activities that succeed or fail, but you want to keep putting yourself in that realm of possibility. Meisner himself said that the design of the independent activity was to put you into a puzzle box with no solution, and to watch you twist in it. So, do you engage with your partner or focus on the activity? The answer is both, and sometimes the moment will tip that balance where you'll engage more with your activity and others when you'll engage more with your partner. The only way we'll know where it wants you to go is by allowing it to be a part of the experience."

"You said before that I did something wrong with my activity, some 'fundamental mistake'?"

"You didn't do anything wrong at all. This was a great first attempt. There was one component to the activity that I think would have made your life harder given the conversation a few moments ago. It has to do with tuning the instrument. Had you gotten to the tuning stage, there would have been a real challenge to both completing the activity and dealing with Sam. It's very hard to properly tune an instrument while also engaging in a repetition exercise, so one or both of you would have needed to stop repeating for the tuner to work."

"But wouldn't that have been the demand of the moment?"

"That you both collectively agree to be silent while you tune the instrument?"

"Yes."

"There's nothing in Sam's circumstances that says he needs to be silent. Sam's job is to prepare, knock, and then observe and respond. So that's where it would have become complicated. There's no surprise instructions that are introduced haphazardly, all of the criteria are given beforehand, so that's why adding one last minute would have made the exercise harder, rather than easier, for you."

"I see."

"Before we finish, I have one final question for the both of you. It has to do with the collective bewilderment that seemed to take hold when the timer went off."

"That's when the exercise is finished," Sam replies.

"Is it?"

"Isn't it?" Sam repeats, ribbing me. I chuckle back.

"Okay, fair enough. But we do want to ask, then, where in the instructions does it say the exercise has concluded when the timer goes off?"

"Nowhere," Beverly says, considering it.

"So even though in this case you would have failed at the activity, this could have brought up a lot of things for you. Especially when the consequence is going strong, succeeding or failing at an activity can bring out immensely deep things. The countdown tells you whether or not you've finished the activity in time, but as far as our exercise goes, there's nothing that says the repetition can't continue, now informed on one end by the preparation and on the other by the success or failure of your activity."

"So you still will let us know when the exercise is over?"

"Of course. There's no value in insisting the actors determine that. Look at some of the rich moments you both could have explored, for example. The only exception to the repetition continuing after the activity is if leaving the room is built into your circumstances. If you have to finish your activity in the time you've set, for example, because you need to travel somewhere and you know that finishing in that time gives you just enough time to get to your destination, then as soon as you've been successful, get your ass out of the room immediately. Please come back in afterwards, but that's the one general exception to the possibility of the exercise continuing after the timer goes off."

The Unspoken Depths

Chris and Mike volunteer to work. Chris will be doing his activity while Mike goes out to prepare. Chris asks for a moment to set up. From a bag he pulls some tape, a picture frame (he's remembered my cautionary request from the previous session and the frame is plastic as opposed to glass), a stick of glue, and then a paper bag. He gently tips the bag over, being incredibly careful, as what seem to be dozens- if not more- shreds of a torn photo sprinkle onto the table. He sets the timer on his phone, asks someone in the class to hold it for them, and then lets me know he is ready. On a brief side note, leaving your timer elsewhere in the room is not a bad idea, especially if there's any concern about it accidentally falling. An egg timer is one thing but, if it's your phone or an expensive device, setting the timer and then asking a colleague to hold it for you and push 'Start' when you're ready is more than fine.

As soon as Mike goes out to prepare, the timer begins and Chris is off. He frantically begins to sort through the torn photograph. It seems he is trying to find the corner pieces, anything to give him a reference point. His hands shake, and his face goes red.

"Fuck, fuck, fuck," he mutters under his breath, and then goes silent. He manages to find the corner pieces as the knock comes. Like a bolt he's out of his seat, and opens the door. Mike stands there, looking slightly annoyed.

"You knocked," Chris says, rushing back to his chair.

"I knocked," Mike replies, and comes in.

"You knocked." Chris is already at the pieces again, trying to put them together.

"Your hands are shaking," Mike observes, keeping his distance.

"My hands are shaking," Chris says. He's found two matching pieces and is trying to put them together with a sliver of tape. He is struggling, and exclaims, "Dammit!"

"Your hands are shaking," Mike says, coming to Chris's side and taking the tape. He tears off a small sliver off and hands it to him.

"You're still," Chris says.

"I'm still."

"You're still," Chris manages to get the two pieces conjoined, but begins to be overwhelmed by the sheer number of pieces left.

"Help, help," he says, offering the pieces to Mike, and they both begin sorting.

"You asked for help," Mike replies.

"I asked for help."

"You asked for help."

"I asked for help," They manage to get a third of the photo done, but Chris is getting more desperate, and Mike begins to get frustrated at so many small pieces. In his irritation he quickly reaches for the glue and some pieces fall to the floor.

"No!" Chris shrieks, and shoves Mike hard. Mike is caught off guard and Chris dives to the floor, looking for the fallen pieces.

"You pushed me," Mike says.

"I pushed you," he says, searching.

The timer goes off. Chris stops speaking altogether, and wilts on the floor.

"You folded," Mike says.

Chris says nothing.

"You're quiet," Mike says.

"I'm quiet," Chris repeats, shaking his head. An air of absolute defeat engulfs him.

"You're quiet." Mike approaches him, sits on the ground next to him.

"You're sitting with me," Chris says, finally looking at Mike.

"I'm sitting with you," Mike repeats, putting his hand on Chris's shoulder.

"You're sitting with me."

"Your eyes are red," Mike observes.

"My eyes are red." Chris inhales, nodding sharply.

"Your eyes are red."

The repetition continues for a while longer. Mike continues to comfort Chris, while Chris slowly begins packing up his activity. When he is finished they both sit by the table, and it seems to me that is a good moment to stop the exercise.

"Alright you two, well done," I say. The room is charged; everyone is still processing what they've seen. In the span of roughly eight minutes we've gone on a journey of the human experience, filled with hope, despair, loss, compassion, and so many other unique elements. Looking at both actors, I can tell they are still very open and vulnerable. This is why starting with talking about the activity itself is a great way to give them a cool-down period before we get to the feedback for their processes. "So," I say to the group, "was that physically engaging?"

It's almost as if everyone has choreographed their nods to make it seem like a giant collective "Yes."

"Seems like the consensus leans towards yes," I say, and we all laugh, Chris and Mike included.

"How about difficult to complete in the time he gave himself?"

"Yes," Sam says.

"I agree. Was that too little time for you, Chris? It seemed like you both were making some headway."

"I think in retrospect I would have given myself maybe a minute or two longer, but it was close."

"I agree, your behavior seemed to tell me throughout that you kept believing getting it done was a possibility."

"Yes."

"Great. So what about urgency. Did it seem like it had to be done now and not later?"

"Oh God yes," Sam says.

"I agree, but why do you say that?"

"Everything. He just kept shaking and swearing, it was like Mr. Pacino over there." That sends chuckles through some of us, me included. As much as I admire his work, a Pacino joke here or there never hurts.

"There was a lot of evidence in his behavior that this could not wait. One of the places it really stuck out to me was when he begged Mike for help. On a technical note, asking someone to help might not be an example of strong repetition, but you might remember we talked about moments breaking the rules of an exercise and the value of grabbing those pivotal moments as they arise. Chris blurting out "help me" wasn't great repetition, but it was wonderful acting because it was so true in the moment. With good technique Mike took that in stride and made it part of the repetition. What didn't happen, which thrilled me, is the exercise didn't descend into improv. Mike didn't see Chris's request as an offer of sorts, replying, 'Why yes, I'd be glad to help,' to which Chris would have said, 'So here we'll begin with this side of the photo,' and yada yada yada. You both stayed truthful and didn't let a chaotic moment derail your work or the repetition itself. That's strong technique.

"Now, fourth criterion, did it seem like there was a consequence to not getting this done in time?"

"Are you serious?" Beverly asks me, and everyone laughs at this.

"Very, very true," I say, "that consequence was alive within you. Can I ask who the photo is of?"

"My girlfriend. In my scenario we had a fight and I'd torn it up, but I just got the call that she was in a car accident and . . . I just want her to see it before . . . that I didn't mean it . . ." Chris stops, beginning to tear up.

"Hey, you don't need to share anymore, Chris. We all saw the consequence was so alive in you, we don't need the details. And look, it's over, right?"

He nods, wiping his eyes, and taking a deep breath.

"That's the beauty of using essentially a fantasy instead of asking you to relive a memory. At the end of it you know it never happened, and that removal from reality helps keep everyone emotionally safe in this work. It's what allows you to go to such deep places in the activities and know you are okay afterwards. A particularly powerful activity might shake you up a little, but it's way easier to come back from that and feel confident you can go to that level of meaning again. Re-enacting a memory might produce some profound results, but it can be much more difficult to climb out of that, and to feel confident going there again. So, a truly great activity. That was a pleasure to watch."

I make sure Chris knows I'm being sincere. It takes real courage to work with openness like that, and I want him to know that whether he has as successful or not an activity next time, that courage will always be welcomed in the room.

"Great, so, let's have some individual feedback. Mike, how did your preparation go?"

"Honestly . . . eh," he says, holding out his hands.

"When you came into the room it seemed to me you were more annoyed than anything else."

"I was pretty irritated."

"What type of preparation did you do?"

"I tried a memory."

"And it didn't go too well?"

"It worked a little. I started to feel . . . I guess irritated is the only way I can describe it. Just really irked, like something was getting under my skin, but then it stopped. I figured I would just knock when that happened."

"So the memory gave you something but just didn't really yield a strong preparation?"

"Not really, I wouldn't use that memory again."

"When you came into the room and saw Chris in the state he was in, did your preparation dry up?"

"Immediately. I looked at him and thought, 'The hell did I miss?'"

"That can happen even with a strong preparation, but it almost always happens with ones that don't catch fire. So the frustration that came up later, when you were helping him, was that the preparation coming back or just what was going on in that moment?"

"Just in that moment. I was getting so annoyed at all the little pieces, and the tape wasn't working so well, so I decided to reach for the glue."

"And that's when it all fell apart."

"Yeah, you could say that . . ." He looks to Chris, and they both laugh.

"We'll talk about the pushing in a moment, but for now let me ask you, when you were helping, did at any point you have an impulse to do something else?"

"What do you mean?"

"Well, he asked for help. There's no requirement in the exercise that if someone asks for help you have to do the polite thing and always help. But you seemed to have a genuine impulse to help him. Just because you start helping, however, doesn't mean you need to keep helping. I wondered if when you were getting frustrated you had the impulse to just swipe everything off the table."

"I didn't have it then . . . but I could have seen it going there."

"Fair enough, and thanks for letting me know. I just want you to know that if that had been your impulse, though that would have been a huge action with potentially big consequences, that's a fairly gained impulse. But what I also want to be clear about is I didn't just encourage you to go and be provocative in the exercise. When you work next in the future, if someone has an activity and you think, "Well, the teacher said I could go and mess with it if I wanted too," then disregard that immediately. There's absolutely no benefit to being deliberately provocative in this work. Provocations in other approaches to learning acting may be fine, but not in an exercise that lives on observe-and-respond. Bringing in the agenda to deliberately stir the pot, especially at this stage, is a great way for the exercises to become dangerous.

"In the previous sessions we talked briefly about what keeps the exercises safe in the Meisner technique, but we needed to get to activities to have more context for how that happens. Now that we are working with extremely meaningful circumstances, strong technique is more important than ever. The reason we could have a moment where Chris shoved Mike and it didn't descend into some brutal slugfest is because, even though Mike was shocked, he observed that Chris's behavior came out of his pain. That doesn't mean, by the way, that Mike might not have shoved him back, but here's where the mechanics of the exercise work to keep everyone safe. Repetition exists within a fifty–fifty balance. Fifty percent of your time is spent is in observation of your partner, and the other half is spent responding to them. The process works by making an observation, responding to it, and then immediately observing your partner again, even if the call doesn't change, to see what they are doing. This is that constant give and take of living truthfully.

"If the balance of repetition tips too far in any direction problems will occur. Let's start with the more benign example. If the exercise sways too far in the direction of observation, then the energy dries up. Both partners enter into a type of staring contest where depth becomes impossible. It's both boring to watch and be in, but that's about as far as the issues there go. On the other side, however, if the balance tips too far in favor of responding, that's when safety issues can appear. In this type of dynamic one actor observes, responds, then responds again, and again, and again, all without ever actually seeing what is happening with their partner. If Mike for example had come in solely to mess with Chris, he might have gotten more than just a hard shove. I would have stopped it immediately if violence broke out of course, but as a preventative measure it's not the best idea to continuously provoke somebody in a highly agitated state who has been told they should express their impulses in the moment.

"A few sessions ago, when Nigel worked with Lena we talked about the value of channeling a violent impulse and expressing it without harming your partner. That still applies, but especially in the independent activity, impulses are going to be coming up fast and hard. Chris would have done his best not to hurt Mike, we all know that, but the definition of an impulse is that it is out before you even know it. Remember that exercises have gone to deep, intense places filled with aggression at times, and nobody has been hurt. That's because when you honor that fifty–fifty balance it becomes nearly impossible to descend into a prolonged fistfight. Chris's shove was an excellent example. Even if Mike had pushed him back, the likelihood is that the urgency of the activity would have pulled Chris back and he would have continued trying to retape his photograph. There will be many moments on offer that don't veer into any physically confrontational territory. That, combined with the knowledge that you can always stop the exercise if you feel uncomfortable, and I'll stop it without hesitation if I do, means we can go to thrilling places that sometimes have the feel of danger without ever actually being in real danger."

Winner Winner Without the Dinner

Independent activities are true enigmas in many ways. There is a set of criteria that guides them, but what they will actually end up looking like is nearly impossible to predict. That's why there is so much value in doing as many activities as possible. A colleague of mine who teaches this work in Europe says her primary goal is to get her actors to the independent activity as soon as possible and remain there for as long as possible. The independent activity is the complete package deal in the Meisner technique. It trains you how to live truthfully under a given set of circumstances using what gives your life meaning as fuel.

As I wrote at the beginning, there are several different approaches to the independent activity. In my own work I start actors with using the Impulse Company model you've just seen. It offers a clean, simplified way to fully immerse yourself in the experience. With actors who are more seasoned in this work, we then graduate to the independent activity used by Larry Silverberg, the person I consider my other true Meisner teacher alongside Scott Williams. Larry's approaches to both the independent activity and preparation are to me the most profound and relevant versions for your long-term acting needs. You won't be encountering them in this book for several reasons. Firstly, finding our feet with his version of the activity would add many more steps and a new range of observations and concepts. Secondly, while there are four criteria to this activity, there are nine in Larry's, and they require much more time to develop and absorb. Thirdly, the bridge those variations offer into text work is completely different than the Impulse Company's model. Consider then that if you enjoy the independent activity, for further study look into the work of Larry Silverberg to take it to the next level.

Now that you've seen a pair of examples, enough to get a sense of the working possibilities within the independent activity as well as common errors made early in the process, while also getting a taste of some of the deeper feedback on offer, here are the criteria I normally place at the beginning of the chapter.

Exercise: The Independent Activity

Set-up: There is a table with one chair.

Instructions: Seated at the table, one actor begins their independent activity once the other actor has gone out of the room to prepare. For the person doing the activity, there are four criteria to be met: intricacy, difficulty in a set time frame, urgency, and an extremely meaningful consequence. The actor preparing has five preparations on offer, including physical and non-physical preparations such as memory, imagination, fantasy, and spin. The actor preparing releases their preparation into the knock at the door, which begins the repetition portion of the independent activity.

Summary

Progress in meditation is holistic, involving a gradual accumulation of experiences alongside moments that seem to almost punctuate, or break through, the daily experience of reality as we know it. While there is no "fast-track" option to these latter moments, and encountering them can take just as long as a more routine practice, a form of Zen known as koan practice can offer insights into our own practice that are designed to facilitate moments of awakening. Koan practice takes time, requiring patience and openness, but it offers insights that parallel with moments from the lives of awakened teachers. The selfless nature of insight also finds its expression in Meisner's independent activity, the ultimate training tool for living truthfully under a given set of circumstances. Coupled with preparation exercises, independent activities offer actors a glimpse into the deepest parts of their process, where the pressure of circumstances can elicit surprising behaviors and impulses we never knew we had. It is this authenticity in one's acting while working under a given set of circumstances that the independent activity trains, a skill that will be of immense value when beginning text work in the next session.

13
One Bright Pearl

Ordinary Life, Extraordinary Moment

On the subject of the extraordinary, Zen has very little to say. It would seem that from the many schools and meditation disciplines that exist, Zen is the most boring. It has almost nothing to comment on the subject of reincarnation, for example, which is easily one of the sexiest esoteric ideas that, to some, bridge the gap between practice and religion. What it does have to say on the matter of reincarnation, from everything I've encountered, is boringly scientific. Upon death, the cells of your body break apart and your molecules and atoms enter the greater span of the world, becoming rain clouds, trees, the earth, and so on. I find it beautiful in one sense, but there's no mention of any type of consciousness or soul-like entity carrying on, coming back as another human, dung beetle, or something else entirely. The karmic recycling that is so part-and-parcel to many views found around meditation practices just doesn't appear that often. It's not that Zen wouldn't have something to say on this – it just doesn't seem to care enough to. To be fair there are many branches and sects of Zen practice, and so I'm sure there are some deeply vested in these topics, but I've yet to find anything in my practice or research on them. By and large, it seems the moment something starts to veer towards the grand, cosmic, or extraordinary, Zen develops a severe allergy to it.

What Zen does seem to be interested in is the ordinary. Instead of ten thousand reincarnated lives it would much rather you focus on this one, particularly this moment. That is perhaps what makes it so unique, as well as compatible with many other belief systems. Regarding what goes on beyond this life, Zen has no input. On how you handle yourself within your day-to-day goings, it can offer practical wisdom and tools. Its romantic interests, so to speak, have to do with ordinary moments in our lives serving some lesson or purpose. Instead of you becoming a master at complex meditations, it would prefer to see you master being present with the average elements of your life. Consider this koan:

> A student went to visit master Joshu.
>
> "Master," he said, "I've just entered the monastery. Please tell me what to do, teach me."
>
> "Have you had your rice gruel yet?" Joshu asked.
>
> "Yes, I did."
>
> "Then wash your bowl."

This koan has been the subject of much in-depth analysis to try to get at what is *really* going on in it. Lin Jensen, a Zen teacher and writer, does a wonderful job of summarizing this analysis. The master's question about breakfast is actually code for, "Have you found enlightenment yet?" to which the arrogant student's reply actually has nothing to do with porridge but an assertion that yes, he has indeed attained enlightenment. The master's comment about washing his bowl then is the Zen equivalent of the Ghost of Christmas Future warning Scrooge to change his ways before it is too late. Relinquish your pride, foolish student: you haven't found true enlightenment yet.

That's all a very creative way to read it, but for a practice system that trades so deeply in the obvious it might be *too* creative. The alternate possibility is that asking you to clean the bowl is the lesson itself. No deeper metaphor, no hidden answers: just engagement with ordinary life. Have you had breakfast yet? Yes. Then let's do the dishes. Have you paid the water bill this month? Not yet. Then let's take care of that. Both mindfulness and Zen practice restore a level of clarity so that we can engage more presently with our life. Washing the car, paying the bills, commuting to work – these are the mundane facets of life; yet consider how much we attempt to get away from our reality with distractions, avoiding doing things. If there is a hidden truth to Zen, and it's a big "if," it may be that embracing the ordinary once more is one of the most extraordinary things you can do for yourself, that enlightenment is more in taking the car for a service than some great epiphany that dawns on you and leaves you in a state of perpetual bliss.

Today, we'll focus on two meditations interested in the extraordinary nature of ordinary living. The first is another meditation from Douglas Harding and later Richard Lang's work on your experience of being headless, and the final is another koan.

Exercise: Meditation 12

Set-up: Set up your practice.

Part one instructions: In this meditation you'll be working with exploring your headless experience but with eyes closed. You'll be engaging with a series of micro-experiments, and so will be coming back here frequently. It might help then to place a bookmark on this page or use a pen to mark where you are. I'll number the steps to take for the first part.

1. Close your eyes, then open them again.
2. You're now going to close your eyes again, but this time as your eyes are closed, ask yourself if you really close your eyes. When I close them, the entire room disappears into darkness. This isn't like what happens when I see anyone else closing their eyes. It's like a pair of theatre curtains descend fully and the entire room is swallowed up. Try now, and see if this is your experience.
3. Now open and close your eyes a few more times. Notice how when your eyes open the room reappears, and all of the colors and sights associated with it. Likewise, at will, you can close your eyes and plunge it into darkness. Notice also that the space of consciousness where both happens doesn't change. Try this a few more times, and see what it really is like to "close your eyes" from your first-person perspective.
4. For a final time in this part you'll close your eyes, and this time spend some moments investigating the darkness. How big is it? How near or far? Where are the borders, outline, or corners of it? What can you compare it to to discover these answers?

Part one notes/questions: The simple act of closing our eyes is one we take for granted. We make assumptions that the space in which both the opening and closing, the disappearing and reappearing of our visual field, is the same as everyone else's experiences. Yet the next time you see somebody close their eyes, even for a moment, you'll realize it has nothing to do with what your experience is like. To you it looks as if they are lowering and raising a small bit of skin over some round objects. When you do it, however, the whole world vanishes, and then reappears, all at your own will. Of course from the point of view of somebody else if they saw you closing your eyes it wouldn't change the world for them in such a dramatic way. That's the power and uniqueness of your own individual first-person experience. It's very true that most of us have the capacity to open and close our eyes, provided we have eyes and they function for us as they should, but your experience is entirely your own, entirely unique, and a wonderfully powerful one that shouldn't be taken for granted.

Step two instructions: Set up your practice again if necessary. Set a timer for 5 minutes. In this exercise you are going to continue exploring the darkness of your closed eyes. First notice if your visual field is actually completely gone, or if you can still see some traces of light. Notice what sounds arise and how long they remain for. Notice sensations in the body, and as they arise focus on them. If the sensation comes from your head, for example, what is the shape of your head that you feel? If yourself getting lost in thought, take a moment or two to look at the thought itself, then return to your practice. When you are ready, start your timer, close your eyes, and begin.

Step two notes/questions: Though meditation practice with eyes open is common, the more you investigate this space of awareness without visual stimuli the easier you might find that boundaries once believed to be concrete dissolve. Consider a sensation in the hand. To investigate it, you focus on the shape, or outline, of your hand, and yet the more in depth your attention becomes the more your hand begins to lose the feel of its shape, dissolving instead into a pure sensation. It may seem paradoxical, but this is your exploration of a space you rarely spend time focusing on. We've had a lot of sessions and conversations to be able to reach this point, going at the idea of self as part of consciousness rather than dominating it.

Consider this question: are you in your head? For many of us, before beginning a practice, the obvious answer is yes. We tend to geographically place ourselves somewhere behind our eyes. Now, however, we can start to answer the follow-up question never considered. Are you inside your head, or is your head a sensation that appears within consciousness? Are you in your body, or is your body inside you? The more we investigate our first-person experience, the more we discover that all of the elements of our body we identify with, as well as the sensations within and sounds around us, are all just manifestations within consciousness. Consciousness is the space that can be discovered, explored, and re-discovered time and time again using these tools. It is the constant, while every other experience is a temporary phenomenon. That's a rather profound and beautiful thing to discover not just in theory but in practice from within your first-person experience.

Exercise: Meditation 13

Set-up: Set up your practice.

Part one instructions: Set a timer for 5 minutes. In this meditation you'll be working with the koan, "The entire universe is one bright pearl." You may recall in Chapter 10 we worked with noting the breath using a longer and shorter phrase. In the case of longer koans, you can repeat the entire koan, or it can also be shortened. Where it will be shortened, however, depends on what is resonating more with you. For some of us the latter part of the koan, "one bright pearl," might emerge as the object to repeat, or "the entire universe" could be what calls out to you. The important thing is to listen to what emerges in the moment, rather than trying to pick the part that sounds the most interesting. The whole koan might demand to be worked with, or only part. The final note here is about the breath. In the previous session you would inhale and then on the exhale silently repeat the koan to yourself. Feel free to broaden that range of possibilities so that the koan either coincides with the breath or follows its own rhythm. Again, there's no need to try to make the repetition more interesting or exciting, so listen to how the koan wishes to find its own pattern. If you find yourself getting stuck or too distracted, then attaching the koan to the exhale can be a helpful orienting point. When you are ready, start your timer, close your eyes, and begin.

Part one notes/questions: You may recall in the very first chapter of this book a story about a monk who, dissatisfied with his practice, set out to leave the temple and return to his old life. Along the way, he violently stubbed his toe, and despite all the blood and anguish, experienced a moment of deep awakening. This is just a part of the story of Gensha, who returned to the monastery after this incident, continuing to practice and eventually teaching. In his later years one of his favorite koans to use was this one: the whole universe, and everything contained within it, is one bright pearl. We often think of the experiences in our lives as separate. We see our joys as separate from pain and anxiety, the good events separate from the unpleasant ones. But Gensha suggests in the koan that all of these seemingly separate, sometimes unrelated experiences, are a part of a greater whole, this one bright pearl of total reality we find ourselves constantly in.

Step two instructions: Set up your practice again if necessary. Set a timer for 5 minutes. In this next half, you'll continue to work with the koan, "The entire universe is one bright pearl." You can either couple it with your breath, or let the repetition find its own pace independent of the breath. When you are ready start your timer, close your eyes, and begin.

Step two notes/questions: By its very nature mindfulness practice is interested in this moment above all else. This doesn't mean that it ignores that you have a past, or that you're planning for a future, but enriching your experience in this moment with clarity and attention is the only solution to the woes and suffering we endure or create for ourselves. The past is gone, it cannot be relived for a solution, and the future is yet unknown. This moment, ever changing and developing, sometimes for reasons we love, others we dread, is our only opportunity to adjust the course of our behavior. The immense range of potential the present moment carries is vast, filled with too many variables for us to comprehend.

That's the totality Gensha refers to, the entire body of possibilities within this universe captured in one tiny moment. Our hopes for the future cannot be divorced from our realities in the present; we must work with what is in front of us to realize those better avenues we seek for ourselves. The present is filled with things we wish to change, but it is also filled with many more we don't need to change, and acknowledging this can bring a great amount of clarity and, on occasion, a feeling of peace. Lao Tzu wrote in the *Tao Te Ching*, "Everything is perfect. Why? Because it is perfectly itself." To introduce any change in the now, we must work with things as they are, and the ability to see with a level of clarity offers a profound starting point.

Since we are nearing the end of our journey in these pages, a final book that can offer immense value on koans is *The Gateless Gate*, specifically Kōun Yamada's translation. For further reference beyond these pages, my koan understandings are primarily based on the work of Seung Sahn, who wrote a marvelous book called *Dropping Ashes on the Buddha*, as well as Henry Shukman's Zen teachings.

The Excitement of a Broken World

In the previous session, you took your first steps in training living truthfully under a given set of circumstances using Meisner's independent activity. Dedicating only one chapter to it feels strange, given that actors in an extended Meisner training program will spend hundreds of hours, if not longer, on this one exercise alone. At the end of it, you would walk away with a developed sense of what has meaning for you, and how to use that meaning for your acting in a safe, productive, and reliable way. At the Impulse Company we would liken this to developing musculature, with your actor muscles being at their peak after enough time with activities.

It's those muscles that you will be importing into text in this session. Yes, we're finally here, onto scene work. Scene practice brings up questions such as where to begin, and how to ensure that these values remain with you even once you begin working with text. You have most likely brought with you many habits for text work, and the likelihood is that the majority stand in direct contradiction to the values you've worked so hard for up until this point. This isn't a criticism, more a recognition that we all bring with us a plethora of "what if" tools when it comes to text. What if I do this action on this line, say the words this way, or what if I give it my all and bring so much emotion into this section, and so on. What-ifs are generally a problem. Each asks you to take control of the delivery of the text, the actions within it, and the responsibility for acting it well. This all involves putting the responsibility for the experience onto your shoulders and pre-empting the future before it has even arrived. These are the habits we have to begin breaking, and the Meisner technique has the perfect exercise to do it.

Before I introduce it, I want to give you a sense of the format shift of this chapter. The exercises here and in the following chapter don't particularly lend themselves to case studies or hypothetical examples. There are instructions for how to do them, but there's no way I can capture in writing what a successful example looks like. To be frank, at this stage I don't think you need one anyway. I know that's a big statement to say, but if you've followed the training up to this point your living truthfully muscles are so developed that I believe you are capable of grasping the basic concepts and making them work for you. If you go to a Meisner training class, see examples, and realize you had been in error on some things, the correction process will be minimal, as opposed to a major overhaul. Your technique and capabilities are far stronger now than on day one.

In this chapter I'll introduce the exercise and its criteria. You'll have three scenes to practice them on. I've selected scenes for one man and one woman, two women, and two men, but the gendering of the parts doesn't matter much, so feel free to practice on all three. You'll also notice that I've used scenes from older texts. This is in line with how Meisner would start his actors on text work, with poems from a beautiful early twentieth-century book called the *Spoon River Anthology*. Meisner had several reasons for using this particular text, but one reason that crosses over with our work is that with older texts there generally isn't much risk of you having read them beforehand. It's best to start this work with a fresh set of eyes. It's impossible obviously for me to predict what you have or have not yet encountered, but there's enough variance among these scenes to hopefully provide exposure to at least one piece of writing you haven't seen before.

I also want to use this chance to dispel the notion I've encountered that Meisner is best suited for contemporary, rather than classical, texts. Your technique can be applied to any medium in any genre of any age, and so let's start with the seemingly more challenging works for your technique. At the end of the three scenes will be some further general guidance, tips, and clarification on the exercise. Let's dive in and have our first encounter with a proper given set of circumstances.

Exercise: Breaking the Back of a Scene

Set-up: Two actors sit facing one another in chairs. Their knees are close but not touching. This gives the dynamic of no starting contact but being "in each other's space."

Instructions: This is a first reading of a scene with your partner in which you will both break the back of the text. To properly break the back of a scene, several criteria must be met.

1. Don't read ahead. When you receive your scene, quickly identify your first line for reference and then don't read further.
2. When you speak the words, hold the page high, in sight of your partner's eyeline. This way you can have easy equal access to both the words and their face.
3. Hold the script with one hand, and with the other place your index finger on the line you are currently on. This prevents the issue of you losing your place in the scene and having to struggle to find your line, all of which is unnecessary time wasting.
4. When you read your line out loud, pick up only a few words at a time. Two to four is an ideal starting amount. This prevents you having to worry about remembering the whole line or paraphrasing. Look at your partner, speak the words you've picked up, and then go back for some more, until your line is finished.

As an example, if your line is, "Would you like some breakfast? I made eggs," your reading of that line might be:

> (*looks at page, then at partner*) Would you like . . . (*looks at page again, then partner*) some breakfast I (*looks at page, then partner*) made eggs.

You'll notice a few key things with this example. One, any concern about the logic, punctuation, or flow of a line is gone. Two, you chop the words up solely for one ultimate reason: so you can spend more time with your partner. When it comes to most actors I have seen who don't use this approach, especially at table reads or early rehearsals, 90% of the time is spent with your nose in the page and only 10% looking at and connecting those words with the people you will say them to. We want to reverse that, so the majority of the time is spent observing and responding to your partner and only a small amount is on the page. Take only a few words at a time, don't rush, they aren't going anywhere. Your partner is still the key recipient in this equation.

5. When you do speak your words, say them flat. In the beginning, this means monotone. Yes, you'll impose a monotone inflection on all of your lines. Like a hot iron removes wrinkles, this will iron out any desire you have to impose something on the text not generated by your partner. Down the road, as in after having done this exercise a few times with different scenes, you can begin to release the monotone inflection slightly, but we'll talk about what this means after the scenes.
6. Ignore all stage directions, overlaps, interruptions, or notes on how you should inflect or emote. We'll deal with these later, but they aren't relevant at all to this exercise. This also includes movement and blocking, so stay in your chair for the entire read.
7. When you are done speaking a line, keep your attention fully on your partner. No glancing at the script, no reading ahead: your attention and eyes are fully on them while they are speaking their line. How will you know when it's your turn to speak? They will simply stop talking. What this also means is that even if the scene is filled with suspense and urgency, don't worry about that here. It doesn't matter how brutally you break up the flow or rhythm of the scene, or drain it of meaning. That can be rebuilt. The core of importance is to begin this work with our values of living truthfully. That's why this exercise is often called "a repetition exercise with a piece of paper in your hand."

Here are three scenes for you to work on. The first is from a 1921 short play by Pendleton King called *Cocaine*, the second from Shakespeare's *All's Well That Ends Well*, and the third an adaptation I've done of Dion Boucicault's 1841 *London Assurance*. Together with your partner, select any scene and choose a character without reading the scene first. Break the back of the scene, and then reference the section at the end for input on some of the deeper values of this exercise, as well as how to use and keep developing it, for your current and future needs.

Cocaine by Pendleton King (1M, 1F)

    JOE: Nora, 's 'at you?
    NORA: I didn't mean to wake you up. Go on back to sleep.

JOE: I haven't been asleep. What time is it?

NORA: *[takes off hat]* About four o'clock.

JOE: You're pretty late.

NORA: *[takes off jacket]* Had to walk from uptown.

JOE: How far uptown?

NORA: O, way up town. I let a crowd shake me like a fool. *[Sits in chair at foot of bed and fans herself.]* And didn't have sense enough to get car fare. Whew! You don't realize how hot you are till you sit down.

JOE: Poor kid.

NORA: You must have had the gas lighted to make it as hot as this in here. Lord, I'm so glad to get home.

JOE: *[gently]* You didn't bring in nothing?

NORA: Not a cent, Joe. *[Gets up and goes to bureau.]* I don't know what's the matter with me. *[Looks in glass.]* It's that darn fever blister. If I had only had sense enough to get some camphor that first day.

JOE: But it's most well now. Can't hardly notice it any more.

NORA: Of course it's perfectly well. There won't be a trace of it tomorrow. I oughtn't to have tried to go out those two days the first of the week when it was so bad. Everybody was afraid of me and it made me feel like a leper. I lost my grip in some way and now I can't get it back. It all depends on yourself. *[Picks up candle.]* If you're sure of yourself you have luck; if you aren't, you don't. That's all there is to it. *[Crosses with candle, which she puts down on trunk.]* If I'd had a wee bit of a sniff tonight I'd have got some money out of that crowd. *[Sits on foot of the bed.]* But drinks don't brace me up somehow.

JOE: Hum. 'sright.

NORA: Poor old boy. Have you been lying here all night in this heat waiting for me? It's hard luck on you, Joe. Oh, I thought I'd go crazy tonight! My nerves are just all to pieces. I did think I was going to get some money this time.

JOE: Why don't you take your clothes off and come on to bed?

NORA: *[gets up and takes a packet of cigarettes out of her jacket]* I swiped these for you, anyway. Here. *[Throws him the box.]*

JOE: *[catching it]* Gee! Ta!

NORA: Joe, I wish you wouldn't say "Ta." *[Goes up into recess.]* I don't know why I hate it so. *[She begins to undress.]*

JOE: All right, Missis. *[Gets up to light his cigarette with the candle.]* Common stuff, uhm?

NORA: *[undressing]* No, it doesn't matter. I'm just nervous and irritable. Don't pay any attention to anything I say. If I don't get some money tomorrow I just don't know what I'll do. It's terrible to be so dependent on *anything* as that.

JOE: *[lies down again]* Four days.

NORA: No, tonight's Saturday.

JOE: Well, that's four days, ain't it? We finished up that last deck Tuesday night.

NORA: That's right. I wouldn't have believed I could go so long. I don't see how you stand it, Joe, all night like this, doing nothing.

JOE: I been out. Don't worry about me. I can git on without de stuff for a while.

NORA: *[comes down in kimono]* I can't. *[Takes cigarette.]* But then I've been using it so much longer than you have. *[Lights cigarette at the candle.]*

JOE: I been goin' it some little time – a month or so before we took up together last summer.

NORA: To think. *[Sits on bed.]* Only a year. I wonder what would have become of you if I hadn't found you?

JOE: What becomes of all de other poor bastards who gets knocked out and can't get back in de ring? I don't know.

NORA: That's the trouble with you boys. You are brought up with only one idea – to fight – and if anything does happen to you, you're not fit to do anything else. You're only twenty-four, and you're done.

JOE: Be twenty-four in October, I guess.

NORA: Lord, it makes me feel so old. That's how you stand the strain the way you do. You are as firm and strong as you ever were, and look at me!

JOE: Well, if a fellow has to do as much trainin' as I used to, he more or less keeps in condition, I guess.

NORA: *[lies down beside him]* I feel so old, and tired, and discouraged, Joe. If I didn't have you I don't think I'd go on with it.

JOE: *[tightens his arm about her]* I'm stickin' to you, see?

NORA: I never thought of your leaving me. *[She puts her arm up about his head and strokes his hair.]* I love you too much, Joe. I love you more than anybody else will ever love you if you live to be a thousand years old.

JOE: I don't reckon anybody'd love me much if I was that old.

NORA: *[laughs]* I should. But you're only a baby now. A little old infant. *[She snuggles up to him and presses her cheek to his.]* Joe?

JOE: Um?

NORA: *[in a whisper]* My darling. *[He gathers her closer. Long pause.]*

JOE: Tired, kid?

NORA: No, not now. I get strength from you. You've got plenty of strength for both of us, haven't you?

All's Well That Ends Well by William Shakespeare (2F)

Countess

> Even so it was with me when I was young.
> If ever we are nature's, these are ours.
> This thorn Doth to our rose of youth rightly belong;
> Our blood to us, this to our blood is born.
> It is the show and seal of nature's truth,
> Where love's strong passion is impress'd in youth.
> By our remembrances of days foregone,
> Such were our faults, or then we thought them none.
> Her eye is sick on't; I observe her now.

Helena

> What is your pleasure, madam?

Countess

> You know, Helen, I am a mother to you.

Helena

> Mine honorable mistress.

Countess

> Nay, a mother,
> Why not a mother? When I said "a mother,"
> Methought you saw a serpent. What's in "mother,"
> That you start at it? I say I am your mother,
> And put you in the catalogue of those
> That were enwombed mine. 'Tis often seen
> Adoption strives with nature, and choice breeds
> A native slip to us from foreign seeds.

You ne'er oppress'd me with a mother's groan,
Yet I express to you a mother's care.
God's mercy, maiden! does it curd thy blood
To say I am thy mother? What's the matter,
That this distempered messenger of wet,
The many-color'd Iris, rounds thine eye?
—Why, that you are my daughter?

Helena

That I am not.

Countess

I say I am your mother.

Helena

Pardon, madam;

The Count Rossillion cannot be my brother:

I am from humble, he from honored name;
No note upon my parents, his all noble.
My master, my dear lord he is, and I
His servant live, and will his vassal die.
He must not be my brother.

Countess

Nor I your mother?

Helena

You are my mother, madam; would you were—
So that my lord your son were not my brother—
Indeed my mother! Or were you both our mothers,

I care no more for than I do for heaven,
So I were not his sister. Can't no other,
But, I your daughter, he must be my brother?

Countess

Yes, Helen, you might be my daughter-in-law.
God shield you mean it not! "daughter" and "mother"
So strive upon your pulse. What, pale again?
My fear hath catch'd your fondness! Now I see
The myst'ry of your loneliness, and find
Your salt tears' head, now to all sense' tis gross:
You love my son. Invention is asham'd,
Against the proclamation of thy passion,
To say thou dost not: therefore tell me true,
But tell me then 'tis so; for look, thy cheeks
Confess it, t' one to th' other, and thine eyes
See it so grossly shown in thy behaviors
That in their kind they speak it. Only sin
And hellish obstinacy tie thy tongue,
That truth should be suspected. Speak, is't so?
If it be so, you have wound a goodly clew;
If it be not, forswear't; howe'er, I charge thee,
As heaven shall work in me for thine avail,
To tell me truly.

Helena

Good madam, pardon me!

Countess

Do you love my son?

Helena

Your pardon, noble mistress!

London Assurance by Dion Boucicault (2M)

SIR HARCOURT: Cool, is breakfast ready?

COOL: Fresh and ready, Sir Harcourt.

SIR HARCOURT: Ah. I neglected to mention that I expect Squire Harkaway to join us this morning.

COOL: I'll call for him right away.

SIR HARCOURT: And also that you must prepare for my departure to Oak Hall immediately.

COOL: What? Leave town in the middle of the season, Sir Harcourt? When are you leaving?

SIR HARCOURT: IMMEDIATELY.

COOL: But you've never done this before.

SIR HARCOURT: I know, I know. I hate going south. The air is still humid and gassy at this time of year, the roads perfumed by the open sewer ponds springing daisies. Yes, I confess, it is unusual. There is only One Power that could bring about such a miracle to get me out my house.

COOL: The Divinity Church holding another fundraiser for their "Find the Jesus" Easter picnic?

SIR HARCOURT: No. And they really do need to stop hiding little iron spikes in the grass. The tetanus rates are through the roof.

COOL: I think the roof is where they get the nails.

SIR HARCOURT: Quite. No, it is divinity of a sort, Cool, but in female form. I am about to present the world with a new Mrs. Harcourt.

COOL: Marriage, sir? Again? But the last one went so well.

SIR HARCOURT: I'm unsure of that, Cool. If I can be frank, I'm not sure she even liked me.

COOL: No!

SIR HARCOURT: It was after the now-former Mrs. Harcourt had been stampeded by that small group of freshly castrated bulls whose pen had been left open by that drunken rouster that I attended her side. As she prepared to give herself unto the Lord, her final grace for this world was the parting words: "Thank God, bloody hell, thank God. Finally. Thank God."

COOL: I'm sure it was in relation to the gates opening to receive her eternal soul.

SIR HARCOURT: Possibly. But no matter. This one likes me, Cool. And I like her. A blushing bride, just what I need to clear out the cobwebs in my old bullpen, if you know what I mean! She's a paragon of beauty but, even better, I have her bank details and have seen the numbers. All the apostles sit on an iron spike: she's a goddess with an account.

COOL: The new Lady of the house should be nothing less.
SIR HARCOURT: Despite my expectations on your intellect, it seems this morning your manners rise above your station.
COOL: I thank you kindly. Might I ask the name of your new Venus?
SIR HARCOURT: Grace.
COOL: Amazing.
SIR HARCOURT: Yes.
COOL: (*sings sweetly*) Amazing Grace . . .
SIR HARCOURT: That's enough.
(Cool stops)

SIR HARCOURT: She's the niece of my old friend, Max.
COOL: And tell me, what does she look like?
SIR HARCOURT: Well . . . I've got her portrait around here somewhere . . .
COOL: Have you never seen her, sir?
SIR HARCOURT: Oh don't be daft, Cool, of course I have. It's just . . . it was a while ago.
COOL: Has she changed that much since then?
SIR HARCOURT: Well, she's certainly developed!
COOL: Might I ask her age when you two did meet?
SIR HARCOURT: Well, I've been in the States for the past seven years, and she's now at the ripe age of eighteen–
COOL: Eighteen? One-eight?
SIR HARCOURT: Yes, yes, so that would have made her . . . (counts)
COOL: She was eleven?
SIR HARCOURT: Yes.
COOL: This ain't gonna age well.
SIR HARCOURT: Her father you see was a business colleague of mine. Miserly, a dirty old man who knew how to play the markets. A real little shit. We got along swimmingly. At the time my finances were, shall we say, just generating in the womb of capital venture, and he ended up bankrolling me for a while.
COOL: Nothing wrong with taking help for a few months.
SIR HARCOURT: A few months, seven years, it's all water under the proverbial. When his liver finally erupted from his medicinal habits, he left in his will his wish that I be the one to marry his daughter when she came of age.
COOL: Just like that.
SIR HARCOURT: Well, not like that. Being the scum of Satan's bootheel he made a wager in his will. If she would consent to marry me at the age of 19 then I would receive the entirety of his fortunes.

If she didn't, well, then uh, well, you see this house, and all your fine clothes?
COOL: You told me they were hand-me-downs from the local cemetery.
SIR HARCOURT: And no living man sports them better than you.
COOL: I'm to take it then she hasn't said yes yet.
SIR HARCOURT: No.

Unhappy Campers

One of the earliest workshops I taught in my career involved a co-teach between myself and a colleague who is also a dear friend. His interest is in working with writers, and while I have taught this technique for writers I mostly prefer working with actors, directors, and producers. The benefits for actors are obvious, but directors tend to benefit from this training because it gives them an insight into how to speak to an actor's process and get the results they want. Producers tend to love it because it sharpens their eye immensely for the types of talent they should be looking for, and gives them more insights into creating other elements of the production. My friend and I, however, both thought that we could have a little crossover day. He had been working with a group of writers, using his own Meisner-inspired approach, and the cohort I'd been training was mostly actors. The day we were to work on breaking the back of a scene was approaching, and we thought, "Wouldn't it be cool if we used scenes the other group had written, so that the actors can work with original material they've for sure never seen and the writers can see how actors in this technique begin working with their scripts?" All of the writers contributed two-hander scenes from their repertoire and on a brisk Saturday morning everyone gathered in the same room, the authors watching the actors break the backs of their scenes one by one. And I must say, a couple of writers saw the value in it.

The rest, however, were completely horrified.

From their perspective, what they saw were actors mangling their works of art, pieces some had been developing in one form or another for years. It seemed the actors were deliberately kicking the scenes into the ground, desecrating them for the sake of it. I'm sure it felt as if we were mocking them. Writers aren't generally the best-treated bunch in the industry, particularly in film and television (though that certainly is shifting today somewhat), and I have no doubt that this seemed like an extension of the torture writers endure when their words are pummeled into oblivion by careless actors.

I do have some sympathy for them and their anxieties, but it runs limited. In a request I gave to the writers group, I asked, "Come back to the next session. What you are seeing today is only the first encounter with the text. Come back to see how we build on it and honor what you've written." Only a few did, the rest undoubtedly scared that we were going to do further diabolical experiments on their works. As mostly older, seasoned writers, however, I had hoped for better from them. They knew who Sanford Meisner was, and they knew some of his most famous alumni like Gregory Peck, Diane Keaton, and Sydney Pollack were renowned for how they could take a script and find their way into such surprising and profound nuances of the given circumstances. In the next chapter you will also discover what the next steps are, so I say this for anyone who is worried at this stage: this training is very much about honoring the text, and breaking the back of the scene is perhaps one of the highest salutes we can pay to protecting the writer's words.

Though this might sound paradoxical, given what we've just done, it has to be considered what the alternative looks like. A word I've steered as far clear from as possible in this training has been the dreaded c-word: choices. We hear so much about the need for actors to make clever, inventive, and powerful choices in their acting. I hope we've at least driven some holes into that argument, demonstrating that the moment and your partner make far better choices for you than you do for yourself. A similar value applies to text work. If we just sat down to read the work, and I encouraged everyone to make bold choices, then we would be imposing before we even found our way into the world of the story. After all, a choice in one scene might undermine an important moment in a later scene, and without a full-spectrum understanding of the dramaturgical importance of that choice we wouldn't see those consequences until later, then having to go back and undo decisions we once thought sound.

It's important to recognize that, when it comes to the last sentence in the previous paragraph, none of that is your job. Understanding the impact of decisions across scenes is the job of the director, the dramaturg, sometimes stage manager, and the hopefully sharp producer. Your job is to leave the writer's choices alone, instead asking yourself, "How am I going to live this journey out in this moment?" That's where we want to begin, not with interpretation or figuring out what you like or don't like, or where you can do something inventive. You have a much bigger task on your shoulders. At Impulse we would often say actors are not creative artists, but artists of the experience. Connecting your sensitivity to the moment as well as your ability to observe and respond truthfully to the other actors and the words you are speaking is more important than any creative choice you will make. Living truthfully is the foundation of your training, and it becomes the foundation of your work with a given set of circumstances. You can layer on all of the accents, gestures, walks, and so on onto your character that are called for, but if that foundation of authentic truthfulness is missing, no degree of technical skills, costumes, or special effects will save your work. The only way to honor the text is to ensure you have done the necessary groundwork for you to thrive while speaking the lines the writer has worked so hard to create. Your first encounter with the text must begin with truthfulness.

Words, Words, Words

Breaking the back of a scene has a double meaning. It first relates to the moment when a brand-new book is opened for the first time, when the glue on the spine is creased, or broken. That gives us the first major hint: this is for a first reading of the text. It's not how things are meant to sound during dress rehearsals or the final take. It offers a strong means for how, when you first encounter a text, you can import your truthfulness directly into the lines while leaving out all of the habits that don't serve you as much. This is where the second meaning comes in. Breaking the back is a recognition that, even though we've done extensive training, we can't safely assume we're out of the woods yet when it comes to those deeply ingrained habits of attempting to predict the future and make plenty of creative choices. Those are habits that need to be broken, and what better way to put a stop on your tendencies than to break the text up beyond recognition, ignoring any stage directions, chopping the lines up, and putting a scalding flat iron to the words by making them completely flat. That may sound like drastic measures, but for a lot of actors that temptation to immediately begin making a meal of the text is so large it can't be restrained with just some feedback. We need an entirely new way to begin your work.

Perhaps the most jarring element for actors is the monotone inflection. Breaking the sentences up so as to spend the maximum time with your partner has a functionality to it, as does not worrying about stage directions for a first read. The alien tone, however, rattles the cage. In the directions I called breaking the back of a scene a repetition exercise with a piece of paper in your hand. How in the world is speaking like robots to one another for the duration of the read anything like repetition? The answer has to do with how the inflection is handled in the long term. If you are an actor who cannot help but put on cadences, give the words musicality, or any other self-generated impositions then the monotone tool is your best friend. Eventually, you'll begin to associate your desire to be creative with the words as immaterial to beginning work on a text. It may only take a few runs with this exercise across different scenes, but sometimes actors need longer to begin re-orienting their relationship to a text. The same is very much true of gestures. If I suddenly see hands flying all over the place, and there is nothing in your partner's behavior prompting those physical actions, then inhibiting those movements becomes paramount. If you always have to express yourself through movement when you begin a script, train yourself to stop doing that until later. This is still a living relational experience, not an exercise in connecting your body to the words. Connect yourself to your partner, and let the words be a part of that experience.

After some time, when those habits have been altered, you can slowly start releasing your grip on the monotone element. This does not mean that suddenly your voice will take on John Gielgud's range of colorful inflections, or break out in five different accents in the course of one go. It simply means that what's going to come back is your "normal" voice, and by normal we simply mean your voice in relation to sitting closely with another person and speaking with them. No actor voice, no booming pipes that would rattle the Vatican's organ. Rather than sounding robotic the exercise shifts to the appearance of two people having a conversation. In repetition you don't monitor or censor your voice. It flows in accordance with the demands of the moment, and the moment is largely determined by your partner. Whether you're repeating "You're wearing a hat" or now speaking Shakespeare doesn't matter, that innate value is still the same. Eventually, you'll be able to observe and respond speaking the words of Shakespeare fresh off the page with as much ease as you would any other observation. That is the path you are working towards with this exercise, but if your vocal habits are so strong they prevent you from accessing that experience, then the robotic inflection is of immense value for as long as you need it.

A question that many actors ask at this point is what happens after the first read. Several answers can be found here. The Meisner technique offers additional text exercises in this vein, such as the mechanical and working readings, but breaking the back provides a solid introduction to how to begin approaching text in your work. After you've broken the back of a scene, text analysis can follow (yes, there is a form of analysis in this work, which you'll encounter in just a couple of pages), but as far as line learning goes, a version of breaking the back can be used for this purpose. Using this type of approach to learn lines is fairly common in some approaches to actor development, not just Meisner. David Mamet's Practical Aesthetics training, for example, encourages actors to learn their lines flat. Here, however, is where some challenges in interpretation can arise.

During my MA at the Royal Central School of Speech and Drama, one of my colleagues invited me to see him play Macbeth. I may be biased from having been his colleague, but he really is a knockout actor, and I felt the casting was a superb decision. At this point I had already begun training with the Impulse Company, the two programs of study overlapping, and I had shared some of the exercises and tools with my classmates, him included. When I saw my colleague perform, however, I was very surprised. It felt the whole time as if he were deliberately speaking flatly, as if he were reining in the many impulses and moments coming up for him. I thought it was more strange than anything else, a vibrantly expressive actor toning down where he didn't need to, and so I chalked it up to some conceptual decision the director had made. After the performance I went to congratulate him on his work. Completing a gauntlet like Macbeth is always worthy of praise, and despite my confusion at his intonation, his work was strong. When I let him know how great his acting was he looked proud.

"I used Meisner in my process this time," he said.

"Really? How did you do that?" I asked, genuinely curious.

"I learned all of the lines flat," he said. "'Even in rehearsals I would speak them flat, so when we got to performance I could just let them come out any way they wanted to."

This explained a lot, and while it would have been totally inappropriate to correct my colleague in that moment, coming fresh off of a demanding performance, this unfortunately is not using the Meisner technique to learn lines. He had seen and worked with the breaking the back of the scene exercise a couple of times and had heard it was a tool that could be used to learn lines. What got lost in the translation, however, were several key elements. Firstly, breaking the back as you have seen is generally intended for the first read of a scene. Secondly, the monotone or flat inflection is only used in the beginning to help an actor iron out their habitual text-infusion tendencies. Thirdly, if you wish to use this approach for learning lines, then the monotone element has to be relaxed. This essentially means you speak the lines neutrally as you learn them, when alone picking a single point such as a mark on the wall to look at, and not adding anything onto them, allowing them to come out in your natural voice. Another way to describe it is learning the lines with a quality of ease in your speech, not pressured to do anything with the words and keeping your attention on whatever fixed point you chose.

What my colleague and friend had done, unfortunately, is memorized a flat intonation, and though his acting work was rich and thorough he couldn't fully shake off the inflection he had learned. This is why we spend so much in this training time considering habits, and that when one is replaced by another it's conducive to doing better work rather than making life more challenging for yourself. Where we put our attention early in the process is not necessarily where we will end.

Summary

Actors' lives are filled with challenges. It can be easy to crave escape from the present moment, or to frame your career in terms of getting away from your present circumstances. While having aspirations and working to change our present is important, it is only by engaging with the ordinary elements of life that we can fully connect with what is happening around us in the now. Zen practice, from which both the headless exercises and koans stem, orients itself around reclaiming clarity in the present moment. Habits are in some ways the greatest challenge to an actor's process because, once ingrained, they can be immensely difficult to let go of. Meisner's breaking the back of a scene, intended for the first read of the text, exposes the many habits actors bring that don't aid them in discovering the circumstances of the text they are being asked to live out. Breaking the back of a scene encourages partners to infuse the words with the process of living truthfully, of connecting the first read to the most important variable in both honoring the text and engaging with the world of that story: the other person. Eventually, breaking the back can be utilized as an effective line-learning tool, though caution must be taken to ensure it is adapted properly.

14
The Two-Dimensional Reality

The Warmth of a Shared Practice

Looking back on the process of writing this, from its first days germinating as a "What if we did this crazy thing of putting Meisner and meditation together?" idea to being now close to my final submission, it feels very much like a journey has been taken. I suspect in context of the meditation sessions, you may feel the same way. From just counting backwards from 15 to explorations of headlessness, seeking the thinker of our thoughts, and breakthrough moments of awareness facilitated by koans, a lot of territory has been covered. Woven throughout have been discussions of your self-identity as an actor, the nature of consciousness itself from your first-person perspective, and what is unique about your experience of reality as opposed to anyone else's. The waters of these meditation practices are simple but deep, offering a window of insight into yourself that isn't handed down to you from outside but uncovered and explored from within.

What you also might have gathered is that we've barely scratched the surface of the many forms of practice on offer to you. Though numerous threads connect the three separate approaches to practice we experimented with, each has much more content than we are able to cover here. There are hundreds of koans yet to be explored, new types of experiments with headlessness, and more mindfulness training on offer to you to develop your attention and attune it to the present moment. Throughout I've done my best to give you various references and names, like Thich Nhat Hanh and Sam Harris for mindfulness, Douglas Harding and Richard Lang for headlessness, and Seung Sahn and Henry Shukman for more koan practice. If any or all of this content has sparked inspiration and relevance, then I encourage you to take your practice deeper by going to these sources. The potential on offer to you extends well beyond the pages of this book, and the more you explore the more you may find that they don't only apply to either your acting or personal life. The whole package blends together into one unique, integrated whole, with the insights and lessons that are applied across your life, regardless of how we categorize a certain experience.

These last two meditations can be practiced all in one go, or feel free to return to them at different times or days even. In additional online content on the publisher's website you will encounter further koans and supplementary exercises to the Meisner training, but for now, this is the last time we will practice together. It's a moment that touches me thinking about it but, my sentiments aside, I hope you will find these a useful round-off to our time in meditation. They certainly won't answer all of your questions, but hopefully will continue to point towards further development and depth on offer to you.

Exercise: Meditation 14

Set-up: Set up your practice.

Instructions: Set a timer for 10 minutes. For this session, simply allow all sensations. Whether it is feelings of pressure or other sensations in the body, the sounds that arise in the room, or even unpleasant feelings like any pain or anxiety, sit with them, notice them, and let them come and go. Even allow your thoughts to be a part of this process. Let them rise and come. If at any point you feel any judgments towards yourself, restlessness, and so on, let these too be a part of your experience. Notice them as they pass through you. Let yourself be the space of conscious awareness they arise and disappear within. When you are ready, start your timer, close your eyes, and begin.

Notes/Observations: In allowing yourself to be truly still, perhaps for the first time in a long, long while, you give yourself permission to not attach to the flow of experiences constantly bombarding you, whether it is the emotions of a given moment, thoughts, or sounds arising. All of these phenomena, whether they seem to come from within you or from outside, are experiences within consciousness, that space of awareness in which you encounter everything within the world, your self included. In being still, you become a mirror: filled with clarity rather than muddiness, present instead of swept away, no longer swallowed up in the many distracting thoughts that used to be able to dominate your attention. As you go throughout your day, and as you build on this practice, continue noticing. Your own mindfulness practice holds the key to alleviating many of the challenges you struggle with as an actor, your attention and attunement to your experiences the true guide rather than the words of a guru, system of thought, or even a book.

Exercise: Meditation 15

Set-up: Set up your practice.

Part one instructions: Set a timer for 5 minutes. In this meditation you'll be working with a koan from Master Yunmen, who said, "Medicine and disease correspond to one another. The whole world is medicine. Where is your true self?" The koan for practice here is "the whole world is medicine." You can either attach this koan to your exhale or let the repetition have its own rhythm independent of the breath. Again, there's no need to try and make the repetition more interesting or exciting, so listen to how the koan wishes to find its own pattern. If you find yourself lost in thought, then turning your attention to the breath for a few moments can be helpful before resuming the repetition of the koan. When you are ready, start your timer, close your eyes, and begin.

Part one notes/questions: In commenting on this koan, Henry Shukman takes care to remind the listener that while koans have a historical element, in that they tend to involve stories hundreds or thousands of years old from masters long dead, they are not historical parables locked in their own time. I think this is an incredibly valuable point: koans are for us in the present moment. They might originate in a different historical setting but their worth is how they can comment on and guide us in our current circumstances. We don't need to put ourselves into any mentality, or to attempt to appreciate koans as historical tales of wisdom. So this brings up the question, how is the whole world medicine for you? That disease and medicine depend on one another is clear. Lao Tzu, in the *Tao Te Ching*, wrote, "Without beauty there is no ugliness. High and low depend on one another to exist." But Yunmen is suggesting that the whole world, and everything within it, is medicine. Without disease there is no medicine, so what is our illness then if that is the case? Rather than try to work it out analytically, let's sit with this koan a bit longer.

Step two instructions: Set up your practice again if necessary. Set a timer for 5 minutes. In this next half, you'll continue to work with the koan, "The whole world is medicine." You can either couple it with your breath, or let the repetition find its own pace independent of the breath. When you are ready start your timer, close your eyes, and begin.

Step two notes/questions: We have all been through an extremely challenging few years. For readers encountering this well past what is considered the "post-pandemic" phase, you can certainly consider not only the ripple effects of the time these words were penned in but also the trying moments in your life. But even if these factors never existed, I'm going to say something with no sarcasm or cynicism intended: you're a working actor, the chances are you've had a rough year, or couple of years. This is a challenging field to thrive in, even when the jobs and money become fairly stable or abundant. Both your tragedies and anxieties exist within the world. Yet Yunmen looks to the world and sees healing everywhere. He isn't ignorant that pain and suffering exist, but says that these too can be medicine for us. It's hard to believe Yunmen's point then that even the worst things in our lives can be medicine, a treatment for our growth and healing.

What we have to ask, then, to get an insight into this koan is this: if our healing is everywhere, then what is making us sick? One perspective Zen offers is our belief in the idea of a separate self, that somehow we are separate from the world we find ourselves in. It is true that we each have a unique perspective and experience of life, but we are not separate from reality itself. That is, however, how we often see ourselves. My needs versus others', my pain versus theirs, my goals, my dreams, and so on. Having goals and ambitions is fine, healthy even, but it is when we lose the recognition that we are not separate from the rest of the world that our suffering compounds. Yunmen's koan hints that if the illness comes from our misconceptions, and that all of the world has healing within it if we can recognize it, then there is a totality on offer. Our pain can also be a source of lessons, growth, and healing.

Rather than look at it in terms of some sort of cosmic balance, you can see it as the rollercoaster of life. It is possible the more we try to see ourselves as separate from the rest of reality that we can begin to make ourselves sick with delusion. Your trials as an actor are linked to your successes. If you did not continue to go through the challenges, the pain of the rejections, you wouldn't accomplish the goals you already have, and if you don't continue to go through the challenges, the new ones that await you won't come to fruition. These are both part of the human experience. The wounds you've gained offer lessons for growth and healing. Our need to separate ourselves can make us ill, but recognizing that as an illusion can restore a degree of wellness, to remind us that even though there is pain and suffering, the whole world can be a treatment for the separateness that ails us.

In the previous chapter we explored how Zen is concerned much more with the ordinary than the extraordinary, and this koan can highlight that. In practice you go through a journey to learn about yourself and the world, only to return to this present moment. Zen is not about leaving your present circumstances for some grand life elsewhere, but rather connecting you with the peace that comes from embracing this moment, of recognizing and working with your life as it is happening rather than living in the delusion that surely it is just waiting for you elsewhere if some magic force would simply teleport you there. Winning the lottery doesn't change the perspective you wake up in every day. Despite all the pain of the recent and the long-term past, the solutions for your growth and healing might have always been in front of you, the whole world being your medicine for the disease of separation.

Brain Fog

Analysis in the Meisner technique is a challenge. By nature it takes place within your head, the place we've continuously attempted to direct your attention away from. Facilitating and keeping the integrity of truthfulness in your acting is a priority, but equally valuable is ensuring that you have filtered your truthful impulses by connecting them to the circumstances. There are multiple approaches to text analysis in the Meisner technique, and so we are going to begin by using a simpler but more powerful one. This method of analysis is used by Scott Williams at the Impulse Company. It has one function only, which is to put a fire inside you that is directly related to the given circumstances. Rather than forcing your analysis to work, you'll be testing it, the same way you've done with preparations or circumstances in activities. Together with your partner you'll explore whether your analysis is on the right track in practice. To analyze text using this exercise, you'll want to ask and answer three questions. Let's take a look at the components and clarifications around them, and then you'll try it out for yourself.

Exercise: Text Analysis

Set-up: By this point the scene has already been read at least once, using the breaking the back of the scene tool. Before it is read again, you will now analyze the character you are reading. A successful analysis asks and answers three questions accurately. To do your best work, there are some guiding suggestions that can maximize your time and results. These suggestions will be explored after each question is introduced. The only guidance worth suggesting up front is to make sure that when you analyze you have something to write your answers down on. It could be a piece of paper and pen, an app on your phone, or something else, but you do not want to try to keep track of all these answers in your head, because it will become too much information and some will be inevitably forgotten.

Here are the three questions you will be looking to answer:

1. *What is the Knowledge of the Character Before the Scene Begins?*

When we talk about knowledge, we are simply referring to basic facts about the world and people this character knows are true. This is very different from objective, or dramaturgical, facts about the world. Sometimes characters will believe things to be true that turn out to be false, and vice versa. You are wanting to find the facts your character knows from within their point of view. List only knowledge before the scene begins, not discoveries made during the scene. If, for example, it is your character's knowledge that their partner has been faithful to them for three decades of marriage, and in the scene their partner drops the bomb that they've had a separate family for years, then your knowledge would be:

- They've been married for thirty years.
- Their partner has never cheated.

As you can see, information doesn't need to be written as complicated, in-depth sentences. It is best summarized into bite-sized chunks. You'll also notice that the information is worded in the third person. This is because I don't recommend you personalize your character by writing, "I know this . . ." or "My spouse's name is . . ." Keep it in the third person. This is an unnecessarily contentious point among actors, so I have to be a bit more plain about my reasons. To start, you're not analyzing yourself. You are not the character. You are an actor being asked to live out a set of circumstances form a particular point of view. You're never going to be shifting identities, changing eye pupil and shoe size, and metamorphosing into a different human. Your circumstances leading up to this moment have been wildly different from your character's, and so there's no value in trying to personalize the analysis. Refer to them by their name or the pronouns they identify as in the world of the story.

I'm paraphrasing this story a bit, but an actor in one of Sanford Meisner's classes was doing a scene with his partner. During the scene he looked out the window, suddenly ceasing to speak. It seemed he was really wrapped up and connecting with some vibrant, imagined image. Meisner got up from his seat, making his way over to the actor with the help of his cane. Together they looked out the window.

"What do you see?" he asked the actor.

"I see . . . the Swiss Alps. There's a ski slope, with a family going down it. At the base of the mountain is a small cabin, and through the window I can see someone making hot chocolate, laughing with joy . . ." and on and on.

Once the actor had stopped talking, Meisner peered through his thick glasses out the window. "I see bricks," he said.

Sticking with reality is the value we've encouraged since the very first day when you listened to sounds and experimented with investing in the reality of doing. A piece of paper like a script doesn't change the reality you are in. See the bricks, recognize you're not analyzing yourself, and refer to your character in the third person when analyzing.

Another aspect is that no piece of information is too basic, simple, or obvious. Sometimes what we might consider unnecessarily obvious at the outset becomes the piece of information that unlocks a reveal. Does your character know their own name? Include that. Do they know what day of the week it is? In your quest for answers, any piece of information becomes evidence, and a good detective won't throw evidence away.

The final note about this first question is to leave out anything that you aren't sure about or might force you to speculate on whether it is actually knowledge. If you take as an example Lady Macbeth's infamous scene with Macbeth in which she cautions him to not hesitate, to "screw your courage to the sticking place," let's ask a simple question: is it her knowledge that she loves Macbeth? It's very possible, after all. She's risking an immense amount to come out on top with him, and certainly taking huge risks on another person can be a sign of love. But we also know that she is ambitious, and while she might trust in Macbeth's competence, love may not be a factor in her decision-making. The beauty of this form of analysis is that we don't need to make a decision on things we aren't sure of. If it seems unclear, or forces you to guess, leave it out. It only strengthens the analysis to have a list of facts you are confident the character believes is true.

2. What is the Character Literally Doing in the Scene?

Now we turn our attention to what happens in the scene. This question solely has to do with physical actions. For these you will mostly reference the stage directions in your script. If you are working with an older scene that has no stage directions, then you'll have to infer any essential actions from the text. For example, if your character's first line is, "Good day to you," and then their next line is, "Hark, I am slain!" there probably was a literal action that occurred – most likely involving sharp and pointy objects – you'll want to include in your analysis.

Not all actions are created equal for our purposes, however. Before we get into the weeds on what types of actions are worth including, a major piece of advice I can give that can help you, similar to the previous question, is to word your actions as simply as possible. For example, this action:

> She opens the pantry door, removes the coffee grounds, closes the pantry door, sets the coffee on the counter, goes to the cabinet, opens the cabinet, retrieves a French press, etc, etc.

Can be summarized as:

> She is making coffee.

Simplicity will be your friend in writing the actions out.

Now, for the way to determine what pieces of action are relevant to your analysis, include any that are essential to the action happening. One way to think about this is that if the action did not happen, a portion or the entirety of the scene could not be completed. Likewise, sometimes in film, but particularly in theatre, authors think it is their job to tell you how to act a scene. Any inessential actions, or pieces of direction whereby the author is telling you how to do your job, can be promptly cut out for your analysis. You didn't tell the author how to write their scene, they don't need to tell you how to act it. For example, and of course there are exceptions so judge based on the material in the scene, if your stage direction reads, "Flings himself angrily on the chair," feel free to leave that out. If it says, "Takes out knife and stabs him," I would recommend keeping that in your analysis.

As a final hint, with extremely rare exceptions, there will always be two pieces of character action that are very easy to miss. Rather than me telling you here, see if you can spot them in your analysis (if you miss them don't worry, you'll discover later what they are). Using the information obtained in steps one and two, you're now going to treat them as evidence, employing your powers of deduction to answer the third and final question.

3. What is the Need of the Character in This Scene?

Needs are markedly different from objectives. Objectives ask you to consider how you are going to execute something. For example, if playing a businessperson your objective might be to convince another character to invest in your company. To achieve your objective, you will employ tactics, such as being charming, seductive, persuasive, or possibly even actioning your lines. All of this is integral to many approaches to how you will live out the scene, but here is where we come to a challenge using this method. Rather than deciding what your objective and tactics are, we want you to discover them as you go. The tactics and objectives might remain the same across performances or takes, but there is a risk some actors run into, which is that they end up focusing more on executing their tactics rather than letting them adapt to the actor they are working with. If your colleague in a scene is normally quite energetic, and tonight they seem more down and slower, you might choose to ignore that if working with what they are giving in the moment won't harmonize with your tactics. Some approaches that utilize tactics are aware of this, and have adapted the concept of them to accommodate the unique variables between rehearsals, takes, or performances, but we want to move away from these risks altogether.

Though it might be controversial to say, objectives are by and large more useful for writers than actors. Rarely do we go through our day contemplating a master objective for a span of time. There are times we attempt one, such as focusing on what you need to get from a particular meeting or job interview, but just as easily life throws wrenches into our plans that derail our objectives. It's a great help for a writer to know what their character's objective is, but as an actor it's far too literary. We need to find a way to honor the organic values of living truthfully while rooting you right into the given circumstances and letting the objectives and tactics arise without any need for you to think about them beforehand. The "need" in this approach to analysis is that solution.

One helpful way to begin thinking about needs is that they are a layer deeper than the objective. They are more primal, rooted closer to the essence of the human experience. Needs give rise to objectives, and so one means you can employ to find the need of the character is by beginning with their objective. If your objective is to convince the other character in the scene to invest in your company, then we can ask why that is important to your character. What is valuable about it occurring? Let's say you reference your knowledge of the character and discover they haven't had a big win in decades. They've been struggling along, with their colleagues saying they're washed out and need to retire. What does this win mean for them? In need terms, you might say their need is to "be the big dog on the block."

Needs are often worded abstractly, as metaphors. They capture what is most meaningful in a visceral sentence. There is no clear way to act them, but they connect you with that primal fire inside the character related to their circumstances, which allows you to act truthfully with your impulses being filtered by the given set of circumstances without too much pre-empting. Needs are not entirely subjective either. If two people analyze the same scene they might word them differently, but should arrive at similar conclusions about the territory of the need.

Now that you have your three questions, we're going to look at a scene from the previous chapter, from Pendleton King's *Cocaine*. Pick either Nora or Joe to analyze. You can analyze both eventually but for now start with just one. You've already broken the back of the scene, so quickly refresh yourself by reading through it again here. At the end I'll give some additional suggestions and then you can begin analyzing. Whenever you are ready, go ahead read the scene again.

Cocaine by Pendleton King

>   **JOE:** Nora, 's 'at you?
>   **NORA:** I didn't mean to wake you up. Go on back to sleep.
>   **JOE:** I haven't been asleep. What time is it?
>   **NORA:** *[takes off hat]* About four o'clock.
>   **JOE:** You're pretty late.
>   **NORA:** *[takes off jacket]* Had to walk from uptown.
>   **JOE:** How far uptown?
>   **NORA:** O, way up town. I let a crowd shake me like a fool. *[Sits in chair at foot of bed and fans herself.]* And didn't have sense enough to get car fare. Whew! You don't realize how hot you are till you sit down.
>   **JOE:** Poor kid.
>   **NORA:** You must have had the gas lighted to make it as hot as this in here. Lord, I'm so glad to get home.
>   **JOE:** *[gently]* You didn't bring in nothing?

NORA: Not a cent, Joe. *[Gets up and goes to bureau.]* I don't know what's the matter with me. *[Looks in glass.]* It's that darn fever blister. If I had only had sense enough to get some camphor that first day.

JOE: But it's most well now. Can't hardly notice it any more.

NORA: Of course it's perfectly well. There won't be a trace of it tomorrow. I oughtn't to have tried to go out those two days the first of the week when it was so bad. Everybody was afraid of me and it made me feel like a leper. I lost my grip in some way and now I can't get it back. It all depends on yourself. *[Picks up candle.]* If you're sure of yourself you have luck; if you aren't, you don't. That's all there is to it. *[Crosses with candle, which she puts down on trunk.]* If I'd had a wee bit of a sniff tonight I'd have got some money out of that crowd. *[Sits on foot of the bed.]* But drinks don't brace me up somehow.

JOE: Hum. 'sright.

NORA: Poor old boy. Have you been lying here all night in this heat waiting for me? It's hard luck on you, Joe. Oh, I thought I'd go crazy tonight! My nerves are just all to pieces. I did think I was going to get some money this time.

JOE: Why don't you take your clothes off and come on to bed?

NORA: *[gets up and takes a packet of cigarettes out of her jacket]* I swiped these for you, anyway. Here. *[Throws him the box.]*

JOE: *[catching it]* Gee! Ta!

NORA: Joe, I wish you wouldn't say "Ta." *[Goes up into recess.]* I don't know why I hate it so. *[She begins to undress.]*

JOE: All right, Missis. *[Gets up to light his cigarette with the candle.]* Common stuff, uhm?

NORA: *[undressing]* No, it doesn't matter. I'm just nervous and irritable. Don't pay any attention to anything I say. If I don't get some money tomorrow I just don't know what I'll do. It's terrible to be so dependent on *anything* as that.

JOE: *[lies down again]* Four days.

NORA: No, tonight's Saturday.

JOE: Well, that's four days, ain't it? We finished up that last deck Tuesday night.

NORA: That's right. I wouldn't have believed I could go so long. I don't see how you stand it, Joe, all night like this, doing nothing.

JOE: I been out. Don't worry about me. I can git on without de stuff for a while.

NORA: *[comes down in kimono]* I can't. *[Takes cigarette.]* But then I've been using it so much longer than you have. *[Lights cigarette at the candle.]*

JOE: I been goin' it some little time – a month or so before we took up together last summer.

NORA: To think. *[Sits on bed.]* Only a year. I wonder what would have become of you if I hadn't found you?

JOE: What becomes of all de other poor bastards who gets knocked out and can't get back in de ring? I don't know.

NORA: That's the trouble with you boys. You are brought up with only one idea – to fight – and if anything does happen to you, you're not fit to do anything else. You're only twenty-four, and you're done.

JOE: Be twenty-four in October, I guess.

NORA: Lord, it makes me feel so old. That's how you stand the strain the way you do. You are as firm and strong as you ever were, and look at me!

JOE: Well, if a fellow has to do as much trainin' as I used to, he more or less keeps in condition, I guess.

NORA: *[lies down beside him]* I feel so old, and tired, and discouraged, Joe. If I didn't have you I don't think I'd go on with it.

JOE: *[tightens his arm about her]* I'm stickin' to you, see?

NORA: I never thought of your leaving me. *[She puts her arm up about his head and strokes his hair.]* I love you too much, Joe. I love you more than anybody else will ever love you if you live to be a thousand years old.

JOE: I don't reckon anybody'd love me much if I was that old.

NORA: *[laughs]* I should. But you're only a baby now. A little old infant. *[She snuggles up to him and presses her cheek to his.]* Joe?

JOE: Um?

NORA: *[in a whisper]* My darling. *[He gathers her closer. Long pause.]*

JOE: Tired, kid?

NORA: No, not now. I get strength from you. You've got plenty of strength for both of us, haven't you?

Fires That Burn Both Hot and Cold

Now that you've had a chance to refresh yourself on the scene, it's time to analyze. Using a pen and paper or a writing app, choose either of the characters and answer the three questions about them. For a refresher those are: What is the knowledge of the character before the scene begins? What is the character literally doing in the scene? What is their need in the scene? When you are finished with your analysis, come back here for the next steps.

I've also done an analysis of each of the characters in this scene, so let's compare notes. Rather than starting with the character you chose, begin by reading my analysis of the other character. If you analyzed Joe, for example, start by reading what I've done with Nora, and if you notice any major differences or realize you have made a mistake go back and tweak your analysis. I've included notes after each question to support the reasons for my analysis.

Joe

What is Joe's knowledge before the scene begins?

> His name is Joe.
>
> He lives with Nora.
>
> They are in a relationship.
>
> He has been asleep.
>
> He knows Nora has been out.
>
> Nora has been out earning them money.
>
> They have a mirror.
>
> Nora has a visible fever blister.
>
> She has had it for a few days.
>
> They use candles.
>
> Nora uses cocaine.
>
> It's Saturday.
>
> He smokes.
>
> He uses cocaine.
>
> He and Nora finished their cocaine four days ago on Tuesday.
>
> They've been together over a year.
>
> He began using cocaine a month before they took up together.
>
> He was a fighter who was knocked out in the ring.

He's twenty-three.

His birthday is in October.

Notes on Joe's knowledge: One of the biggest challenges for me when deciding what was knowledge was trying to field the line of how much Joe's addiction impacts his truthfulness. There's nothing to indicate in his relationship to Nora that he would be deliberately dishonest with her, but addiction can blur the lines between when to be truthful and not. Joe says he and Nora finished their deck four days ago, but has Joe had any since that Nora wasn't aware of? Without speculating, I'm just not sure, and so I don't include it as Joe's knowledge that he hasn't had any cocaine for four days.

This is what we mean by the line between speculation and knowledge. Most of the time it will be fairly clear what can or can't be supported based on what the text is giving us, but if you encounter moments in a gray area when you're not sure about the level of evidence presented then make your best judgment on the strength of the evidence. If you argue Joe hasn't had any cocaine in four days due to his lack of money and no clear reason to lie, I don't think you would be in the wrong in including that as knowledge. For me, while I'm confident saying that it is his knowledge the shared stash was finished four days ago, and also his knowledge that Nora hasn't had any for four days, whether he has something going on the side makes it too speculative for me. We know that Joe has been using for more than a year, and Nora even says he doesn't seem to get withdrawals, so this also is what I used to support that knowledge as speculative and not worth including.

It's also this question of truthfulness that makes me wonder about Joe telling Nora he is sticking with her. That very well could be knowledge, and from Joe's limited dialogue it is hard to tell, but the impression I get is that Nora is far more invested in sticking with Joe than Joe is with Nora. There's nothing in Joe's behavior to support him being dishonest or manipulative, but is there enough evidence to support him being committed to a long-term relationship with her? We know he's had a pretty major setback in his career, his dreams of being a prize fighter failed. Nora even acknowledges she was there to pick up the pieces. It's not the kindest thing, but people do depend on others for emotional comfort when in a dark place only to move on when their life improves or they have a change in perspective. I'm confident of Joe being in a relationship with Nora as his knowledge, but I'm not as sure in his mind that he knows he is going to stick with her regardless of whatever trouble comes their way or if their circumstances begin to improve.

What is he literally doing in the scene?

He is smoking.

He is talking to Nora about her earning money for them, her face blister, the last stash of cocaine they finished, how long they have been using cocaine, his failed career as a fighter, and him staying with her.

He is listening to Nora talk about walking all the way uptown, not earning any money, her face blister, her nerves falling to pieces, swiping cigarettes for Joe, being dependent on cocaine, how long they have been using, Joe's youth, Joe's fighting, how tired and discouraged she feels, his figure, and how she will love him even if he were a thousand years old.

Notes on what Joe is literally doing: Joe has some blocking written out for him. Times when he moves, puts his arm around Nora, and so on. None of that really leapt out to me as essential to the circumstances. Even when he is holding Nora, that appears to be more a staging desire on the author's part than an essential action for the circumstances to continue. There are many ways to show the tenderness and desperation I believe King is attempting to capture at the end of the scene, so the only pieces of action that seem important enough to keep are Joe's smoking, as well as what he is talking about and hearing Nora speak of. Talking and listening are the two pieces of essential action that will almost be in every scene you analyse, and being specific about the content of each can greatly assist you in determining what the need of the character is.

What is his need in this scene?

Joe's need is to be man enough.

Notes on Joe's need: We know that Joe has had a rough patch. He had dreams of being a prize fighter and was stopped before he could go as far as he wanted. He began using cocaine, ending up living in impoverished conditions with Nora, an addict who genuinely cares for him, but an addict nonetheless. Nora constantly tells Joe how strong he is, strong enough emotionally for both of them. It is revealed later in the play that Nora works as a prostitute, and to me this all paints the picture of a man who had very different dreams and aspirations for himself than what he is currently living through. Since we are analyzing this to understand Joe's point of view, we have to leave our judgments at the door about how healthy his dream was, the ethics of how he may or may not see Nora, or how he might be contributing to the toxicity of the situation. From Joe's perspective, life was going on one track, and now it's derailed into a darker place full of major compromises and no clear way forward.

I have to be honest and say I've never had a relationship with the concept of masculinity. I've never had to worry whether I was man enough, or felt I did things that specifically were "guy things." It seemed to me I was always just doing my thing, following my interests regardless of the label placed on me or other people's judgments about what I wanted to do with my life. I have known lots of men, however, for whom questions of masculinity are a real concern. I imagine that if a lot of these things happened they could be a real challenge to a man's sense of confidence and identity. To go from a strong man full of promise to an addict living in poverty with another addict would crush a lot of men's conceptions about a man and his role in relation to both his life and a woman. The prostitution element I imagine especially would sting for a lot of men, to know their spouse is sleeping with others, even if it is out of desperate financial need.

Still, living with all of these setbacks, Joe does seem to make something of an effort. He treats Nora with kindness, helps her keep track of when she misremembers things, listens to her, shares his feelings with her, and assures her of his commitment to her. It's easy for us to sit back and judge these as not very important, but from within those circumstances even small acts of kindness, listening, and affirmations of commitment can be huge. It seems to me that on some level Joe is still making an effort to show Nora he is still a man and man enough for her. Considering those factors and the evidence we've gotten from the scene, I think Joe's need in this scene is to be man enough.

Nora

What is Nora's knowledge before the scene begins?

> Her name is Nora.
>
> She lives with Joe.
>
> They are in a relationship.
>
> She owns a hat and jacket.
>
> She has been uptown trying to earn money.

It is nearly 4 a.m.

She tried to solicit within a crowd with no luck.

She didn't earn a cent.

She has a fever blister.

Camphor can treat a blister, and she didn't take any.

She went out with it for two days and people looked at her like a leper.

The blister has gotten better and will be gone tomorrow.

She uses cocaine.

She hasn't had any today.

She obtained some cigarettes for Joe.

Joe says "ta."

She is dependent on cocaine.

It's been three days since she and Joe finished what they had.

Drinks don't brace her up like cocaine does.

She's been using for much longer than Joe has.

Joe was a fighter who couldn't get more work.

Joe is twenty-four.

She "found" Joe after his career had failed.

Notes on Nora's knowledge: For analysis purposes, Nora's knowledge is filled with some great examples of character knowledge that may not map onto true facts in the world. It is her knowledge they finished their cocaine three days ago when it has been four, and that Joe is 24 when he is actually 23. Her knowledge is also filled with personal facts she knows to be true about her point of view: she knows she is dependent on cocaine, she knows alcohol doesn't work for her in the same way, and she knows that she has been using for much longer than Joe, even if in reality the differences between their started uses might not be that great. It also is her knowledge that her blister is better and should be gone by tomorrow, even if Joe doesn't share the same view. It could be wishful thinking out of desperation on her end, but I think there's enough evidence to support her believing it to be true.

There are also examples of speculative knowledge we didn't include. When she becomes irritated at Joe for his use of "Ta" instead of thanks or thank you, she says, "I don't know why I hate it so." Is it possible that she has always hated it when Joe uses "ta," or is it a facet of his speech that only now sounds annoying because of her withdrawals? We don't know, and so we don't need to include it as knowledge. She also makes a fair number of comments about how strong Joe is, but whether she believes this or is just trying to boost Joe's confidence is unclear. Even her saying, "I love you," brings up some questions for me. There's no question to me that Nora is a kind soul, and she's kind to Joe and has immense compassion for him, but the desperation, fear, and tiredness of a wearied life weighs heavily on Nora. Does she love Joe for who he is, or does she love that there is another human who isn't cruel to her and shares the pain of her circumstances? The answer at the end of the day is that we don't know, and so not including her loving Joe as knowledge is to me the safer bet.

What is Nora literally doing in the scene?

She is getting ready for bed.

She gives Joe his cigarettes, and later lights one.

She is talking to Joe about being uptown, how hot it is, not being able to make any money from the crowd, her struggles with the blister on her face, her nerves, withdrawals from the cocaine, being dependent on it, how long they have been using for, Joe's attitude towards himself, how tired and discouraged she feels, and how she loves Joe and that he is strong enough for the both of them.

She is listening to Joe ask her about her night, coming to bed, how long he has been using, how long they have been together, his failed fighting career, and how he is sticking with her.

Notes on what Nora is literally doing: Nora has a few more actions than Joe in this scene. There are quite a few directions related to the timing of her changing into her bedtime clothes, as well as when she disappears from view and whatnot. All of that to me reads as how the author wishes to see the scene staged rather than occurrences essential for the circumstances to progress. We can reduce all of the complications King imposes to a simple action: she's getting ready for bed.

Talking and listening are both actions that you will encounter in almost every scene you analyse. Being specific about the content of what the character is saying, as well as what they are listening to, can greatly aid you in assessing evidence for the need.

What is her need in this scene?

Nora's need is to live in hope.

Notes on Nora's need: One thing about Nora keeps jumping out to me when I read this scene: she's tired, and keeps communicating that. I believe she is physically tired due to the long walk, but I think as well she is tired in her soul, weary of the pain that comes from being a slave to the drug as well as having to sell her body to feed her habits. Once someone is caught in that cycle, I imagine it's easy to begin believing it's unwinnable, that there is no clear way to climb out of that situation. We might know of people who beat their addiction, but it seems to me it's much harder once we find ourselves in the same situation, able to rationalize that the people who beat it were just somehow stronger than us.

Fighting a battle like addiction is never easy, but it feels easier when you have the economic means to seek support and treatments. Without any such privilege to aid her, Nora is very much aware of how alone she is. Joe is her rock, a balm for her pain, but I wonder if she also recognizes that Joe is trapped in troubled cycles of his own, not only related to the cocaine but narratives about his life he has come to believe. He is 24 (in her mind), and yet he's bought into the view that his life is over and he's helpless. Joe might be a support unit for her, but he's also another person she has to take care of when she can barely handle herself. Nora is a person fraying at the seams. Her anxieties might be related to the cocaine, but also perhaps the inevitable terror and despair her circumstances are fueling.

Based on the evidence we have, Nora hasn't given up hope yet, but she might be close. Rather than any one specific thing, she needs to believe that life as a whole will get better, that things will turn around for her, and that Joe will recognize his own potential and be the support unit she truly needs. In the grips of such despair, her deepest need is to live in hope. Fewer things drive this home for me than when, in a moment of such tender pain and longing, she says to Joe, "I get my strength from you. You've got plenty of strength for the both of us." I don't find support for the idea that she's saying that because Joe is that amazing; rather, she's saying those words to herself to keep alive what little embers of hope for the future and a better life still flicker.

Now that you've come to a possible conclusion about your character's need, the question becomes what do we do with the need in the next reading? Do you treat it like an objective and try to orient your performance around making it happen? As you've probably guessed, forcing the need into existence loses the many values of this work. Instead, in your next reading, your goal is to test the need. Remind yourself of the need, put your attention on your partner, and then see what happens. Testing the need is very similar to how you test the strength of your circumstances in an independent activity, or gauge the strength of preparation. The moment is what will tell you when you've arrived at a need that is true. That answer, however, is never set in stone. Each subsequent reading, whether it is in rehearsal or in performance, is re-testing of your need. Every time before you work ask yourself, "Will the need be true today?" and then actually seek the answer. It may be true every time, but at the end of the day we'll never know the answer until it arrives.

Exercise: Character Koan Practice

Testing needs within the given circumstances can keep you busy enough. Each time you enter those circumstances there is a vibrant world of trial-and-error on offer, discoveries to be made by letting your scene partners take you on the ride of living truthfully. Some actors do find that for them testing the need is helpful but, particularly after a long run of rehearsals, performances, or takes, they may need more support in reconnecting with the need. To be clear, this is different from if I said, "They need more helping in making the need happen, of juicing more life and energy out of it." This is more about going deeper into a need, of giving yourself some verbal summary that exists even beneath the need that you can repeat to yourself in between reads or even use in a meditation practice to see if it reveals any further insights. You are going to experiment with finding the koan of your character.

We've explored how koans are glimmers from moments in the lives of awakened individuals. These people found a level of clarity and insight into the nature of their reality. The koan you'll extract is a sliver of your awakening to the deeper reality of the individual you are analyzing. To find a koan, add a fourth question directly related to the need: why? Why is this their need? This doesn't mean to look for backstory, but it does ask you to investigate meaning. Why does living in hope mean so much for Nora, or being man enough matter as much as it does to Joe? The koan is the extraction of the why. It would be a moment of awakening for these characters if they realized the cycle of the life narrative they were caught in, and you are after a verbal summary of that realization.

The koan of your character can be worded anyway that resonates with you. Koans that we've seen in meditations can be as simple as, "What am I?" all the way to, "The entire universe is one bright pearl." Wording them in a way that personally resonates with you connects you further to the meaning driving your character. It can offer you another route into igniting the fire of exploring the circumstances. Let's say that I ask myself, why is it important for Joe to be man enough? What does it mean to be not enough of a man? Well, to someone for whom this is a need, it would mean weakness, not measuring up. Why is that a big deal? Because, to me exploring this point of view, it means then you aren't fit to live, that you'll just be walked on by everything like some worm. That image hooks me, that within Joe's fear of being so miniscule the world sees him as more insect than man. This seems to be what could fuel such a need. I write down this small sentence:

> Small Grub Crawls Through All the Shit

This for me resonates in a unique way. When I sit with it in a meditation practice I feel a level of humiliation and fear. I also, however, uncover another feeling, a bizarre type of contentment. If being at the bottom of the ladder means you have nowhere to go, that too is a type of stability. The more we climb upwards, filled with ambitions and dreams, the harder we fall. I go back to Joe, wondering if this dynamic of being willingly trapped at the bottom mixed with disgust at oneself is what drives his need. This is as speculative as I can get about it, the farthest my boat can be pushed out without inventing new details, but in future reads I test it to see if it resonates with his need.

Working with Nora, I reflect on the value of needing to live in hope. Hope is seen somewhat differently by certain schools of meditation. Thich Nhat Hanh would caution against using hope as a crutch to prevent ourselves from dealing fully with our present circumstances. To constantly tell ourselves, "It will get better someday," without identifying what is causing our pain in this moment and then actively working to transform it places us within a passive experience, our eyes closed and hoping that the problems we face will magically go away. Being optimistic about the future is a virtue, but hope without the engagement can quickly turn toxic, prolonging our suffering. Yet at the same time, someone like Nora depends on there being hope, that the only way she can cope with waking up in the hell she lives in is the deeply rooted feeling that one day it will get better. Why does this matter so much? Hope can be a fire to some, it can act as a guiding light that encourages us to keep our heads down and continue to push forward. Imagine somebody in such dire predicaments waking up to find that light suddenly extinguished, the familiar companion of hope abandoning them to the cold pain of their daily existence. No warmth of possibility in the future, no second chance, or redemption for all the pain one has endured. That's enough to make someone cling to hope as if it is a partner who could leave them. A sentence comes to me:

Blue Waves Crash Against Splintered Doors

Sitting with this koan, I sense the double nature of hope. There's a fragility deeply intrinsic to hope, a recognition of the seemingly overwhelming odds and our desire to call on the enigma of the future for relief. The prospect of the future becoming better is a beautiful one, akin to a cerulean wave on the sea, but the future can also be a source of more pain and fear. I think of the fragility of Nora's situation, how desperately she is fighting to keep things going for her and Joe, a slave to the force of her addiction and yet equally desperate to believe that somehow, by some means, things must get better.

One clarifying point that I want to give is that this isn't meant to be an analytical or creative writing exercise but a visceral one, and unlike needs the likelihood with koans is our expressions of them will end up in totally different territories. You might determine different things give rise to a character's need than I do, and on that front this is more than fine. What we are doing is exploring our own sources of meaning to get a deeper grasp on the need and why it arises in that scene. We are after a bit of the essence of this human and what fuels their needs. You might word your koans as questions, single words, or several sentences. This is entirely up to you, dependent on your personal expression. Nor do you need to sit with your koan in a meditation like I do. The koan can be used in meditations but also repeated in downtimes during rehearsals or on set. Equally important is to not try to look to it for meaning, but rather to use it for insight and clarity. Let it work on you and see if nuance emerges as you live truthfully under the given circumstances. If the koan doesn't do anything for you then it doesn't mean you analyzed it improperly or are doing something incorrect. It is one more tool in your work on text that can provide further insight into the event and point of view you are being asked to live out.

What Trips Us Up

Some actors like to write backstories for their characters, inventing entire narratives the authors never intended. I can remember in some of my Stanislavski classes writing literally dozens of pages about my character, what their childhood was like, favorite foods, and so on. Over time I have come to think of this as problematic for several reasons. Firstly, if the writer felt further details were necessary they would put them in. Secondly, generally writers don't think of recreating a character's biography. Even biographical scripts are structured around a series of events. Script writers trade in circumstances and events, the best writers giving an actor everything they need to live out that journey. My suspicion is when an actor adds additional story elements this tends to be done out of fear, from concern that they don't have enough material to study and so they need to invent more to further inform and flesh out their performance. Writing the story of how Macbeth had a pet cat as a child and they went on to have wild adventures might have great sitcom potential, but as far as helping you act out his journey it's superfluous.

Every decision made about your character must be clearly supported by the text. Infusing your performance with unsubstantiated choices can derail things, adding details that don't organically fit within the world of that story and so seem confusing to an audience. This is certainly not to say there isn't room for interpretation or uniqueness. My favorite theatre company hands down is Cheek by Jowl, who is renowned for their ability to find the most unique interpretations in any script they work with. I've never spoken to Declan Donnellan or Nick Omerod, the two visionaries behind the company, but I think I can guess one criterion when it comes to creating a show: any decision about what to do with a given set of circumstances must be supported by the circumstances themselves. The world of that story must have some element already there that supports the vision. Audiences can sense when a concept is in line with the world of the story and when it is not. The same is true for any discovery you make as an actor.

Text analysis in this work isn't interested in transforming you in any way. You won't ever look unrecognizable, having so many tics of voice and movement that people go, "I had no idea it was you!" It won't make you a living magic trick with a reveal at the end. To be clear, lots of characters call for accents, mannerisms, and patterns of walking. Those are all given circumstances, and of course you'll include them in your work. But many actors invent mannerisms, gestures, and patterns of speech not called for by the script. If that's what you are after, there are other schools interested in that type of approach, but I have to caution you: regarding how much they actually work, there are major questions, doubts, and debates. You don't need to be constantly ladling extra things onto your work. If there is one virtue the Meisner technique can instill that will carry you so far, it is that your own authenticity is enough.

The Sad Sweetness of Parting Ways

I believe a progressive Meisner approach will deliver significant results in the coming years. It lines up so well with more reliable theories about brain, behavior, and impulses emerging from the cognitive sciences. At the end of the day acting techniques are living ones, and the best ones adapt to our newest understandings of human biology and psychology, leaving behind tradition in favor of new knowledge. I think this version of the Meisner technique, already vastly different in some respects from the classical one, lines up better with things we know about the environment and how human behavior can be replicated. Its emphasis on a holistic process, in which tools can be integrated across disciplines including other approaches to acting and even non-acting ones such as meditation, make it more relevant to the unique needs of the coming years, as digital mediums and new ways of working phase out old approaches to doing things. Those are the circumstances not found within a text you must nevertheless adapt to.

At the same time, in twenty or thirty years, I hope the Meisner technique looks different than it does now, elements of it or the entire thing having been replaced with new knowledge and keeping its claims better in line with the results it produces for the needs of contemporary actors. I think the best piece of advice on what you do today to find the answers you need comes from someone I look up to very much for his dedication to seeking relevant knowledge and better means of doing things, the enigmatic Bruce Lee: "Absorb what is useful, reject what is useless, add what is essentially your own."

As an actor, keep what works. Discard what does not. Above all else, research your own experiences.

15
Maybe So. Maybe Not. We'll see

Instead of doing the right thing, do the thing right now.

—Scott Williams

If you're not fully doing something, you're not really doing anything at all.

—Larry Silverberg

When I first encountered Meisner, it was by working with a particularly special individual who teaches a novel take on the technique. Scott Williams was not only a magnificent teacher to me but a genuinely wonderful human being. I joined his full-time Meisner training sessions at the Impulse Company in London, remaining with him for five modular years, totaling more than a thousand hours of training. Towards the end of that time period, I decided to undertake a deeper investigation of the Meisner technique, this time more closely to how Meisner himself taught it. This led me to another name in the Meisner world: Larry Silverberg. Larry's style, as well as his ways of working with actors, is far more traditional, in line with how Meisner himself worked. What was perhaps most shocking to me were the results he got from his actors: equally as strong and powerful as Scott. He is brilliant and intense, and treated me with such patience and compassion for my many questions and struggles in an entirely new approach to Meisner.

As is often the case with opposites, complimentary points could be found. The reasons why Larry's and Scott's work is so different and yet yields such good results is a can of worms not for this book. What is most relevant for you to know is that the Meisner you've worked with is my own synthesis of Scott's and Larry's approaches. It's not a Frankenstein-for-novelty's-sake method as much as taking the elements of each one that I've found pair more cleanly with the exercises from mindfulness and Zen.

I've been blessed to have done a lot of training in my life. What these experiences gave me was the chance not only to explore and deepen my own process but as well to get a better understanding of the actor's process from different angles. It sounds simple on paper, but it's profound when the penny drops and you actually see it happening in front of you: we are not all the same, and we all need different tools tailored to our unique paths to thrive. Before I came to Meisner, training such as Eugenio Barba's old-school Grotowski approach was a wonderful environment for me to discover this in practice, and after my Meisner studies so was my training in Bruce Lee's Jeet Kune Do concepts under Sifu Clive Whitworth, an absolute genius in his field and a dear mentor.

There's both an equally human comedy and tragedy woven throughout our expectations of the future. The content of those moments can never be known until they finally arrive. When they do, we can only do our best to embrace and work with them. Sometimes our trusted tools see us through, while at others they fail. That's the learning process for life. Meditation is designed to help you work with chaos, uncertainty, and anxiety; a strong practice can handle the peak times of life, the moments when all seems to fall apart, and everything in between. This book was written through an unexpectedly chaotic time in my life, and so reminded me of these lessons. We don't get to be immune to life, but we can learn to recognize it clearly and respond to it authentically. That seems to be the better outlook than wandering through it blindly, wondering why painful things happen but lacking the clarity to see them and recognize our role in those events.

The past few years have been challenging, and while the next few don't look as though they will have the same problems, there will be many impacts to come. In statistics there is a term known as "regression to the mean," and in psychology this has been used to describe the phenomenon of when we mistake things getting better for the norm. Somebody who has suffered from untreated mental illness, for example, might find a new medication improving things. The difference may be so stark that they believe they are "normal" again, when in reality they are still a long way from finding the stability and levels of interaction they need to function at a basic or even optimum level. There's a lesson here for all of us. Just because our industry is returning, shooting schedules picking up and theatre doors reopening, doesn't mean we've found the old norm. It just means we're so glad for a taste of it.

Even in 2027, however, and beyond that point, ripple effects from the coronavirus pandemic will still be felt in the industry. We can't lose sight that our biggest number of workers, both talent and crew alike, have faced untold economic and personal hardships. This is a group largely on the fringe, desperately fighting poverty and attempting to stay healthy to support their art. Even as we regress to the mean, discovering a norm again, we cannot forget that a large number of gifted artists have either been set back or fallen by the wayside, or that there will be ones who leave the industry over the next few years, burnt out over battles with health, exhaustion, debt, lack of opportunity, inflation, mental health, housing crises, and more.

Finding solutions is not going to be easy. From my perspective, a meditation practice oriented around connecting with your experience of reality is a way to develop some of that authenticity so valued in great acting, even when your other resources are limited. Exploring it in conjunction with the Meisner technique gives you access to a formal training system and set of values deeply intrinsic to the industry today. These solutions, however, don't cover the whole picture. There are numerous areas of need for actors today that have not been addressed, so many avenues of support that must be opened in light of the realities of 2020 onwards. My hope is that people with expertise in these relevant areas continue to research and recognize the problems modern actors are grappling with. Most importantly, I hope we continue to talk about them, bringing these topics into multiple circles of knowledge and awareness, and that this conversation is not silenced by our very human, and understandable, desires to find our norm again.

Bearing the weight of many global factors, it seems almost disingenuous of me to suggest something good can be found in the pandemic as well as the systemic problems within the industry that existed before it. We're a planet nearly six million short and counting because of a single disease, and tens of millions more now grapple with debilitation from long COVID-19. Even more have been sidelined or economically derailed by the numerous global shutdowns, some of which were handled far better and more intelligently than others. While previously we may have felt clarity, the future now seems murkier than ever. Looking at our own membership in an interconnected world, we've come to recognize how fragile a way of life can be, even one riddled with problems. I think we are all feeling the anxiety about the many new unknowns that have been created just over the past few years, and this is a set of challenges that was ladled onto a reality already filled with systemic injustices and imbalances. It's hard to find something positive to say about things.

Still, without needing to deny these realities, others also emerge. In times of greatest distress, the arts find ways to survive and sometimes even flourish. The pandemic has invited us to rethink our safety protocols about how we handle rehearsals and working with one another. Within these confines, new approaches to rehearsals, auditions, and even entire productions have been invented. The digital age of acting may bring its own unique set of challenges, but the access it provides can be a greater aid to connecting actors across the world with productions, contacts, and new opportunities. We've also seen a rise in new and established voices interested in topics of social justice, including within the industry itself. Breaking conventions, exposing flawed ones, and creating new avenues of dialogue and action all reaffirm our own valuing of life and the right every artist has to fair opportunities. Lockdowns and restrictions may have been torturous, but they also have offered more time than usual to reflect, and ideas borne of this solitude have found their way into our industry. It is possible that in addition to new problems we are also carrying new solutions going forward into the future, antibodies buried within the DNA of the arts to ills both new and old. The possibility that we hold the cure to our own challenges isn't a new concept, but rooted deeply in traditions as old as Zen, including the koan *"The whole world is medicine."*

When I first submitted this book for consideration, one of the requests I received was to write on how actors can keep going when things get hard. I was deeply touched by this for a number of reasons. In addition to hopefully making some kind of case that you can continue to develop and create professional tools even when your opportunities are restricted, even if it is just enough to gain a foothold in the industry, I hope the tone and spirit of this book supports the very real fact that there are many ways for actors to adapt and survive. A large part of the ability to keep going depends on the knowledge that there is some likelihood of surviving. If you are an actor established in the industry, or considering entering or re-entering, there are many people actively interested in how to make your life easier, whether it is by creating more efficient techniques, developing support programs, or combatting the social hurdles you have come into. This is something we often forget: the industry is filled with challenges, but it is also filled with allies you may not have known you had.

For your acting process, the best gift that the Meisner technique can offer you is the habit of staying open, flexible, and adaptable, to become, as Shambala master Pema Chödrön writes, "comfortable with uncertainty." There are many theories and values acting techniques base their tools on: emotional realism, the power of imagination, psychophysical embodiment, and so on. The Meisner technique certainly isn't the only approach that values the moment, but I've yet to find a technique that staked so much on its consideration of the moment and creating exercises constantly concerned with it. I have no crystal ball, but I suspect this is what will keep the Meisner technique going for many, many years to come. As an actor you have so many uncertainties about what you'll encounter on set or in production. In an ocean, water remains the only constant, and in an ocean of possible experiences, the moment is the only continuous variable. The moment will always be there in your acting and, as long as you know how to work with it, you will always have a relevant skillset. It simply, though not always easily, asks that you be mindful of it.

When I teach, I often tell actors that the most important quality for an artist to have is the ability to endure. Questions of skills, opportunities, or rough patches can all be worked through if you hold this core trait. That, in itself, is possibly one of the great ironies: it seems that in the face of hardship we keep going by keeping going. When in the midst of contentment and success, challenges await around the corner. When holding our own against fear and desperation, unexpected opportunities and joys arise. If you cannot know the future, the only constant worth holding onto and nurturing is that you will be there and, whatever the wave brings, you can stand on your own two feet to meet it head on, and get back up when knocked down. If we look closely, there's no greater attribute for an artist to have.—

One day, the farmer awoke to news: his prized horse, so vital for many of his needs, had run away. Though he and his neighbors searched high and low, it could not be found.

"This is terrible!" his neighbors exclaimed. "What bad fortune!"

"'Maybe so. Maybe not. We'll see," the farmer replied.

A few days later, the horse returned, and what it brought shocked everyone: it had found a family of wild horses, and led them all back to the farm. Not only had the farmer regained his prized horse, but now had five more to call his own. Hearing of this unprecedented luck, his friends and neighbors all said, "What great fortune you have!"

"Maybe so. Maybe not. We'll see," the farmer replied.

A week later, the farmer's son was working with one of the horses, attempting to train it. The animal became startled and, without warning, violently threw the son off. He fell hard against the ground, shattering his leg. It would be months before he would be able to walk properly again, costing the farm with his lack of ability to help work the fields and tend to the animals.

Hearing of this devastating news, friends and family said, "This is terrible! What bad luck you've run into!"

"Maybe so. Maybe not. We'll see," the farmer replied.

Nearly six weeks later much had changed. A violent war with a neighboring country had broken out. Needing to mobilize and train soldiers quickly, the emperor instated a draft. An official went from house to house, property to property, under order to bring back any able-bodied men for immediate training. When he arrived at the farmer's property, he found the farmer's son, barely able to walk and only with the support of a stick for a few minutes at a time. He thanked the farmer for his time, wished his son the best, and went in search for more men who could fight in the coming war. Of the many drafted from that region, barely any would return home alive. The son's seemingly great misfortune had saved his life.

Index

acting career: career planning *vs.* artistic growth 5, 7; difficulties 33, 48–52, 54, 64, 118; impact due to COVID-19 pandemic 3, 6, 7
actor training 14, 92, 166–171, 181–189
All's Well That Ends Well scene 253–255
analysis: in actor's process 126; in mediation 110, 121, 212–213; in the Meisner technique 118, 142, 183, 261; text analysis exercise 268–287
anxiety: in acting 41, 61–62, 70, 142, 161; due to COVID-19 pandemic 6, 290; in flow research 129; role in meditation 28, 33, 81, 125, 141, 210, 254, 273, 289
auditions: impact by COVID-19 pandemic 4, 6, 291; technique 10, 30, 37, 46, 129

Barba, E. 42, 166, 289
Bates, K. 124
Boucicault, D. *see London Assurance* scene
Brando, M. 124

character backstory tool 286
Cheek by Jowl 286
Cocaine play: analysis of 273–283; scene 250–253; scene exercise 283–285
cognitive science 12, 287
COVID-19 1–3, 8, 289–290
Csikszentmihalyi, M. 128

Davis, V. 124
depression 6, 27, 125
digital acting 4–6, 47
digital age 5–8, 287, 291

film, acting in 24, 44, 123, 174, 181, 271
film industry 3–4, 6, 258
flow, experiences and psychology 127–131, 140, 212
fourth wall technique 42–45, 47

Gensha 2, 246–247

Harding, D. 83, 105, 125, 140, 243, 264
Harris, S. 264
Hawthorne Effect 43–44
headlessness 84–85, 104–106, 121, 125, 264

imagination: use in actor's toolbox 26, 29, 81, 171, 291; use in Meisner training 120, 172, 183, 220–221

Kathakali 17
King, Pendelton *see Cocaine* play

Lang, R. 83, 105, 107, 243, 264
London Assurance scene 256–258

Meisner, S. 7, 36, 42, 45, 71, 119–121, 270
mental health 6, 27–28, 34, 54, 290
method acting 7, 17, 152, 164, 171
Metta meditation 20

naturalism 42
New York Times 4
Noh theatre 17, 139–140

Odin Teatret 23, 42, 166

pandemic *see* COVID-19

Sahn, S. 247, 264
Shakespeare, W.: acting 8, 172, 261; pedagogy in teaching 188–189; scene (*see All's Well That Ends Well* scene)
Shukman, H. 214, 247, 264, 266
Silverberg, L. 218, 240, 288

Stanislavski, system and person 17, 42–45, 171, 212, 286

theatre industry 3–4

Watts, A. 166
Williams, R. 124
Williams, S. 24, 46, 70, 148, 216, 268, 288

Zoom 6

Taylor & Francis eBooks

www.taylorfrancis.com

A single destination for eBooks from Taylor & Francis with increased functionality and an improved user experience to meet the needs of our customers.

90,000+ eBooks of award-winning academic content in Humanities, Social Science, Science, Technology, Engineering, and Medical written by a global network of editors and authors.

TAYLOR & FRANCIS EBOOKS OFFERS:

- A streamlined experience for our library customers
- A single point of discovery for all of our eBook content
- Improved search and discovery of content at both book and chapter level

REQUEST A FREE TRIAL
support@taylorfrancis.com

For Product Safety Concerns and Information please contact our EU
representative GPSR@taylorandfrancis.com
Taylor & Francis Verlag GmbH, Kaufingerstraße 24, 80331 München, Germany

www.ingramcontent.com/pod-product-compliance
Lightning Source LLC
Chambersburg PA
CBHW071805300426
44116CB00009B/1207